LINGUISTICS TODAY

LINGUISTICS
TODAY

Edited by
Archibald A. Hill

BASIC BOOKS, INC., PUBLISHERS
New York   London

SECOND PRINTING

© 1969 by Basic Books, Inc.

Library of Congress Catalog Card Number 68-54149

Manufactured in the United States of America

The Authors

JOHN B. CARROLL is Senior Research Psychologist for the Educational Testing Service, Princeton University. He was the Roy E. Larsen Professor of Educational Psychology at Harvard University from 1960 to 1967. He is author of *The Study of Language* and *Language and Thought*.

J. C. CATFORD is Acting Director of the University of Michigan Center for Research on Language and Language Behavior. He is a frequent contributor to professional journals and is author of *A Linguistic Theory of Translation*.

DAVID DECAMP is Professor of English and Linguistics, University of Texas, Austin. He was Senior Linguistic Specialist and Chief of Party for the Administration for International Development-sponsored Language Advisory Group in Taiwan. His books include *A Collation of Checklists Used in the Study of Jamaican Creole*.

PAUL L. GARVIN, Manager of the Language Analysis and Translation Section, Data Sciences Department, in the Defense Systems Division of the Bunker-Ramo Corporation, is author or editor of more than 100 professional publications.

ERIC P. HAMP is Director of the Center for Balkan and Slavic Studies at the University of Chicago. He specializes in Indo-European, Sanskrit, Baltic and Slavic, and Celtic. He has been recipient of numerous awards in the field of languages and linguistics.

EINAR HAUGEN, Victor S. Thomas Professor of Scandinavian and Linguistics at Harvard University, has received the Order of St. Olaf (Norway) and the Order of the North Star (Sweden). He is a member of the American Academy of Arts and Letters, the Icelandic Academy of Science, the Royal Norwegian Scientific Society, and the Oslo Academy of Science.

CURTIS W. HAYES is Assistant Professor in the Department of English at the University of Nebraska. He has done extensive research on the prose style of Samuel Johnson and has published several articles in linguistics journals.

ARCHIBALD A. HILL, Professor of English and Linguistics, University of Texas, Austin, is Secretary-Treasurer of the Linguistic

Society of America. He is the author of *Introduction to Linguistic Structure* and *The Oral Approach to English.*

CARLETON T. HODGE is Professor of Linguistics at the University of Indiana and Director of the Intensive Language Training Center. He is a frequent contributor to professional journals and is a member of the Linguistic Society, Oriental Society, American Schools of Oriental Research, and the Linguistic Society of India, among other professional groups.

HENRY M. HOENIGSWALD is Chairman of the Department of Linguistics at the University of Pennsylvania. He has held fellowships from the American Council of Learned Societies, the Guggenheim Foundation, the Newberry Library, and the National Science Foundation.

HARRY HOIJER, Professor of Anthropology at the University of California, Los Angeles, has been an officer of Sigma Xi, the American Anthropological Association, and the Linguistic Society of America. He is Chairman and American Council of Learned Societies Representative on the Committee on Research in Native American Languages.

FRANCES INGEMANN is Professor of Linguistics and Chairman of the Linguistics Committee at the University of Kansas. She has specialized in Cheremis and Mari. Her current research involves a study of Ipili-Paiyiala.

MARTIN JOOS is Professor of Linguistics and Director of the Centre for Linguistic Studies at the University of Toronto. He is a member and officer in numerous linguistic societies and has contributed extensively to technical journals.

HANS KURATH was Professor of English at Michigan University. He edited the *Linguistic Atlas of New England, Middle English Dictionary, A Word Geography of the Eastern States,* and *A Phonology and Prosody of Modern English.*

SYDNEY M. LAMB is Professor of Linguistics at Yale. He has worked extensively in the field of mechanical translation and has published *A System for Analyzing Russian Texts* and *Outline of Stratificational Grammar.*

WINFRED P. LEHMAN, Chairman of the Department of Linguistics, University of Texas, Austin, is chief investigator for government-sponsored research programs on machine translation and the development of a linguistic computer system. He is author of several books in linguistics and of textbooks, including a grammar of formal written Japanese.

RAVEN I. McDAVID, JR., is Professor of English and Linguistics at the University of Chicago. He is Editor of the *Linguistic Atlas of the Middle and South Atlantic States* and is President of the American Dialect Society.

NORMAN A. McQUOWN, Professor of Anthropology and of Linguistics at the University of Chicago, has been Editorial Supervisor for *Konsulan Inglizce* (*English for Turks*), *Spoken Maya*, and *Spoken Quiche*. He is author of *Spoken Turkish* and of *Tzeltal Hablado*.

ALBERT H. MARCKWARDT is Professor of English and Linguistics, Princeton University. He is Director of the *Linguistic Atlas of the North Central States* and author of the *Scribner Handbook of English*. In 1961 he received the University of Michigan's Distinguished Faculty Achievement Award.

WILLIAM G. MOULTON is Professor of Linguistics at Princeton University. His special interests are Dutch and German dialects, dialect geography, and the application of linguistics to teaching foreign language. He is author of *A Linguistic Guide to Language Learning*.

THOMAS PYLES is Professor of English and Linguistics at Northwestern University. He is author of *Words and Ways of American English* and *The Origins and Development of the English Language*.

HENRY LEE SMITH, JR., Acting Director of the Program in Linguistics at the State University of New York in Buffalo, is also Professor of Linguistics and English there. He was founder and first Director of the School of Language and Linguistics of the Foreign Service Institute.

ROBERT P. STOCKWELL is Professor and Chairman of the Department of Linguistics at the University of California in Los Angeles. He is author of *Some Old English Graphemic-Phonemic Correspondence* (with C. W. Barritt) and *Sounds of English and Spanish* (with J. D. Bowen).

WAYNE TOSH, Chief of the Descriptive Linguistics Group, Linguistics Research Center, University of Texas, Austin, is the author of *Syntactic Translation*.

FRANCIS WHITFIELD is Professor of Slavic Languages and Literatures at the University of California in Berkeley. He translated Louis Hjelmslev's *Omkring Sprogteoriens Grundlaeggelse*) *Prolegomena to a Theory of Language*) and wrote *Beast in View* and *A Russian Reference Grammar*.

Preface

This volume would seem to need only a small preface, since the last chapter, that contributed by the editor, has been designed as an overview of the present state of language science in the United States and, at least in part, elsewhere. Yet it can be added here that the state of our science at the moment is one which particularly calls for two types of summaries and syntheses. First, the impact of linguistics on other activities, practical and theoretical, is great and growing and consequently calls for extended discussion. Second, the great upsurge of interest in theoretical linguistics has led on the one hand to great advances in knowledge and on the other to development of many varied schools and approaches. Synthesis of these various schools may be neither possible nor finally desirable, but it is certain that it will be accomplished, if at all, only by reasonable presentation and patient discussion. The writers represented in this book have, in spite of the varied views they hold, a common devotion to discussion and an ability to differ without excessive heat.

It is true of this volume (from another point of view) that it is unique among books on linguistics in what is not in it as well as what is. Almost all books in this field necessarily exhibit the content and structure of the phenomenon studied — human language. This book does not. It substitutes a full and, one hopes, profitable discussion of what linguists of various kinds do when they are practicing their science. Thus, this book is essentially an answer to a query which every linguistic analyst has met, and been frustrated by: "What is linguistics, and what on earth is it good for?"

The chapters in this book stem from a series of lectures broadcast by the Voice of America in its Forum series.

November 1968   Archibald A. Hill

Contents

LINGUISTICS TODAY

I THE NATURE AND HISTORY OF LINGUISTICS

William G. Moulton

The ability of human beings to talk — to use language in order to communicate with one another — is so universal and seems so natural that most of us never bother to think much about it. We take it for granted that every normal human being can talk, just as we take it for granted that he can eat, sleep, or walk. This common attitude toward language is in part entirely correct: every normal human being beyond infancy *can* use language to communicate with his fellow human beings. It is precisely this ability that distinguishes man as "the talking animal" most sharply from all other beings. This is not to say that other living beings do not communicate with the other members of their species. They do of course; and a few of them have communication systems that are complex and flexible enough to deserve the name "language." The research of recent decades has shown us, for example, a great deal about the remarkable language of bees; and we are just beginning to realize that dolphins use a language that is perhaps even more remarkable. Nevertheless, none of these animal languages even remotely approaches the complexity, flexibility, and elegance of every human language. Man's ability to use language far surpasses that of any other living being.

Though it is true that every normal human being is able to use language, it is misleading to compare this with his ability to eat, sleep, or walk. All of these abilities are passed on to us by genetic transmission: we receive them by way of the genes that we inherit from our parents. In the case of language, however, it is only the *ability* to talk and understand that we inherit genetically; the particular language or languages that we speak are passed on to us not by genetic transmission but by cultural transmission. That is to say, a language is something that we learn and are taught, not something that we know by instinct.

When we say that a language is culturally transmitted — that it is learned and not inherited — we mean that it is part of that whole complex of learned and shared behavior that anthropologists call "culture." This might lead us to believe that a simple culture would make use of a simple language, that a complex culture would make use of a complex language, and so on. In fact, this does not seem to be true at all, except in a very trivial sense. There are so-called primitive cultures in the jungles of the Amazon and on the island of New Guinea, and there are so-called advanced cultures in Europe, Asia, and Africa; but the languages of these cultures are all equally "advanced" and complex. The trivial sense in which some languages are simpler than others concerns only matters of vocabulary: it is obvious that a language whose speakers talk about philosophy and science will contain more words than a language whose speakers are engaged primarily in hunting and fishing. With this one exception, it is quite wrong to suppose that a "simple" culture will also have a "simple" language. The grammar and sound system of such a language may turn out to be more complex than that of many an "advanced" culture; and even its vocabulary will run to many thousands of words and may include subtle distinctions which strike outsiders as very complex indeed.

Linguistics is the branch of learning which studies the languages of any and all human societies: how each such language is constructed; how it varies through space and changes through time; how it is related to other languages; and how it is used by its speakers. Fundamental to all branches of linguistics is the basic question: What *is* language? How does it work? What happens when a speaker says something and a hearer understands him? If we look at a typical act of communication by means of language, two aspects seem quite clear. First, it is obvious that language makes use of *sound*. Second, this sound is used to convey *meaning* from speaker to hearer. We might therefore be tempted to say that a language is a communication system consisting merely of sound and meaning.

If we look a little further, however, it becomes clear that this is not even a first approximation of the way language works. Language does indeed involve sound and meaning; but itclearly involves much more than this since we can easily think of situations in which we can hear the sound and know the meaning and yet really understand nothing of the language. Consider the following example. Suppose that we are in Japan and that we see two people talking together. The first one makes the sounds "Nañ-zi desu ka?" whereupon the second pulls out his watch, looks at it, and then makes the sounds "Ni-zi desu." Here two messages have been transmitted. We have heard all the sounds in each message, and we can easily guess at the meanings: the first speaker was surely asking what time it is, and the second speaker almost surely answered that it is two o'clock — since our own watch tells us that this is the time. Yet though we have heard the sound and know the meaning, we do not yet really understand anything of the Japanese language. To learn this we must investigate the connection between sound and meaning. We must find out what parts of the sound correspond to what parts of the meaning, how the first sentence is marked as a question and the second as a statement, and so on. Sound and meaning are not language, but only the external, observable aspects of language. Language itself, in the narrower sense, is neither of these observable things but rather the connection between them — which can be observed only indirectly, by inference.

In order to understand a little better how sound and meaning are connected so as to yield language, let us consider a typical speech event in which a speaker says something and is understood by a hearer. How does the speaker formulate his message? How is it transmitted to the hearer? And how does the hearer understand it? There seem to be 11 different stages in the whole process, and we can consider them briefly one by one.

1. *Semantic encoding*. The first thing the speaker must do is to formulate his message in the semantic units his language uses. Since this is like putting a message into proper shape to fit the code in which it is being sent, we can call this stage "semantic encoding."

If the situation we have just described had taken place in an English-speaking country, we would have heard the sounds "What *time* is it?" — "It's two *o'clock*." In the question we use the semantic unit *time*, the same unit that also occurs in such sentences as "I don't have *time*" and "I saw him last *time*"; and in the answer we use the curious unit *o'clock*, which occurs only in sentences of this sort. Where we must use two different semantic units, *time* and *o'clock*, a Frenchman can use the same semantic unit in both the question and the answer: "Quelle *heure* est-il?" — "Il est deux *heures*" (with singular *heure* and plural *heures*). This semantic unit *heure* is the one which corresponds in other sentences to English *hour*, a unit of time. A German would also use the same semantic unit in both the question and the answer: "Wieviel *Uhr* ist es?" — "Es ist zwei *Uhr*," though his semantic unit *Uhr* does not correspond to English *hour* (for this the Germans use the unit *Stunde*), but rather to what we call a *clock* or a *watch*. A Dutchman handles the matter still differently. He says: "Hoe *laat* is het?" — "Het is twee *uur*." His word *laat* corresponds in other sentences to our English *late*; that is to say, his "Hoe *laat* is het?" corresponds to the English question "How *late* is it?" The semantic unit *uur* he uses in his answer is similar to French *heure* in that it corresponds in other sentences to English *hour*; but, unlike French *heure*, it can be used only in the answer and never in the question. A Japanese uses the same semantic unit, *-zi*, in both the question and the answer: "Nan-*zi* desu ka?" — "Ni-*zi* desu." This unit, however, is quite different from English *time*, French *heure*, German *Uhr*, and Dutch *uur*: it is never used *except* in asking or telling time, and has no other uses.

As the above examples show, each of these five languages encodes the same situation in ways that are semantically quite different. Metaphorically speaking, every language gathers together various bits and pieces of the things people talk about and symbolizes them with its own particular set of semantic units. In English we use the same unit, *time*, in such sentences as: "What *time* is it?" "I don't have *time*," and "I saw him last *time*."

On the other hand, in equivalent sentences, French employs three different semantic units: "Quelle *heure* est-il?" "Je n'ai pas le *temps*," and "Je l'ai vu la dernière *fois*." Any instrument used for telling time can be referred to in German by the semantic unit *Uhr*. In English, however, we make a sharp distinction depending on whether the instrument is usually portable: if it is, we call it a *watch*; if it is not, we call it a *clock*. Every language, in short, has its own particular set of semantic units; and any message which is to be sent must first be encoded into the particular semantic units of that language.

2. *Grammatical encoding.* Once a speaker has chosen the proper semantic units for the message he wants to send, his next task is to find the corresponding grammatical units and to arrange them in the way required by the grammar of his language. For example, if we want to make an English message out of the semantic units *boy*, *buy*, and *watch*, we can encode them grammatically — among other ways — as *The boy buys the watch*. As we do so, our language forces us to add some further elements of meaning to the message — the kind of meaning that is customarily called "grammatical meaning." In English we are forced to specify whether *boy* and *watch* are singular or plural: *boy* vs. *boys*, *watch* vs. *watches*. We are also forced to classify both units as either definite or indefinite: *the boy* vs. *a boy*, *the watch* vs. *a watch*. And we are forced to specify whether the buying takes place in the present or the past: present, *The boy buys the watch*; past, *The boy bought the watch*. Further, if we make *boy* singular, we must add the grammatical element *-s* to the unit *buy*. *The boy buy-s the watch* — though English does *not* force us to do this if we choose past *bought* rather than present *buy*.

What name should we select for the grammatical units that are used at this stage of the encoding process — for example, for the six units in the sentence *The boy buy-s the watch*? The customary name for each such minimal grammatical unit is, in English, the term "morpheme" (from Greek *morphē*, meaning "form"). Some morphemes are words: *the*, *boy*, *buy*, *watch*; others are smaller than words: the *-s* of *buy-s*, or the *-ing* of *buy-ing*. Some morphemes clearly correspond to semantic units: *boy buy*, *watch*; with others the semantic connection is far less clear: *the*, *a*, or the *-s* of *buy-s*; still others do not seem to have any semantic connection at all, such as the *to* of *The boy wants to buy a watch*.

Where the basic *unit* of grammar is the morpheme, the basic *device* of grammar is that of *construction*: putting two (or more)

7

grammatical forms together so as to produce a larger form. For example, if in English we put the morphemes *boy* and *the* together in the order *boy the*, we have added nothing: the whole is no greater than the sum of the parts. But if we put them together in the order *the boy*, something *is* added and the whole *is* greater than the sum of the parts. Put together in this way they form a construction; and the added element of meaning is the constructional meaning.

A very striking feature of human language is the fact that all grammars are so designed that a speaker can say and a hearer can understand sentences that they have never said or heard before, and that there is no theoretical limit to the number of sentences that can be produced. How do human languages attain this marvelous flexibility? All of them seem to do so by means of a number of very ingenious grammatical devices. First, every language groups its words into a number of different classes — traditionally called "parts of speech" — which are specialized in certain specific grammatical functions. In English, for example, nouns function (among other ways) as the subject of a sentence, and verbs as the main element in the predicate. This means that, given 1,000 nouns like *fire*, *water*, *snow*, and 1,000 verbs like *burn*, *boil*, *melt*, we can make 1,000 × 1,000 — one million — sentences like *Fire burns*, *Water boils*, *Snow melts*. The only limitations are semantic ones. At the moment we can make no use of the sentence *Snow boils*, though some day we shall perhaps need it. If so, we shall be able to say and understand it, even though we have never heard it before.

Though all languages use specialization in this way, they also have devices for avoiding the dangers of overspecialization. English, for example, permits a noun like *girl* to function not only as the subject of a sentence, as in *The girl sings*, but also as the object of a verb, as in *The boy loves the girl*. This means that, given only 1,000 nouns and 1,000 verbs that can take an object, we can form not just 1,000 × 1,000 sentences, but 1,000 × 1,000 × 1,000, or one billion, sentences — since every noun can function in either of two ways. Of course, if we allow a noun to fill more than one grammatical function, we must then add something to the grammar that tells us when it is functioning in which way. In the example just given, English does this by means of word order. In *The boy loves the girl*, word order tells us that *the boy* is functioning as the subject of the sentence; but in *The girl loves the boy*, word order tells us that *the boy* is functioning as the object of the verb.

Another device through which languages gain flexibility is that of *embedding*: arranging morphemes and words not just in simple sequence, with one merely following the other, but rather in successive layers of construction, with one inside the other — theoretically without limit. Even so simple a sentence as *The boy loves the girl* contains three layers of embedding. At the highest level this is a construction made up of *the boy + loves the girl*; at the next level these consist, respectively, of the constructions *the + boy* and *loves + the girl*; and at the third level these latter consist of the constructions *love + -s* and *the + girl*:

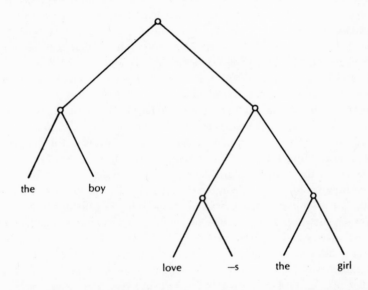

Still another device which all languages seem to use to gain flexibility has recently come to be called *transformation*. Consider, for example, the grammatical structure which underlies the sentence *The boy buys the watch*. If to this underlying structure we apply a passive transformation, we get *The watch is bought by the boy*. An

9

interrogative transformation gives *Does the boy buy the watch?* A negative transformation gives *The boy does not buy the watch.* A combination of interrogative and negative gives *Doesn't the boy buy the watch?* One type of embedding transformation gives (*the boy*) *who buys the watch.* Another type of embedding transformation gives (*the watch*) *that the boy buys.* Still another type of embedding transformation gives (*it was easy*) *for the boy to buy the watch.* Since successive embeddings, theoretically without limit, can be added to a sentence, there is no such thing as a "longest sentence": no matter how long it is, we can always add more to it by means of further transformations.

3. *Phonological encoding.* Once a speaker has given the proper grammatical encoding to his message, we can assume that it consists simply of a string of morphemes. (We know, of course, that this "string of morphemes" may show a complex internal structure in terms of layers of embedding; but at least on the surface the morphemes merely follow one another.) What the speaker must now do is to convert this string of morphemes into sound so that the message can be transmitted to his listener. The simplest way of doing this would be to go directly from morpheme to sound, converting each unit of grammar (each morpheme) into a unit of sound. A sentence such as *Boy loves girl* would then require four different units of sound: one each for the morphemes *boy, love, -s,* and *girl.* If a language had only thirty or forty morphemes, this would be a delightfully simple way of sending messages. In actual fact, of course, every language has many thousands of morphemes, and a more ingenious method of sending has to be used. What every language does is to convert each unit of grammar (each morpheme) not into *one* unit of sound but rather into *one or more* units of sound. Such units of sound are customarily called *phonemes* (from Greek *phōnē,* meaning "sound"). For example, in English we encode the morpheme *if* into two phonemes, /if/; the morpheme *cough* into three phonemes, /kof/; *shift* into four phonemes, /šift/; *thrift* into five phonemes, /θrift/; *glimpse* into six phonemes, /glimps/; and so on. A few morphemes, by chance, are encoded into only one phoneme — for example, the /-z/ of /baiz/ *buys,* or the /-t/ of /koft/ *coughed;* but this is not a necessary part of the system.

This device of encoding each grammatical unit (each morpheme) into *one or more* phonological units (one or more phonemes) is extraordinarily efficient and economical. If each morpheme were encoded into only one phoneme, then the number of morphemes in a language would be limited by the number of sounds that the human ear can easily distinguish from one another. But when each morpheme is encoded into one or more phonemes, the number of available morpheme shapes is far larger than will ever be needed in any language. If a language has, for example, thirty phonemes (a relatively modest number as the languages of the world go), and if it permits morphemes no larger than five phonemes in length (again a modest limitation), it would allow — theoretically — for over 25 million different morpheme shapes.

When we examine the way the phonemes of any language are turned into audible sound, and the way they are used in encoding morphemes, we find that they show two types of structure. First, no language permits its phonemes to occur in any and all possible sequences. In English, for example, we find that morphemes can begin with /pl-/ (*play*), or /bl-/ (*blow*), or /sl-/ (*slow*); but English does not permit us to encode morphemes beginning with /tl-/, or with /dl-/, or with /θl-/, or with any of many other possible sequences of phonemes. Every language shows strict limitations of this sort. As a result, no language allows its speakers to use more than a small fraction of the morpheme shapes that are theoretically available. At the same time, every language also provides for far more morpheme shapes than its speakers actually use or need. In English we use the shapes *tab, tube, tub*; but we have not yet made use of such further permitted shapes as *teeb, tib, tabe, teb, tob, tobe, tibe*, and *toyb*. They are there, ready and waiting, whenever we should want them.

Every language also shows a great deal of structure in the ways in which it converts its phonemes into audible sound. Our English phoneme /p/, for example, is phonetically a voiceless labial stop. Corresponding to it we also have a voiced labial stop, /b/; a voiceless labial fricative, /f/; a voiced labial fricative, /v/; and a labial nasal, /m/. That is to say, these five phonemes are not converted into sound in a random way; instead, they form a tightly structured system composed of the features "voiceless" (/p/ and

/f/), "voiced" (/b/ and /v/), "stop" (/p/ and /b/), "fricative" (/f/ and /v/), and "nasal" (/m/). The English dental consonants show a similar structure: voiceless /t/ and /θ/; voiced /d/ and /ð/; stops /t/ and /d/; fricatives /θ/ and /ð/; and dental /n/. Very often this sort of neat and economical symmetry occurs in only part of the system. The English velar consonants, for example, include only the two stops voiceless /k/ and voiced /g/, plus the nasal /ŋ/ (as in *sing*); there are no corresponding voiceless and voiced fricatives.

4–8. *Sending, transmission, receiving.* The first three stages in our typical speech event have now been completed: the message has been encoded (1) semantically, (2) grammatically, and (3) phonologically. We are now ready for the next five stages: two for sending, one for transmission, and two for receiving. As encoded thus far, the message consists of a sequence of phonemes. At stage (4) the speaker sends instructions from his brain to his speech organs, telling them what movements to make for each phoneme. At stage (5) the speech organs make these movements and thereby set the air molecules into vibration, producing audible sound. At stage (6) these vibrations fan out from the speaker's mouth and are transmitted to any listener within hearing distance. At stage (7) the vibrations produce corresponding vibrations in the hearer's middle and inner ear. And at stage (8) the energy of these vibrations is carried from the hearer's ear to his brain.

9–11. *Phonological, grammatical, semantic decoding.* At this point the process of decoding begins. As the hearer receives the energy of the message in his brain, he must decode it (9) phonologically, (10) grammatically, and (11) semantically. This, of course, is possible only if he possesses, somewhere inside his head, the same total code as the speaker — that is, if he knows the same language. We shall assume this to be true.

How is this decoding accomplished? To answer this question in detail we would have to look inside the hearer's brain, and this is obviously impossible. Nevertheless, we can make a number of useful indirect observations. Basically what the hearer seems to do is to match what he hears against his own knowledge of the language. In doing this he does not decode the entire message first phonologically, then grammatically, then semantically; instead, he seems to race back and forth from one part of the total code to another, picking up all the clues he can. Let us suppose that he hears, in American English, the partial sentence "He was writing/riding. . . ," with a sound halfway between a /t/ and a /d/. From the phonological code he knows that such a halfway sound is not acceptable; it must be decoded as either a /t/ or a /d/ because the code does not provide for any halfway items. The grammatical code tells him that the word can be either *writing* with /t/ or *riding* with /d/, since both of these verbs occur in English. To settle the matter he must refer it on to the semantic code. If the sentence continues "He was writing/riding *a letter*," he knows that it must be the word *writing* with /t/; but if it continues "He was writing/riding *a horse*," he knows that it must be the word *riding* with /d/.

When a speaker sends a message, it consists of a linear sequence of morphemes which have been converted into a linear sequence of phonemes. It is of course this latter which the hearer hears and tries to interpret. At the same time, because he also knows the grammar of the language, he is able to reconstruct and interpret the nonlinear structures which lie behind what he hears. Suppose, for example, that he hears such a sentence as: "The man is horrified by his son's being accused of stealing." In terms of surface structure, this is a passive sentence consisting of *the man* as subject, *is horrified* as verb, plus the complement *by his son's being accused of stealing*; and this latter consists of the passive expression *being accused* with the modifier *his son's* and the complement *of stealing*. At the level of deep structure, however, this sentence has been put together by transformation from four different active sentence structures: *Something horrifies the man*, *The man has a son*, *Someone accuses the son of something*, and *The son steals*. Because the hearer also knows the language, he is able to reconstruct this series of deep structure sentences; and, from them, he derives the proper semantic interpretation of the surface structure.

In the preceding paragraphs we have described a typical speech event in order to show the various aspects of language with which linguistics is concerned. *Semantics* is the study of the semantic code. *Lexicology* studies the total stock of morphemes — the "lexicon"

— of a language, particularly those items which have clear semantic references (e.g., *boy*, *buy*, *watch*, as against *the*, *a*, *-s*, *to*). (Note the difference between *lexicology*, the study of the lexicon of a language, and *lexicography*, the art of making dictionaries of various sorts.) *Grammar* is the study of the grammatical code. *Phonology* (or, in American usage, *phonemics*) is the study of the phonological code. *Articulatory phonetics* studies the movements of the vocal organs in producing the sounds of speech (the way the sounds of speech are "articulated"); *acoustic phonetics* studies the vibrations of the air molecules; and *auditory phonetics* studies the way the sounds of speech are perceived by the human ear.

Further branches of linguistics are concerned with variations within language, changes in language, and relationships among languages. *Linguistic geography* deals with the way in which a language varies through geographical space — the fact, for example, that the pronunciation *barn* (with /r/) in western New England corresponds to the pronunciation *bahn* (without /r/) in eastern New England — and how this difference in pronunciation came about. Traditionally, linguistic geography also deals with the variations in linguistic usage of different social classes, though work of this type has recently come to be called *sociolinguistics*.

All of these branches of linguistics are commonly referred to as *synchronic linguistics* — the study of a given language at a given period in time. Opposed to this is *diachronic linguistics* — the study of language change through time. Here the two chief branches are *historical linguistics*, which studies the historical development of a language; and *comparative linguistics*, which studies the historical relationships among languages and attempts to group them into families, subfamilies, and so on.

Because language is such a unique possession of human beings, and because it is of such obvious importance to the functioning of human society, it is not surprising that it has been studied for many centuries in many parts of the world. One of the greatest linguistic achievements of all time was also one of the earliest: the highly detailed Sanskrit grammar attributed to the Hindu scholar Pāṇini, which is dated about 300 B.C. Every language changes in the course of time; and this grammatical description — like so many later ones — was written in order to preserve unchanged the language of sacred writings. Many centuries later this same motivation led to the descriptions of Classical Arabic written by Arab grammarians and to works on Classical Hebrew written by Jewish scholars.

Though modern linguistics has been influenced by these early writings, especially those of the Sanskrit grammarians, it is based primarily on the scholarly traditions of Europe. Like so many other branches of modern science, it had its origins in the philosophical speculations of the ancient Greeks. As early as the fourth century B.C. the philosopher Plato raised one of the basic questions of linguistics: Is there any necessary connection between the words we use and the things they name? Though Plato seems to have believed that there is such a connection, his most distinguished pupil, Aristotle, took the opposite point of view: that the connection between the form and the meaning of a word is a matter of convention and of tacit agreement among the speakers of a language. This is the view we accept today. There is no necessary reason why the same animal should be called in English *dog*, in German *Hund*, in French *chien*, in Spanish *perro*, in Russian *sobaka*, and so on.

The Greeks were not interested in foreign languages but confined their studies almost exclusively to Greek; they seem to have taken it for granted that their language represented universal forms of human thought. Though their observations on language were made almost exclusively in abstract philosophical terms, many of their ideas are still accepted in modern linguistics — for example, the theory of parts of speech, the division of the sentence into subject and predicate, and such inflectional categories as gender, number, case, person, tense, and mood.

The Greek approach to language was taken over by the Romans and applied with little change to their language, Latin. Once again grammars were written in order to preserve highly valued forms of language which had already become archaic. Two outstanding examples are the Latin grammars of Donatus in the fourth century A.D. and of Priscian in the sixth century — both written long after classical Latin had ceased being spoken in everyday use.

Even after the fall of the Roman Empire, Latin continued for many centuries to be *the* language of learning in all of western Europe; and the approach to language used in these late Latin grammars constituted for centuries the "linguistics" of the western world.

It is customary to date modern linguistics from the late eighteenth and early nineteenth century, when scholars for the first time worked out detailed scientific methods for establishing relationships among languages — notably those of the Indo-European family. Most of nineteenth-century linguistics was devoted to historical–comparative studies of this sort. Toward the end of the century there were rapid advances in both phonetics and linguistic geography, though scholarly interests were in both cases still in large part historical. Modern synchronic linguistics traditionally dates from the *Cours de linguistique générale* of the Swiss scholar Ferdinand de Saussure, a work published posthumously from lecture notes in 1916. Because Saussure showed for the first time the great importance of structure within language, this approach to the study of language has often been called "structural linguistics." Similar ideas were developed or taken over in many other parts of the world during the following decades, notably by such scholars as the German-American Franz Boas, the Americans Edward Sapir and Leonard Bloomfield, and the expatriate Russian N. S. Trubetzkoy. It is significant that these scholars also extended their studies to many languages which had never been investigated before.

What should we say of linguistics today? First, we find that the diachronic and synchronic traditions have been united in the works of such scholars as the Russian-American Roman Jakobson and the Frenchman André Martinet. Second, there has been renewed interest in the building of comprehensive linguistic theories, notably in the works of the Dane Louis Hjelmslev and the American Noam Chomsky. The latter has done us the special service of reuniting modern grammar with the traditional Greco-Roman grammar of past centuries. Finally, perhaps the most striking development in modern linguistics is the extent to which it has been carried over into related fields. We find this in such joint fields of study as psycholinguistics, anthropological linguistics, and mathematical linguistics; in the new interest which philosophers have taken in linguistics and linguists in philosophy; and in the application of the findings of linguistics to such fields as machine translation and foreign-language teaching. Great strides have been taken in the past decades; but, as with so many other fields of study, the more we learn of our subject, the more we realize how little we yet know.

2 PHONOLOGY: PHONEMICS AND ACOUSTIC PHONETICS

Martin Joos

This chapter will treat two topics: the minor one is acoustic phonetics which will be discussed rather briefly at the end. The major topic is phonemics. For the past forty years phonemics has been the characteristically American way of dealing with pronunciation. Today, many people will say that phonemics has been superseded by the newer treatment used in transformational grammar. But phonemics is still the working method of the great majority of American linguists; furthermore, the history of the development of phonemics cannot be disregarded if we are to understand the various things that Americans say and do about language nowadays.

Phonemics is a part of descriptive linguistics, which undertakes to describe a language, no more and no less than that. There are a great many things that can be done about a language, other than just describing it. But American linguists, ever since the early part of the twentieth century, have been in agreement that all those other lines of work are dependent on an adequate description of the language. This may seem obvious, but in fact it is a new idea, only about half a century old.

Descriptive linguistics, then, comes first; and it begins with a question, namely, What is an adequate description of a language? Before the twentieth century interesting things were said, and published, about particular languages; but the question of what constitutes an adequate description had never been discussed, and therefore it is not surprising that every earlier description (except the description of Classical Sanskrit developed in India about two thousand years ago) leaves us in ignorance about some of the most important things to be known about the language in question. Rather than open up a full discussion of the arguments that led to the beginnings of descriptive linguistics in America in the early part of the twentieth century, I shall simply sketch the sort of description that then emerged. First, it contained a description of the pronunciation system of the language, its phonology; second, there was a description of its grammar; third, some samples of text; and fourth, there was a vocabulary, either in the form of notes to the text samples or else assembled into a glossary at the end. The sequence, beginning with the phonology, was not adopted accidentally or for convenience only; rather, the new theory was that everything else depends on the phonology, so that the phonology must be described first.

So far, however, there was no agreed theory or doctrine on the nature of phonology — that is, there was no general theory of phonology. That came only after World War I, and it developed rather gradually, arriving at last at what has been called "phonemics" ever since the 1920s. In the first years of the twentieth century it had been believed that a scientific description of a phonology must discover and record every little phonetic detail, and as far as possible present all the details in the final description. I proceed, then, to discuss these phonetic details, and what is done about them in phonemics. I take my illustrations entirely from English, but since they are illustrations of general principles, nothing new would be added by exotic examples.

The illustrations are found in a couple of very short English sentences. Here is one: *Please try to remember*. Imagine that I have pronounced it in two ways, nearly alike. One is *Please try/to remember*. The slant line indicates a short pause after *try*. If I introduce the pause, the word *to* is pronounced with a noisy puff of air which is technically called aspiration. A second pronunciation of the sentence would be without the pause indicated above. If the pause is absent, no aspiration occurs on *to*. There is still another variation, since *to* may be slurred to [tə]. We now have three ways of pronouncing the sentence —

Please try /[t'ə] *remember*

Here the mark after *t* indicates aspiration.

Please try [tə] *remember*

This form is without pause and without aspiration.

Please try/[tʻʊ]*remember*

This form has aspiration, pause, and a full form of the vowel.

The second sentence, only slightly different from the first, is *Please try and remember*. This can also be spoken in three ways, in which I give the forms with maximum slurring first, and that with full vowel and consonant last —

Please try [ən] *remember*
Please try [ənd] *remember*
Please try [ænd] *remember*

The meaning is practically the same as in the first sentence. Now the problem of linguistic description can be posed in this form: Do we have just one text here, or two texts, or six texts? Starting out from the meaning, we would be unable to prove that there is more than one text; starting out from the sound, we would similarly be unable to prove that there are fewer than six texts; and yet there are several kinds of reasons, too many to discuss here, for believing that we ought to say there are just two texts, each spoken in three ways.

This is a simple illustration of the central problem that faced the linguists who developed phonemics in the 1920s and a little later. At the beginning of the twentieth century, they had an elaborate phonetic alphabet of several hundred symbols — namely, that many letters, together with modifying marks (like the aspiration mark, for example) — with which the performances of my two sentences could be written in a total of six different ways. As long as the purpose was to describe six performances only, such transcriptions were logical. But such transcriptions did not serve to distinguish between substantive differences in grammar and lexicon (*to* and *and*) and insignificant phonetic details. According to the basic principle of descriptive linguistics, the differences in the grammar and the vocabulary are based upon, and remain dependent upon, the phonetic differences; yet it appeared that grammar and vocabulary are somehow different from phonetics. How were they to be separated?

At about this same period in history, the members of the International Phonetic Association were facing the same problem. The solution they adopted is known as "broad transcription." As a result of this approach, the third word in my first sentence came to be written in two ways only, though there were three pronunciations. That is [tə], [tʼə], and [tʼʊ] became [tə] and [tʊ], by omission of aspiration, so that the first two transcriptions became identical. Then it was pointed out that no transcription can tell absolutely everything about the performance anyhow, and that readers who know English will speak the sentences in normal English ways and other persons will make mistakes in any case: for instance, they will fail to interpret aspiration marks or the absence of such marks correctly when reading narrow transcription.

This whole line of argument seemed irrelevant to many linguists, Americans and others alike. What the Americans in particular wanted was not merely a simple or simplified transcription; what they wanted was a logic for whatever transcription they found themselves using. They were not too much concerned to find the best transcription; what they wanted was an understanding of how transcription works in itself, and from this they hoped to derive an understanding of how language works.

Let me try to make this clear by concentrating on the word *to*, spoken [tə] or [tʼə], without aspiration or with aspiration. The method of broad transcription was simply to erase the difference between the two writings and then point out that the text was not spoiled by doing so. What those Americans finally did was something quite different: they established a third writing /tə/, which equally well represents both [tə] and [tʼə] and is called a phonemic writing; and afterward — several years later, in fact — they invented ways of making sure which of the two performances would correspond to the single writing in particular circumstances. This is a summary statement of what they did, but it deserves a somewhat fuller statement.

The leaders who began this development most conspicuously were Edward Sapir and Leonard Bloomfield. Both had learned not only from the earlier descriptive linguists, especially Franz Boas and the other describers of American Indian languages at the beginning of the twentieth century, and from the nineteenth-century historical linguists and dialectologists of Europe, but also from the book published in 1916 by pupils of the European Ferdinand de Saussure, a synthesis of his university lectures on language, under the title *Cours de linguistique générale*. What they took from Saussure was the idea that phonetic details are meaningless apart from the system in which the details are located; or, to put it the other way around, that each language has its own coherent systems, including a phonological system, and that the phonetic details have to be interpreted from that system as a whole. Then each detail gets its significance from the fact that it is systematically different from each other detail; and it turns out that the system consists of the significant differences among the details, or in other words the system does not consist of the details themselves but instead consists of the differences among them.

This was a radically new idea compared to the earlier treatments of phonetics, for now the phonetic alphabets were shown up as mere lists, and as lists they had no system, no structure. There was also another point of American doctrine which most people took for granted — namely, that each language has its own phonological system, its own structure, different from the phonological structure of each other language, so that an international phonetic alphabet could not by itself reveal the phonology of any single language. Accordingly, there would always have to be a systematic statement of how to interpret the phonological transcriptions, or, in other words, a statement of the correspondences between the phonological writing and the actual speech performances. Let me illustrate this from our two sample sentences, starting out from phonetic details that make little or no trouble and then moving on into more difficult details. We begin by noticing some system, some pattern, which is already clear without the help of phonemic theory, and then we go on to other things for which phonemic theory is urgently needed.

Please begins with a phoneme, /p/, spoken with aspiration as [pʿ]. *Remember* contains the phoneme /b/ [b] and two examples of the phoneme /m/ [m]. These three phonemes are alike to this extent:

22

each of them requires the two lips to touch, and no other English phoneme has that feature. These, then, are the three "bilabial" phonemes of English.

The word *to* begins with the phoneme /t/ [t] or [tʿ]; the word *and* may — or may not — end with the phoneme /d/ [d], and it always contains the phoneme /n/ [n]. This, then, is another list of three phonemes, not bilabial but instead requiring the tongue-tip to touch; they are called "apical." Finally, when listed in the sequence /t, d, n/ they are parallel to the first sequence, the three bilabial phonemes /p, b, m/. In each sequence, the first phoneme listed is a "fortis" stop, so called because whenever it follows another sound it cuts it off abruptly, and when (as in these sentences) it is followed by a vowel it explodes abruptly, strongly. The second one in each list is a "lenis" stop because it only gently and softly cuts off a preceding sound or softly and gently explodes into a following one. (There is a tradition which calls the fortis stops "voiceless" and the lenis ones "voiced," but that tradition derives from French phonetics and is irrelevant to English; in English, fortis stops can be voiced, and lenis sounds are only faintly voiced and often voiceless.)[1] The third members of the lists, /m/ and /n/, are nasals.

Now when the two lists are written one under the other, for instance with /t/ under /p/ and /n/ under /m/, we can see that the six phonemes form a system having three dimensions: (1) bilabial in contrast to apical, (2) fortis in contrast to lenis, and (3) nasals in contrast to stops. This system is only part of the complete system of English phonemes, which has more than two dozen members (instead of six) and more than half a dozen dimensions (instead of three). But it will not be necessary to go any further along this line; it is enough if we understand what is meant by "system," or "structure," and what is meant by "dimensions" in the phonemic system.

Still, we have not taken care of all the varieties of phonetic detail. In particular, there is the fact that the single phoneme /t/ has at least the two varieties unaspirated [t] and aspirated [tʿ]; and remark that the other fortis stops of English, /p/ and /k/, also have un-

---

[1]Other authors in this book follow the traditional voiced–voiceless terminology. [Ed.]

aspirated and aspirated varieties, [p, pʻ; k, kʻ]. Logically, there are two possibilities here: Either these are separate phonemes, making six phonemes instead of the three fortis-stop phonemes which we say that English has (and if we were speaking about Chinese that would be a good answer, for a Chinese aspirated stop has no unaspirated varieties); or else the difference between unaspirated and aspirated stops in English is not the sort of difference we have been calling a "dimension" of the English phonological system. At this point in the historical development, Edward Sapir and Leonard Bloomfield halted, leaving the problem unsolved while they turned to grammar and the rest.

The solution which has been most generally adopted by American linguists, the solution which is most characteristic of American descriptive linguistics, was worked out in the 1930s by George L. Trager, Bernard Bloch, and Charles F. Hockett, of course in discussions with many other linguists. In this solution, we recognize another kind of phonological element, a "juncture," originally called "internal open juncture," written $/+/$. The $/+/$ juncture is not a sound; it is rather a kind of incident in the flow of successive sounds. In English and certain other languages, nearly every word is said to be preceded by this $/+/$ juncture; but certain kinds of words may lack $/+/$, and certain other words have $/+/$ somewhere inside the word, notably those called "compounds," for instance the word *afternoon*, whose two parts are separated by $/+/$ just as the words of the phrase *after noon* are separated.

The $/+/$ is not a sound, but it variously affects the pronunciation, the performance, of neighboring sounds. For example, English fortis stops are aspirated after a $/+/$ juncture. Now consider the sentence *Please try to remember*, spoken without pauses between the words and with a pause. We can now describe these two spoken versions, one with unaspirated [t] and the other with aspirated [tʻ], by saying that the word *to* belongs to a small class of English words which basically begin with $/+/$ but lose their $/+/$ when not stressed (not "accented") immediately after a verb or a preposition. The result is that "Please try [tə] remember" has no $/+/$ between the second and the third word, while "Please try [tʻə] remember" does have: "Please+try to+remember" and "Please+try+to+remember"; and this is what accounts for the unaspirated and aspirated varieties of /t/. This is an economical solution because it eliminates three hypothetical phonemes /p', t', k'/ at the cost of recognizing one new phonemic unit /+/ which is not a sound but a juncture. It is an illuminating solution because it agrees with our intuitive feeling that we are distinguishing between different ways of speaking the same text instead of distinguishing different texts.

Still, it might be argued that the one phonemic unit /+/, because it is without precedent in tradition or for some other reason, is too big a price to pay for eliminating three aspirated stops as separate phonemes of a familiar kind. Then the answer is that the same /+/ will serve equally well to account for several other details of performance that previously had no explanation worth considering seriously. I will mention only two.

One is the notorious fact that in English, and in several other languages which have aspirated and unaspirated varieties of fortis stops, words beginning with /sp, st, sk/, such as *spin*, *stock*, and *skin*, have only the unaspirated varieties, although the aspirated ones are usual before stressed vowels. In the nineteenth and early twentieth centuries, it was customary to say that in those languages the fortis stops /p, t, k/ are basically aspirated, but unaspirated after /s/, and then to suggest that there must be something about the articulation of [s] that inhibits the aspiration. Today we can say that English /p, t, k/ are aspirated after /+/, and that in *spin*, *stock*, *skin*, and the like they remain unaspirated because there is no /+/ before them and thus no occasion for aspiration; instead, they are preceded by something which is not /+/ and just happens to be /s/ — not that it matters.

Another example of what /+/ is good for comes from British English (and is paralleled by the English of our northeastern coast). In such English, the word *remember* when spoken either in *Please try to remember* or *Please try and remember* does not end with any /r/ phoneme. But if another word beginning with a vowel is added *and* is spoken without the least hesitation, as for instance in *Please try to remember it* or *Please try and remember it*, the /r/, the same /r/ that is always there in *remembering*, reappears. If we recognize /+/, the explanation is easy. In such English, /r/ can be spoken only when a vowel immediately follows it, not otherwise; without a following vowel, /r/ is unpronounceable and drops out. Then we observe that British (and northeastern coastal American) English drops out its /+/ much oftener than other English, so that the two words *remember it* are not separated by /+/ and the /r/ is followed by the vowel of *it* without a break. The confirmation of this explanation is found in sentences spoken slowly or hesitantly, in which words are regularly separated by /+/ in all English; in that style of speech, British English has "Please+try+and+remembe(r)+it" and no /r/ is spoken before *it*.

This leads us naturally to a point of quite general interest. As often, a very slight sophistication of phonological theory has made possible a simple and clear discussion of a number of things which, before the development of phonemic theory, could be recorded phonetically but remained without any effective discussion at all. So far, this point has been illustrated only with the /+/. But the same people who introduced the /+/ into American phonemic theory have done still more. They have provided a simple discussion, and a clear way of transcribing, speech melodies — what are called "intonations" in American terminology; and they have shown the utility of recognizing exactly four degrees of "stress" — the technical linguistic equivalent of significant degrees of loudness — in English and certain other languages. They have also been able to correlate these four stresses with the choice of vowels. For instance, they have shown that *to*, when pronounced with any stress except the weakest, has the vowel /u/ as in *two new shoes*. The vowel /u/ never occurs under weak stress unless it is followed by another vowel. As a result *to* under weak stress has the vowel /ə/, that of American *cut up some* — /ə/ is a vowel associated frequently with weak stress. If we return to *Please try to/remember* and pronounce it at various speeds, we find /tə/ in the most fluent pronunciation, and /tu/ in the more deliberate pronunciations, where *to* gets one of the stresses stronger than weak.

At this point in this illustration we begin to see a relation between phonology and grammar; and it is in dealing with such a relation that American phonemics faces its most difficult task. The historical result has been that in very recent years there has been a split into at least two schools of thought. The continuers of the tradition have undertaken to meet the problem by recognizing a systematic relation between phonology and grammar; paradoxically, they begin by regarding the two as essentially separate, independent of each other; therefore the relation between the two has to be recognized and separately discussed; and this relation receives the separate name of "morphophonemics." The innovators, led by Noam Chomsky, deny that there is any essential separation anywhere within the structure of a language, and under the name of "transformational grammar" they undertake to take care of everything from semantics to phonetics by a uniform treatment. See Chapter 24.

ACOUSTIC PHONETICS

Leonard Bloomfield, in his 1933 book *Language*, said that all the phonetic varieties of one phoneme have the same constant phonetic feature, even though this constant feature may be only a small part of all the phonetic features of the phoneme in any single performance, and that this constant phonetic feature is what causes the native speaker to hear all the varieties as the same phoneme no matter how different they may sound. So far, this was only a speculation, though an obvious and attractive one. But Bloomfield went beyond the speculation; he said that the constant phonetic feature could be expected to emerge from phonetics laboratory work in ten years or so, once engineers had developed suitable instruments. What actually happened within ten years was not at all what Bloomfield expected, but it was interesting enough in its way.

Early in World War II, Bell Telephone Laboratories had perfected the sound spectrograph, the instrument which ought to find Bloomfield's constant phonetic fraction — if it really exists. The instrument makes a recording on a special paper, a record which has roughly the same dimensions as printed music; its markings represent intensities of sound at all the instants of time and all the levels of frequency. These recordings, called "spectrograms," are far more illuminating to a phonetician than earlier types of machine recordings, such as the smoked-drum records called kymograms or

27

the types of recordings of air waves translated into electrical impulses, called oscillograms; indeed, it can be demonstrated mathematically that if Bloomfield's constant phonetic feature exists it must be readable from a spectrogram. But, it has never yet been read in a spectrogram; and we are forced to conclude, at least tentatively, that Bloomfield was wrong.

Because of a combination of historical accidents, I was myself the first linguist (though there were phoneticians) to have a chance to use the sound spectrograph, and in fact used it more than two years before any other linguist did — so that the possibilities of using the spectrograph for learning more about phonemics were at first open only to me. I have not departed, even today, from the position I took in my 1948 monograph *Acoustic Phonetics*:[2] the sound spectrograph can teach us a great deal about phonetics but nothing at all about phonemics — at least not in Bloomfield's sense of the term. To this general statement I must add two remarks.

First, phonemics has always been based upon the best phonetic evidence available at the time; and now that the sound spectrograph has improved our understanding of phonetics, we can set up better arguments than ever before to cover the central problem of phonemics, the problem of the relation between phonemic structure and phonetic performance. Further, without the spectrograph evidence, we are frequently forced to recognize two or more phonemic hypotheses as equally plausible, or very nearly equally; with the new evidence, we can quite usually dismiss all but one of our phonemic hypotheses, all equally good from Bloomfield's point of view. We even find that Bloomfield's own choice among hypotheses is often, though not always, confirmed; for example, we can see from the spectrograms that he was right in regarding the "vowel" of stressed or deliberate *to* (as in "Please try [t'u] remember") as compounded of a vowel and a semivowel, so that he was right in transcribing it with two symbols: [uw] in his writing, /uw/ in ours.

Second, we find that what the spectrograms confirm consists mostly of what was added to Bloomfield's phonemics by later workers. Of these additions, I have especially discussed the /+/,

[2]Martin Joos, "Acoustic Phonetics," *Language*, XXIV, No. 2, Monograph No. 23 (1948), 136.

the stresses, and the intonations. Now the intonations are easily read off from spectrograms, though the performance turns out to be much more ambiguous than its phonemic analysis. The stresses are impossible to read off from spectrograms, so that we are forced into auxiliary speculations to account for English stress. And, contrary to all earlier expectations, the /+/, which Bloomfield did not recognize, has turned out to be the one phonemic feature which is more consistently readable from spectrograms than any other.

For more than a decade after /+/ was first recognized and employed in phonemic discussions, its phonetic status was problematical — to say the least. Its presence was manifest in recognizable phonetic phenomena only in quite heterogeneous ways.

It was therefore quite a surprise when a group of linguists, of whom I was one, in 1953 found a constant feature in the English /+/: It adds a practically constant small amount of duration to the neighboring phonemes; it adds quite precisely one-fortieth of a second of time to them (to all of them together). But, and this is the strange thing about it, one-fortieth of a second of extra time cannot be perceived as such — the human sense of time is not delicate enough for that — so that its constant feature cannot be separately perceived and is accordingly not a "phonetic" feature.

3 MORPHOLOGY AND SYNTAX

Carleton T. Hodge

Each language is unique not only in its inventory of sounds but also in the manner in which it employs them in meaningful combinations. The study of these combinations has been traditionally divided into morphology, which is the description of the meaningful forms, and syntax, which is the ordering of the sentence elements. While it is generally recognized that drawing a sharp line between these two aspects of language study is difficult, it is convenient to do so here.

Both morphology and syntax follow the same basic principle of analysis, that of substitution. In order to identify elements and separate them for analysis, the analyst seeks to find utterances which differ in only one respect. If one takes the sentences *I saw the shoreline* and *I saw the lifeline*, they are seen to differ by having *shore* in one and *life* in the other. The meaning is also quite different, and we conclude that *shore* and *life* are different and meaningful pieces of the language. If we compare *I saw the book*, *I saw the books*, and *I saw the booklet*, we conclude that the *-s* of *books* and the *-let* of *booklet* are separate meaningful elements, but we also note that *book* may occur without either of them.

In the same way we may abstract other kinds of structural elements, such as stress and intonation. In *I saw a blackbird*, the person speaking refers to a particular kind of bird. In *I saw a black bird*, the speaker indicates only that the bird was black. It may have been a blackbird but might just as easily have been a crow or a raven. In such a case we can abstract the stress pattern as a meaningful element. This same contrast of patterns occurs in, for example, *the*

White House (where the President of the United States lives) and *the white house* (which indicates a particular house of that color).

On the basis of such substitution we establish forms, or morphs — the smallest meaningful pieces into which we may divide the utterance. These morphs may be roots, such as *book, black, bird, house*; affixes, such as *-s* and *-let*; stress patterns, such as that in *blackbird* which contrasts with that of *black bird*.

Let us now consider a series of verb forms: *I stop, he stops, I stopped, I'm stopping*; and *I slip, he slips, I slipped, I'm slipping*. Disregarding the stress, we have the forms (or morphs) *I, he, stop, slip, -s, -t, -m*, and *-ing*. If we substitute *kick* for *stop*, we get exactly the same forms combining with the new verb: *I kick, he kicks, I kicked*, and so on. If, however, we substitute *describe*, we find some variation: *I describe, he describes, I described, I'm describing*. The phrases *I describe* and *I'm describing* parallel *I stop* and *I'm stopping*, but where *he stops* has *-s, he describes* has *-z*; and where *I stopped* has *-t, I described* has *-d*. (We are, of course, discussing the pronunciation, not the spelling, of these words.) It is easy to find other verbs which have the *-z* and *-d* endings, such as *he squeals, I squealed, he lives, I lived*. By continuing the substitution procedure we find a third form for both the *-s* of *stops* and the *-t* of *stopped*. In *I advise, he advises* there is an *-əz*, different from either *-s* or *-z*. In *I vote, he votes, I voted* there is an *-əd*, also different from its two parallel forms.

It should be kept in mind that in these substitutions the meaning of the respective suffixes has stayed the same, despite the change in form; *-t, -d*, and *-əd* all signify past tense.

If we continue our substitutions and gather as many examples as we can of verbs which have *-s*, those which have *-z*, those which have *-əz*, we are soon able to see that these differences are not haphazard. The *-əz* occurs after sounds that are sibilant, such as *s, z, š, ž, č*, and *dž*: *hiss hisses, rise rises, wash washes, rouge rouges, hitch hitches, judge judges*. The *-z* variety occurs after other voiced consonants, such as *b, d, g, l, m, n*: *robs, rides, hugs, feels, seems, runs*; and the *-s* variety, after other voiceless ones, such as *p, t, k*: *hops, rots, licks*. The past-tense suffix is likewise predictable. The *-əd* occurs after *t* or *d*, as in *rotted, minded*; the *-d* after other voiced sounds, as in *robbed, hugged*; and the *-t* after other voiceless consonants, as in *hopped, kicked*.

The pattern would be a very neat one if these were the only forms we had with these meanings. There are, however, a number of verbs to which these generalizations do not apply. Few verbs diverge in the present tense, though there are some in which the *-s* does not occur in any of its forms (as in *I can, he can*). The past, however, shows a great deal of unpredictable variety. Compare *I sing, I sang; I choose, I chose; I go, I went*. For *sing sang, choose chose*, the difference is not the addition of a suffix, as in *stop stopped*, but the replacement of one vowel nucleus by another: *-i* by *a*, *oo* by *o*. In *go went* we have a normal suffix *-t* for the past (though it occurs after a voiced consonant), but there is total replacement of *go* by *wen-*. All of these morphs — *-t*, *-d*, *-əd*, replacement of *i* by *a*, of *oo* by *o*, and of *go* by *wen-* (plus *-t*) — have the same function, the indication of the past tense.[1] We call each such morph an "allomorph," and all of them together are a morpheme. The identification task of morphology is, therefore, to discover the morphemes and to give their allomorphs, listing the conditions under which each occurs. These allomorphs may have shapes which are predictable from the sounds of adjacent morphs, or the shapes may be completely arbitrary.

Languages vary greatly in the regularity of their morphologic structure. Some, including English and the Indo-European languages generally, show a great deal of the type of complication illustrated by the past-tense suffix. Others are highly regular. Turkish, for example, has a considerable amount of allomorphic variation, but by far the greater part is predictable. The past-tense suffix has eight different shapes, but which will occur depends on the preceding syllable. These shapes, allomorphs, are *-ti, tü-, -tĭ, -tu, -di, -dü, -dĭ*, and *-du*. The allomorphs in *-t* follow a voiceless consonant; the root *kes-* ("cut") has a past-tense form *kesti* ("he cut"). The allomorphs in *-d* follow a vowel or a voiced consonant, the root *alma-* ("buy") having the past-tense form *almadĭ* ("he bought"). Which of the four vowels occurs depends on the vowel of the preceding syllable. After *e* or *i* the vowel is *i*, after *a* or *ĭ* the vowel is *ĭ*, and so forth. Such determination of the vowels is known as "vowel harmony."

Turkish is a good example of a language in which the morphology

---

[1]An alternate analysis of *went*: the final *-t* indicates past tense, and *go* is automatically changed to *wen-* before this suffix. [Ed.]

consists almost entirely of the addition of suffixes to the root. As a more lengthy and quite typical example we may take the word *besliyémiyecektin*, meaning "you were not about to be able to feed" in the sentence *If you were not going to be able to feed me, why did you marry me*? The morphs making up this word are *besli-* ("feed"; the root), *-yé-* ("able to"), *-mi-* (negative), *-yecek-* ("about to"), *-ti* (past tense suffix), *-n* ("you"; singular): *besliyémiyecektin*, "you (singular) were not about to be able to feed."

One category of morpheme in Turkish is the root. This includes morphemes designating objects such as *house, horse, man, book,* and morphemes designating concepts, such as *go, come, cut, write, see.* The roots designating objects may take such suffixes as *my, your, his*; those designating concepts may take suffixes indicating aspect or tense, such as those for continuous action or for completed action. The first class of roots are "nouns," the second "verbs."

An example of a noun root is *göz* ("eye"). Suffixes may occur with it, as in *gözüm* ("my eye"), *gözün* ("your eye"). An example of a verb root is *yaz* ("write"), which may take suffixes peculiar to verbs, as in *yazdí* ("he wrote"), *yázmadí* ("he didn't write"). The noun root *göz* does not take the suffix *-dü* for past tense, nor may *yaz* be followed directly by *-im* ("my"). However, the root *göz* may take a suffix *-le*, and the resulting form, *gözle-* ("look for"), may take the past-tense suffix *gözledi* ("he looked for" or "he expected"). In other words, *göz* is a noun base, *gözle-* is a verb base. There is also the reverse process: the verb root *yaz* may take a suffix *-ar*, and the resulting form is a noun base, *yazar* ("writer"). At this point it is more convenient to use another set of terms, "verb base" and "noun base." A verb base is that form which may take verb suffixes. It may be a simple verb root, such as *yaz-*, or a noun plus verbalizing suffix, such as *gözle-* . A noun base may be a simple noun root, such as *göz*, or a verb root plus nominalizing suffix, as *yazar*.

These examples also illustrate another distinction often made in morphology, that between "derivation" and "inflection." The combining of morphemes to form a base, as *yaz-* plus *-ar* forms *yazar*, is known as derivation. The adding of endings, such as for *my*, *his*, the past tense, as in *gözle-* plus *-di* to form *gözledi*, is known as inflection. In English an analysis of such a word as *unsuitability* would show successive derivational additions; the addition of the endings discussed above, *-s, -z, -əz, -t, -d, -əd*, is inflection.

A great variety of morpheme types is found among the languages of the world. We have mentioned English, which has, among other things, prefixes, suffixes, and internal change. Turkish has mostly suffixes. Swahili, a Bantu language, has mostly prefixes. In Swahili *kitu* means "this" or "this thing." The plural is *vitu*, "these." *Kitabu* is "book" and *vitabu* "books." So we are not surprised to find that the word for "traffic circle," which is *kiplefti* (from English *keep left*), has the plural *viplefti*.

Still other languages rely heavily on internal change or on adding morphemes in the middle of others. In Tagalog, a major language of the Philippines, the word *pí:lit* means "effort." A morpheme *-um-*, meaning "one who did (such-and-such)" may be added within *pí:lit*, making *pumí:lit*, "one who made an effort or compelled." *Sú:lat* is "writing," *sumú:lat* "one who wrote." A morpheme inserted in this way is known as an "infix."

In Arabic, Hebrew, and certain others of the Afro-Asiatic language family, most roots consist of two or three consonants. To these are added vowel patterns and other affixes. For example, the root *k t b* in Arabic signifies "write." It does not occur as a word in its bare root form but is always combined with some vowel pattern and often has in addition a prefix, a suffix, or both. The combination *katab* means "he wrote," *maktuub* is "that which is written" or "a letter," *kitaab* is "book" (the source, by the way, of Swahili *kitabu*, *maktab* "the place where writing is done" it may also be "a school," "an office," or "a desk"), *kaatib*, "the one who writes," that is, "scribe" or "secretary," and so on through many other changes.

In many languages tone plays a morphological role. In Hausa, where tone differences are not a major part of the lexicon, there are nevertheless such contrasts as *yaatàfi*, "he went," and *yaàtàfi*, "he will (probably) go." The first form has the syllable *yaa-* where it is long with high-level tone; the form with *yaà-* shows the syllable with length, and high followed by low tone. There are other possibilities for the same basic syllable. In *wurin dà yatàfi*, "the place where he went," *ya-* occurs with short vowel and high tone. This last example is called a relative form — that is, the equivalent of an English clause with a *wh-* form. Note however, that the relativization falls on a different place than it does in English. The form which means "have him go" is *yàtàfi*, where *yà-* has a short vowel and low tone. Thus tone, together with vowel length, is used to indicate such verbal categories as "completed action," "relative completed action," "indefinite future," "optative mood," and "indefinite future."

Tone as an inherent part of the morpheme occurs in many Asian, African, and American Indian languages. We may draw an illustration from Burmese. Burmese *ca* with low-level tone is "water lily," but *ca* with high-falling tone is "tiger." Words are distinguished just as much by the tones as by the vowels and consonants used.

Morphemes may be classified according to their shape, according to the other morphemes with which they combine, and according to the way these combinations are made. In most languages the possibilities for combination and the order in which the morphemes combine into words are quite restricted. In English, for example, the morphemes composing a word such as *unsuitability* cannot recombine in any other order.

Morphology is, as we have seen, concerned with discovering, by the technique of substitution, the smallest meaningful parts of a sentence or utterance. It is also possible, using this same technique, to discover the structure of larger segments of the language. What are the over-all patterns of the sentence, or the paragraph, or of an entire discourse? These are the questions which the study of syntax endeavors to answer.

Only a limited amount of work has been done on the analysis of paragraphs and discourse as a whole. Enough has been done to make it very clear that there are over-all patterns involved and that discourse may be classified on the basis of these patterns. For example, in the study of Kaiwa, an Indian language of Brazil, three main categories were discovered: indoctrination discourse, instruction discourse, and conversation discourse. Each of these has its own internal structure.

Most syntactic study has been limited to the analysis of sentences. There are what may be called basic sentence types, and more complicated sentences are, in a sense, variations of these. For example, the two English sentences *He's sick* and *He bought a book* are of two different types. The first is a kind of equation: *He is sick*. The second has the elements subject, action, and goal: *he, bought, a book*. If one takes a longer sentence such as *The short man with dark glasses found a newspaper*, it is readily seen to be of the same type as *He bought a book*; *the short man with dark glasses* is the subject, *found* is the action, and *a newspaper* the goal. The sentence *A lady whom I met in the library last night borrowed my car*, though longer, contains exactly the same three elements. Syntax is concerned with the discovery of basic sentence types and with the description of the possible substitutions for each element of the basic types. The order of elements is fixed to a greater or lesser degree, and there are many restrictions on the combinations which may occur. For example, observation of English sentence patterns will uncover many in which a relative clause follows a noun: *the lady whom I saw, the man who bought the car, the small boy who came to the door*. It would be highly unusual to find *the whom I saw lady, the who bought the car man*, or anything of this sort. The English order has the relative clause following the noun. Japanese, on the other hand, regularly has such a modifier before the noun, as in *ano kado ni tatte iru zyunsa* — "the on that corner standing policeman." Order is, then, something which has limitations.

A familiar line from English literature illustrates both certain limitations of the language and its great freedom in possible word order. The line from Gray's "Elegy Written in a Country Churchyard":

> The plowman homeward plods his weary way

may be recombined in nearly every order without change of basic meaning:

> The weary plowman plods his way homeward.
> His weary way plods the plowman homeward.
> Homeward the weary plowman plods his way.
> Plods the plowman his weary way homeward.

One cannot, however, place *the* anywhere except before *plowman*, or *his* anywhere except before *way*.

On the other hand, limitations on the choice of words that may be used are much harder to determine, being largely a matter of meaning. It is also true that what one person finds normal in a given language, another simply would not say. For example, the sentence *The bracelet stolen was returned* might be considered perfectly normal by one speaker but not by another.

In discussing morphology and syntax I have been discussing primarily how one goes about analyzing a language. By making substitutions on both levels, we can isolate morphs, group them into morphemes, and determine which morphemes are alike, either in form or in distribution. We can also determine which words, phrases, and clauses are to be grouped together as similar in form or distribution. Given such facts, linguists differ considerably in the way in which they wish to present them. Some approaches currently being tested may be briefly mentioned.

The approach perhaps least fashionable at present was vigorous fifteen years ago. This was the neo-Bloomfieldian or structural one, which tried to build identification of syntactic entities on their sound, that is, the vowels, consonants, pitches, and stresses used. The attempt was never either as narrowly mechanical as its enemies claimed, nor as successful as its practitioners hoped. But at least it is still true that sentences like *I saw Pa Price* and *I saw Pop Rice* are distinguishable by sound, as *I sâw him búy it*, and *I sáw him bŷ it* are distinguishable by stress. Phonologically based analysis often did a service to the science by pointing out differences of this sort, which had been previously slighted.

Another approach considers the relationships of the forms as describable in terms of units of behavior, or "tagmemes." A tagmeme, for example, may be the subject (or actor) function. This function may be the grammatical subject in one instance, a form with a special "actor" affix or construction in another. For example, the actor is John in both *John ate the apple* and *The apple was eaten by John*. The function "actor" is differently treated by different languages, but one expects to find it somehow expressed. This is not true of many tagmemes. The aim of the tagmemicist is to have a set of tagmemes sufficient to serve the usages of all languages, but any one language merely makes a selection from the group as a whole.

37

A third approach, that of transformational-generative grammar, has laid emphasis on two features of language largely left untreated by earlier descriptive linguists. The first of these is the relationship of one linguistic pattern to another. How is a sentence with an active verb related to one with a passive verb? What, further, is the relationship between *the bad man* and *the man is bad*? The second feature is the construction, the putting together, of the sentence. How does one proceed, not to describe a sentence, but to make one? The purpose of this approach is to write a set of rules — called a "grammar" — which will produce grammatically correct sentences. One may compare the result to a huge vertical maze having two compartments, one above the other. The entrance at the top is labeled "sentence." Beyond the entrance the path divides and subdivides into a number of paths; the choice between them determines the kind of sentence one gets. The morpheme used must be selected to fit properly into this structure. After passing through the first compartment, they enter the second, where they are put into proper order and given their proper shape.

Visualizing such a machine as it might be constructed for English: The sentence path would divide into two, both of which must be taken — a noun-phrase path and a verb-phrase path. As one descends the maze for the noun phrase, he finds he eventually ends up in a path for one of the varieties of form the noun phrase takes (pronoun, proper noun, common noun, article plus common noun). Rules are written so that the morphemes introduced into the maze are screened for fitness to a given path and also for mutual compatibility. One might imagine these morphemes to be blocks of different sizes, multifaced, each face having on it an allomorph. The morphemes assembled to make the sentence are screened by the machine, which allows only a certain size of morpheme to slip into a particular path. There may be thousands of that shape, or only a few. Once the morphemes are chosen and each is in his proper path, they are ready for the second compartment of the maze. Here they are shuffled and given their final order and phonetic shape. Suppose we have as morphemes *the man plural past go away*. The second compartment has a sorter which combines the *man* and *plural* blocks, discarding *plural* and turning the *man* block around so that *men* shows on the face. *Past* and *go* are similarly treated, except that here *past* flips to a side showing *t* and *go* to one showing *wen*. They exchange places, forming *went*, and all the blocks drop to the bottom of the maze, showing *The men went away*.

This is a vastly oversimplified view, as, among other things, the determination of the subclasses of morphemes is a highly complex matter. The idea of a sentence generator has, however, caught the imagination of many scholars the world over.

Syntax was for long an almost neglected area of linguistic study in America because of the reliance on meaning in setting up syntactic categories. Meaning, it was felt, was an insufficiently precise tool. No approach has succeeded entirely in overcoming this difficulty, but each endeavors to control its use of meaning so that the results will be verifiable. The current lively work in syntax, whether from a structural, a tagmemic, or a generative point of view, holds some hope for escaping from the dangers of working with meaning. All approaches share a view of linguistic signals which separates referential meaning (that which can be recognized by pointing to objects or actions, designated by such words as *table* and *speak*) from identity, which can be determined in large measure by what linguistic situations a form can occur in. Since all schools of analysis are now actively working in syntax, the dichotomy between referential meaning and linguistic identity would seem to be useful, and we can now hope for advances in syntax comparable to the advances of the first half of the century in phonology.

4 LEXICOLOGY AND SEMANTICS

Sydney M. Lamb

The area of linguistic structure which is studied under the headings of lexicology and semantics, if I describe it very simply, is concerned with words and their meanings. Some of the phenomena which must be accounted for in this area are these: (1) a word can have more than one meaning. An example is the English word *table*, which can designate either a piece of furniture or a type of display of information on the page of a book. (2) Different words can have the same meaning, for example *big* and *large*. (3) The meanings of some words can be analyzed into components. For example, the English word *mare* can be analyzed into the components *female* and *horse*; similarly, *doe* has the components *female* and *deer*, and *hen* has the components *female* and *chicken*. (4) Certain combinations of words have meanings which are different from the combinations of their separate meanings. An example is *blow up*, meaning "destroy by explosion," as in *the bomb blew up the building*. (5) Some pairs of words have opposite meanings. An example is the pair *big* and *little*. (6) The meanings of some words are included in the meanings of others. For example, the meaning of *plant* is included in that of *tree*, and the meaning of *tree* is included in that of *oak*.

If we attempt to describe these various phenomena more closely, we soon find that the concept "word" is too vague. Consider this question: Is *table* a word? People would generally agree that it is. Now let us consider another question: Is *tables* (the plural of *table*) a word? If so, is it a different word from *table*? Many people would say that *table* and *tables* are two different forms of the same word. But some linguists have defined "word" as a minimal unit that can be said in isolation; that is, a unit that can be said in isolation and that does not consist of parts that can be said in isolation. According to this definition, *tables* is a word, since the plural suffix *-s* cannot be said in isolation; and it is thus a different word from *table*. Consider also another question: Since *table* has two quite different meanings, as in *a book on the table* and *a table in the book*, are these two words — *table 1* and *table 2* — or just one?

It would be a mistake to suppose that the way out of this difficulty is to determine what a word really is, to decide which of several conflicting definitions is the correct one. For in fact each of these different units is important in linguistic structure, and each deserves to be recognized. Let us therefore distinguish the *morphological word*, the *lexical word*, and the *semantic word*. Then we may answer our questions easily. *Table* and *tables* are two different morphological words but they are two forms of the same lexical word. *Table 1*, as in *the book on the table*, and *table 2*, as in *the table in the book*, are two different semantic words corresponding to a single lexical word. The morphological words of a language are specified by its morphological constructions. They are the units which linguists are attempting to specify as the smallest units that can be said in isolation. The lexical word is the basic unit of the lexicon, or dictionary, of a language, and it is also the basic unit of the syntax, the unit whose combinations are specified by syntactic structure. Some lexical words are morphologically simple, such as *sing*, *red*, *table*, while others have an internal morphological structure, for example *woodpecker*, *on account of*, *concerning*, and *computer*. Many linguists have supposed that the morphological word, rather than the lexical word, should be taken as the basis of syntax, but this is a mistake which has led to a great deal of confusion. The term *lexeme*, introduced by Benjamin Lee Whorf in 1938, has often been used for the lexical word, and I shall use it here. Similarly, for the semantic word we may use the term *sememe*, first used in 1908 by the Swedish linguist Adolf Noreen and introduced into American linguistics by Leonard Bloomfield in 1926. As a rough approximation, one may think of a sememe as an element of meaning.

Now let us take a closer look at the types of structural patterning I enumerated as some phenomena to be accounted for. My first observation was that a word can have more than one meaning. Now, speaking more accurately, we can say that a lexeme may be connected to more than one sememe; the lexeme *table* is an example. This relationship is often referred to by the term *polysemy*, which means "multiple meaning."

My second observation was that different words can have the same meaning, for example *big* and *large*, as in *a big house* and *a large house*. In the more exact terminology we would say that different lexemes may be connected to a single sememic unit. This relationship is generally called *synonymy*.

For many years in the recent history of American linguistics, there was a reluctance to recognize the relationship of synonymy, since it was argued that there was no such thing. The common argument asserted that instances do not exist in any language of lexical items which are identical in their meanings and functions. One could argue that *big* and *large* are not truly synonymous, since *he is a big man in this town* does not mean the same as the slightly improbable *he is a large man in this town*, and *she is my big sister* does not mean the same as *she is my large sister*. This conflict of opinions has a very simple resolution. The argument against synonyms is concerned with the notion of absolute or complete synonymy. Absolute synonyms would be lexemes sharing all of the same syntactic functions as well as all of the same connections to the sememic level. It happens to be quite correct that such units do not exist, but this argument does not destroy the concept of synonymy at all, since that concept does not require absolute synonymy. In other words, synonymy is always partial, never complete. The lexemes *big* and *large* are synonymous because they both connect to a single sememe; let us call it *big 1*. But they are not absolutely synonymous, since the lexeme *big* also connects to a sememe, *big 2*, which is not connected to *large* but to *important*, as in *he is a big man in this town* or *he is an important man in this town*.

A linguistic structure is a system with two ends: meaning is at one end and speech or writing is at the other. The linguistic structure is what connects meanings to speech and writing. We may visualize the system as having meaning at the top and speech or writing at the bottom. The sememes of a language are near the top, and the lexemes are below them; still lower are the morphemes. In polysemy there are two sememic units connected to the same lexeme, that is, two units at the higher level connected to one unit at the lower level; while in synonymy there are two units at the lower level connected to the one unit at the higher level.

My third observation was that the meanings of some words can be analyzed into components. More precisely, we may say that some lexemes connect to combinations of sememes. The lexeme *mare* is connected to two sememes, which we may label *horse* and *female*.

But we have also noted that the lexeme *table* is connected to two sememes. Yet these two relationships are quite different. A table is *either* a piece of furniture *or* a display of information; but a mare is *both* a female *and* a horse. An example which exhibits both of these relationships is the lexeme *father*, which can designate a male parent or a priest in the Roman Catholic Church, not to mention still further possibilities; this is an "either-or" relationship, an instance of polysemy. But *father* in its function as designator of male parent connects to two sememes, *male* and *parent*, in a "both-and" relationship — that is, a father is both a male and a parent.

In short, the lexeme *father* connects, in an either-or relationship, to two units, one of which connects, in a both-and relationship, to two sememes. We have thus identified an intermediate unit between the lexeme and the sememe. Let us call it a *sememic sign*. Then we may say that the lexeme *father* connects to two sememic signs, *male parent* and *Catholic priest*, and that the sememic sign *male parent* connects to two sememes, *male* and *parent*.

Notice also that the sememic sign *male parent* leads downward not only to the lexeme *father*, but also to other lexemes, including *daddy*, *papa*, and *old man*.

Now let us consider the fourth observation that certain combinations of words have meanings different from the combinations of their separate meanings. Using the technical terminology, we say that a sememic unit can connect to a combination of lexemes. Such units are usually called *idioms*. In the example *blow up* as in *the bomb blew up the building*, we have one semantic unit connected to a combination of lexemes. This is a relationship of just the opposite direction from that involved in the example of *female horse* and *male parent*. The sememic sign *mare* connects upward to a combination of sememes, *female* and *horse*; but the sememic sign *blow up* connects downward to a combination of lexemes, *blow* and *up*.

Now we have also seen that the sememic sign *big 1* is connected to two lexemes, *big* and *large*. But this is an either-or relationship; the meaning *big 1* is expressed by either *big* or *large*. But the sememic sign *blow up* is expressed by both *blow* and *up*.

The fifth observation was that some pairs of words have opposite meanings. As examples we have *big* and *little*, *high* and *low*. The name *antonymy* has often been used for this type of relationship, and the words of opposite meaning are called *antonyms*. But actually there is more than one way in which linguistic units can be opposite in meaning. Consider the pairs *big* and *little*; *come* and *go*; *male* and *female*. Although they all seem to share the relationship of opposite meaning, each is opposite in a different way. The term *antonymy* for this type of relationship is actually misleading, since it suggests that only one relationship is involved instead of several. In the case of such pairs as *big* and *little*, *large* and *small*, *tall* and *short*, the second member of each pair is a negative of the first; *little* means *not big*, *small* means *not large*, *short* means *not tall*, and so forth. But the same is not true for *come* and *go*. To *not come* is not the same as to *go*. Rather, the difference between these two is one of direction: to come is to move toward the speaker or his point of reference, to go is to move otherwise. One says *come here* and *come to my party*, but *I will go there* and *I will go to Mary's party*. Another pair showing this same relationship is *bring* and *take*. One says *bring it here* but *take it away*. However, *go* and *take* are used not only for movement away from the speaker; they are also more general terms, which cover movement without a specific directional orientation. In the terminology of linguistics, *go* is the "unmarked" member of the pair, and *come* is "marked" — for direction toward the speaker or his point of reference. In the same way, *bring* is marked, *take* unmarked. In providing the structural analysis for these pairs, we would say that the marked member of each pair has an additional sememic component; let us call it *direction toward*. Thus the sememic sign *bring* leads upward to two sememes, *take* and *direction toward*.

Let us now return to the pairs *high* and *low*, *big* and *little*, *large* and *small*. Here also one observes that in each pair one member is marked and the other is unmarked. *Little* means specifically *not big*; and *big*, while it covers the opposite of *little*, is also a more general term. If the speaker of English asks about the size of an object and does not know whether it is big or little, he says *how big is it?* rather than *how little is it?* He does not say *how little is it?* unless he already knows that it is little. In other words, *little* is the marked term and *big* the unmarked. By applying the same test, we determine that *small* is marked while *large* is unmarked, *low* is marked while *high* is unmarked, *near* is marked while *far* is unmarked; and so forth. As before, the marked terms are those which have the additional component; and in this case that additional component means *not*. In other words, *little* is to be analyzed as *not big*, *near* as *not far*, and so forth. But this example involves a lower level of the linguistic network than that of *bring* and *take*. The native speaker of English knows that the opposite of *big* is *little*, and not *small*; that the opposite of *large* is *small*, not *little*. This knowledge clearly does not involve meaning, for according to meaning, *small* and *little* could serve equally well as opposites of *big*. The relationships of *big* to *little* and of *large* to *small* must exist in a lower part of the linguistic structure than the synonymy area, which relates *big* and *large*. Therefore, the components of *little* and of *small* are lexemic components, not sememic components. *Little* is a *lexemic sign* which connects upward to two lexemes, *not* and *big*.

The pair *male* and *female* exemplifies still another relationship. Unlike the other pairs, neither member is complex relative to the other. It is not correct that *female* is merely the negative of *male*. Inanimate objects are not male, but they are not therefore female. The actual relationship of these terms lies in the fact that they are the members of a class which has only two members. The only question we must consider is, What kind of class? found in what part of the linguistic structure? It is in the part that may be called *sememic syntax*. We shall come back to this.

But first let us consider my sixth observation, that the meanings of

45

some words are included in those of others. The meaning of *plant* is included in the meaning of *tree*. Whatever semantic properties *plant* has are all properties of *tree* also; but *tree* has, in addition, various other properties not shared by *plant*. One of the characteristics of this area of semantic structure is that it has a multilevel or hierarchical structure. *Plant* connects downward to *tree, bush, flower*; each of these leads down to further branchings. For example, *tree* leads to *evergreen* and *nonevergreen*. *Evergreen* then connects downward to *pine, fir, spruce*. With each step downward in this hierarchy we encounter terms of more specific meaning. This type of structure may be called a *taxonomic hierarchy*.

This part of semantic structure is not the same for all languages, as only a little investigation shows. Every language has its own semantic structure, and in fact there is considerable variation, in the lower parts of taxonomic hierarchies, from one speaker to another. The hierarchy for trees varies considerably for speakers of English in accord with the variation in their knowledge of trees.

One might suppose that, despite different amounts of knowledge possessed by individual speakers of a language, there is some absolute, true taxonomy given by nature that people approximate to one degree or another, but there is no absolute or universal way of classifying the phenomena of the universe. There are innumerable ways, and each language has its own system of classification. Consider the color spectrum. It extends from red at one end to purple at the other; we know from physics that there are no natural boundaries of any kind within this range, and any way of dividing it into sections is essentially arbitrary. And each language divides the range in its own way. English happens to make more divisions at the first level of the hierarchy than most languages: *red, orange, yellow, green, blue*, and *purple*. By contrast, the Shona language, spoken in Rhodesia, has only a three-way division at its first level. One of its terms covers approximately the range of English *orange, red*, and *purple*, and a small part of *blue*; another covers *yellow* and part of *green*; and the third covers the rest of *green* and most of *blue*. None of the boundaries corresponds exactly to any English boundary.

Some investigators of semantic structure have made the mistake of supposing that taxonomic structure can be analyzed in terms of sememic components; for example, that *pine* should be analyzed into components including all the components of *evergreen* plus a component which distinguishes pines from other evergreens. But such a component would occur only as a component of *pine*. A true sememic component occurs in two or more different sememic signs. For example, *female* occurs not only in *mare*, but also in *doe, sow, vixen, hen, sister, queen*, and so forth. In addition, true sememic components are sememes and as such they participate in the sememic syntax.

The term *sememic syntax* may seem odd or confusing at first, since it is generally believed that semantics and syntax are separate areas of linguistic structure. But investigation of semantic structure has shown that it has its own syntax, quite independent of the more familiar kind. The traditional syntax of a language specifies how lexemes may be combined to form sentences. But there is also a syntax of sememes, which specifies how sememes may be combined. Consider this sentence: *Tomorrow the sleeping table married its jumping lake*. It is nonsensical. Yet it is altogether different from another combination of the same words, *lake table jumping sleeping its the married tomorrow*, which is ungrammatical as well as nonsensical. The first sequence is a sentence, having an easily recognizable syntactic structure. It conforms to the syntactic pattern of English. It is nonsensical in that it fails to conform to the sememic syntax; in this respect it differs from ordinary sentences, which conform to both syntactic patterns. The fact that there are sentences which conform to the lexemic syntax but not the sememic syntax shows that the two syntacuic patterns are independent of each other.

The differences between these two patterns are of several kinds. In the first place, the basic elements are different — in the one case lexemes, in the other sememes. Also, in the lexemic syntax one finds categories like *noun, verb, preposition, adjective*, and so forth. Such classes are not present at all in the sememic syntax. Instead, the categories of sememic syntax are those given by the taxonomic hierarchies, which belong only to the sememic syntax. Examples of categories in the sememic syntax of English are *human, animate, concrete object, movement; plant, tree, evergreen*.

Now let us return to *Tomorrow the sleeping table married its jumping*

47

lake. Why is this sentence odd? Because in several places it violates the sememic syntax. Tables do not sleep, nor do they marry or possess lakes; and so forth. These prohibitions are contained in the sememic syntax, which specifies that certain combinations of sememes are acceptable and others are not. The hierarchy of sememes for actions has connections to the hierarchy of sememes for objects such that only certain classes of objects may perform certain types of actions, and only certain classes of objects may serve as the goals of certain actions. Only animate beings can serve as performers of the action of dying; only foods can be eaten; only songs can be sung.

As another type of evidence for sememic syntax, consider the sentence *John found a book on Broadway.* This sentence is ambiguous: John may have found a book whose subject matter is the famous street named Broadway, or it may be that on this street he found the book. But now consider the two related sentences *John found a bracelet on Broadway* and *John found a book on linguistics.* They are unambiguous. Yet their syntactic structure, according to the lexemic syntax, is identical to that of the ambiguous sentence. The three sentences are equally ambiguous according to the lexemic syntax alone, because in all three cases it allows the prepositional phrase to modify either the preceding noun or the verb. But only the first of these three sentences is really ambiguous, because for it the sememic syntax also allows two interpretations. The ambiguity involves not primarily the two possible syntactic interpretations but the lexeme *on,* which connects upward to two different sememes, one for *location on a surface,* as in *on the floor,* and another which also has the lexemic realizations *about* and *concerning,* as in *a book on linguistics.* The sememic syntax of English specifies that the locational sememe *on* can occur only with members of the category of surfaces; and the other sememe *on* can occur only with members of the category of types of discourse. This category includes objects, such as books, and speeches and actions, for instance talking, as in *a book on linguistics* and *he spoke on linguistics.* The sentence *John found a book on Broadway* is ambiguous because both of these sememic interpretations for the lexeme *on* are accepted by the sememic syntax: *book* is a type of discourse and *Broadway* is a surface. But the sentence *John found a bracelet on Broadway* is unambiguous because the sememic syntax rejects one of the interpretations offered by the lexemic syntax; *bracelet* is not a type of discourse. Similarly, *John found a book on linguistics* is unambiguous, since *linguistics* does not belong to the taxonomic category of surfaces in the sememic syntax.

In this very brief survey I have tried to describe several areas which may be identified within the lexicological and semantic structure of a language. These areas, in order from the top downward, are concerned with sememic syntax, which includes taxonomic hierarchies; sememic components, such as *female*; idioms, such as *blow up*; synonymy, illustrated by *big* and *large*; polysemy, illustrated by *table*; and lexemic components, for example *not* and *big* as components of *little*. Although most of my examples are taken from the English language, the structural relationships I have illustrated are apparently found in all languages.

5 THE ORIGIN OF LANGUAGE

Harry Hoijer

A principal means of reconstructing the prehistory of man and his cultures is archeological research. Such studies provide direct evidence of man's biological evolution and evidence as well of the prehistory of several aspects of culture. But direct archeological evidence of language appears only after the invention of writing, only in written records inscribed on stone, clay, or some other durable material. Since the earliest of these remains date back no further than five thousand years, and since language is certainly very much older, it is clear that early writings can provide no evidence of either the origin or the evolution of language.

During the nineteenth century, scholars developed a method for reconstructing the early history, and in some instances the prehistory, of languages spoken today and those recorded in older writings. Thus it was shown that most of the languages of Europe and some of those spoken in the Near East and northern India were so related to each other as to make it certain that they developed in large part from an ancient tongue no longer spoken and for which no written records existed. The success of these reconstructions led some scholars to the belief that the method might also be applied to the reconstruction of the primeval language or languages of mankind and so possibly solve the problem of the origin of language. Later researches demonstrated, however, that the methods of historical reconstruction, even when applied to ancient languages preserved in writing, yielded a history of only ten thousand years or less, a period much too brief to provide data on origins.

The number of languages spoken in the world today is estimated at more than four thousand. Every human group known, from the tiny tribelets of the California Indians to the great nations of modern Europe, the Americas, and Asia, possesses a language. Comparative studies of these languages reveal that they may be classified into several hundred language families, each of which contains from 2 to 100 or more separate but related languages. Languages so related are said to have diverged from a single ancestral tongue, called a protolanguage, that is now no longer spoken and for which written records are not available. English, for example, is closely related to such languages as German, Dutch, and Swedish, and more distantly ralated to scores of other languages (for example, Russian, Persian, and Hindi) spoken in Europe, the Near East, and northern India. It is not related, so far as we know, to such well-known languages as Arabic and Chinese or to the many less well-known languages of aboriginal America. The large number of unrelated language families points up the great diversity of modern tongues and suggests that language developed very early in man's prehistory, so early that it is quite impossible to recover, by present methods of historical research, any trace of the original language or languages of mankind.

Studies of language during much of the present century have not been confined to the languages of the great civilizations of the modern world. Attention has also been given to the far more numerous languages of primitive peoples, that is, peoples who, like many American Indian tribes, were, until recently, little advanced in culture. In the nineteenth century, before the languages of primitives had been precisely described, many scholars believed that these languages, like the cultures of which they are a part, might be in a primitive stage of development and so might attest to earlier stages in the evolution of language. Later studies, of American Indian languages and of the aboriginal tongues of Australia, New Guinea, and many other regions, failed to confirm the existence of such a primitive speech.

On the contrary, studies of the languages of primitives clearly reveal that these languages, though very different from each other and from the languages of the great civilizations, are fully developed in every essential aspect. Thus, though we can often arrange diverse cultural systems in an evolutionary sequence, there is in language no evidence of a parallel evolutionary development. The most primitive peoples known, whose only tools are of wood, bone, and crudely shaped stones, and who live in very small groups governed primarily by familial relationships, possess fully developed languages that are in every essential respect perfectly comparable to such languages as English, French, German, or Chinese.

It is now clear that the problem of the origin of language is not to be solved by a study of older records or by comparing the languages of the world with each other. We must, instead, approach the problem not only with linguistic studies, but also with the help of the total context of man's biological and cultural evolution. Archeological data provides ample evidence that man and his nearest animal relatives, the anthropoid, or manlike, apes, have a common ancestry. The probable ancestor lived on earth several million years ago, and the lines of divergence that ultimately led on the one hand to man and on the other to the modern anthropoids extend far back, perhaps as far as three or four million years.

Recent archeological discoveries in various regions of Africa and Asia suggest the presence, some two million years ago, of hominoid, or manlike, forms: animals that lack certain of the characteristics, such as brain size, found in modern men, that yet are structurally more advanced than the modern apes. These forms, or some other very like them, gave way to the earliest hominids — forms that belong, like modern man, to the genus *Homo* but to one or more species different from the species, *sapiens*, to which modern man belongs. Evidence also exists that the earliest hominids, and possibly even the hominoids, made and used very crude stone tools and so had acquired at least the rudiments of culture. In east Africa, for example, Professor L. S. B. Leakey found the bones of an exceedingly primitive hominid form, called *Homo habilis*, and, associated with the bones evidence that *H. habilis* made and used crudely shaped stone tools. It seems clear, then, that certain aspects of culture may have begun as early as two million years ago, even though evidence of tool-making and tool use, activities that some have claimed for modern apes, may not be conclusive. Evidence of true cultures, that is, patterned ways of behavior that are traditionally transmitted and cumulative, do not appear until about one million years later, with the coming of the biologically more advanced hominid species. The existence of true cultures clearly implies the existence of language, since language is an obvious prerequisite to the traditional transmission and the progressive growth of culture. The beginnings of language — a stage of evolutionary development that we might call prelanguage — may well have taken place among hominids, but it is likely that true language developed among the hominids much later, and at or about the same time that these forms acquired a true culture. Even then we must remember that both the languages and the cultures of the early hominids were exceedingly primitive; so much so that if today we heard them speak, their speech might sound more like animal calls than human language.

Archeological evidence, although it enables us to set an approximate date for the beginnings of language, offers no evidence from which we can reconstruct its evolutionary development. We must approach this problem by comparing human language as a whole with the communicatory systems of the animals, and primarily with the systems known to exist among the apes.

The communicatory systems of the modern apes, and probably also of the early hominoids, are in essence closed repertories of calls. Man's language, on the other hand, is an open system, a system that is capable of producing an almost infinite number of utterances, some learned but many others formed on patterns common to the speech community rather than learned. Indeed, man's language enables him both to produce and to understand utterances that are completely novel, that have never been spoken or heard before. This property of language, its *productivity*, is apparently lacking in the call systems of the animals.

A second property of language, also absent from call systems, is *displacement*. Displacement refers to man's ability to talk about things and events that are remote in time or space. It is the faculty of displaced speech that enables man to recount events in his past and events that took place long before he was born; to talk about things and events he hopes to achieve in the future; and to create, in myth and fiction, beings, things, and events, natural or supernatural, that have never existed and perhaps never can exist. Displaced speech, it is evident, also gives a continuity to physical experience, and so enables man, alone among the animals, to work out his problems in the absence of the physical situations in which these problems arise.

The utterances of a language consist wholly of a sequence of elementary signaling units — distinctive sounds, or phonemes. Phonemes have no meanings in themselves but serve only to keep meaningful utterances apart, as when the utterance *I hit him* is clearly distinguished from *I bit him* simply by changing the first phoneme of *hit* and *bit*. Language also has a structure in terms of morphemes, minimum meaningful elements, such that a pair of utterances like *he walks along* and *he walked along* are distinguished by the contrast between *walks* and *walked*; more specifically, by the fact that the morpheme written -*s* and marking the present tense appears in the first utterance, whereas the morpheme written -*ed* and marking the past tense occurs in the second utterance.

This design feature of language, whereby morphemes are differentiated by varying combinations of phonemes, is called *duality of patterning*. It is duality of patterning that makes it possible for a language to possess several thousands of morphemes, even though the number of distinctive signaling units, or phonemes, is rarely more than fifty. In a call system, each call differs as a whole from the rest, both in total sound effect and in meaning.

The fourth distinctive property of language, *traditional transmission*, refers to the fact that language is taught and learned; it is not, as appears to be the case with call systems, transmitted by the genes. Human children have no language at birth; they acquire one by hearing and rehearsing utterances made by adults and, later, by inferring from the utterances they hear the meanings of the morphemes and, more importantly, the processes by which phonemes and morphemes are built into complete utterances. Once they have acquired these processes, the children build their own, often quite novel utterances, ones they have neither heard nor rehearsed.

The problem of the origin of language may now be stated more precisely. It is to reconstruct the evolutionary changes whereby a call system, almost certainly possessed by one or more groups of hominoids, developed the properties of productivity, traditional transmission, displacement, and duality of patterning that made it a true language. Such a reconstruction has been made by Charles F. Hockett and Robert Ascher, and I shall present here a brief summary of their work as described in their article "The Human Revolution."[1]

A call system, as we noted earlier, is closed; that is, it contains a finite and usually a small number of calls, each of which is unique in both sound and meaning. At some time in man's prehistory, a hominoid form may have encountered a situation that required him to communicate both the presence of food, let us say, and the presence of danger. It is conceivable that in such an instance the animal would emit a single call that combined part of the food call with part of the call signifying danger. Blended calls very likely occur among modern animals, although such an occurrence has not been observed.

Should such blends become common, it is clear that an originally small number of calls would become larger. Thus, if we assume a closed system of ten calls, and assume further that each of theee is blended with each of the others, the result is an enlarged repertory of one hundred calls. Furthermore, and this point is of far greater importance, each of the blended calls now has two parts, and each part recurs in other blended calls. The habit is established of building composite calls out of meaningful parts of calls, whether or not these occur independently as whole signals. "It is this habit," according to Hockett and Ascher, "that lies at the center of the openness of human languages. English allows only a finite (though quite large) number of sentences only two words long. But it allows an unlimited number of different sentences because there is no fixed limit on how long a sentence may be."

When a closed system of calls becomes open and productive in the manner described, the properties of traditional transmission and displacement must also be developed. The existence of blended calls requires that the young learn to infer the meanings of the parts and the many ways in which these parts are put together to form whole utterances. Such inferences, it is clear, must be drawn from the

[1]"The Human Revolution," *Current Anthropology*, V, No. 3 (June 1964).

contexts in which the composite signals are used and from the resemblances in sound that exist among the composite calls. A premium is therefore placed on whatever capacity for teaching and learning a group may possess, and there results a selective pressure toward an increase in the genetic basis for that capacity.

Teaching and learning result in displaced speech, for teaching and learning, if they are to be effective, must take place apart from the situations in which the utterances that are being taught and rehearsed are pertinent. It is reasonable to suppose that, in prehistoric times as now, much of the teaching and learning of speech took place along with other teaching and learning and that the young acquired not only their patterns of speaking but other patterns of their culture as well. We should expect, therefore, that the properties of language we have called productivity, traditional transmission, and displacement came into being at approximately the same time that much of the rest of culture appeared.

With the development of productivity, traditional transmission, and displacement, earlier call systems, such as probably existed in many hominoid groups, became incipient languages or prelanguages, differing from true languages only in the absence of duality of patterning. Prelanguages, we may assume, became increasingly complex and flexible, since the possession of such communicatory devices had many advantages for the survival of the group. Blending generated an increasingly large stock of minimum meaningful signaling units, or premorphemes, each of which, in the absence of duality of patterning, had to be holistically different from all the others. As a result, some premorphemes became so similar to others that keeping them apart, either in speaking or listening, became too difficult a task for the early hominid vocal apparatus, ears, and brain. Some of these overloaded communicatory systems may even have collapsed and their bearers, as a consequence, become extinct.

In time, however, and with the emergence, possibly one million years ago, of more advanced hominids, the premorpheme came to be heard not as a holistic unit, but in terms of the smaller sound components that occurred in it. Similarly, articulation came to be directed not toward the production of the acoustic pattern of the premorpheme as a whole, but toward an articulation of the smaller

56

sound components sufficiently precise to distinguish each component from others. When this change took place, the premorpheme became a true morpheme, that is, a minimum meaningful unit of speech made up of phonological components without meaning, the phonemes. At that point, the prelanguage became a true language, with all the properties that today distinguish language from the communicatory systems found among animals.

This evolutionary sequence should not be viewed as a sequence of replacements whereby language replaced earlier prelanguage and prelanguage replaced a still earlier system of calls. To quote again from Hockett and Ascher:

> The emergence of true language from a closed call system . . . should properly be thought of . . . as the growth of a new system within the matrix of the old one. Certain features of the proto-hominoid call system are still found in human vocal-auditory behavior, but as accompaniments to the use of language rather than as part of language. The proto-humanoids could vary the intensity, the pitch, and the duration of a single call. We still do this as we speak sentences in a language; we speak sometimes more loudly, sometimes more softly, sometimes in a higher register and sometimes in a lower, and so on. Also, we use certain grunts and cries . . . that are not words or morphemes and not part of language. These various paralinguistic phenomena . . . have been reworked and modified in many ways by the conditions of life of speaking humans, but their pedigree . . . is older than that of language itself.

It cannot be said that all problems connected with the origin of language have been solved, but anyone interested in measuring progress toward a solution need only look at the speculations on language origin wittily described by Max Müller in the middle of the last century — speculations which sought the beginnings of language largely in imitation or else in instinctive cries. These were the theories still remembered by their nicknames rather than their content: the "Ding-dong," the "Pooh-pooh." Comparing these theories with what the work of modern linguists has accomplished, we find that men like Hockett and Ascher have at least greatly narrowed the problem and made it much more precise. The problem of how prelanguage became language is now narrowed to the specific

57

one of the development of duality of pattern. Such a precision of definition is a great advance, yet it can be noted that Hockett and Ascher have succeeded essentially only in pointing out that for language to develop, the transition to duality was needed, simply because proliferation of meaningful elements without it would have been too complex to be useful. They have not been so successful in showing the process by which the need was met.

Nevertheless — even though the process of development is not clear — there is one minor side result which is of fascinating suggestiveness: As Hockett and Ascher have defined duality, its development is so far-reaching, so revolutionary, and so fruitful as to suggest that it was created only once, and in one place. Once created, it would have spread to all hominids irresistibly and speedily. It suggests, in other words, the unitary origin of language, and the unitary origin of language suggests, in turn, that men are cultural as well as genetic and biological brothers.

6 OUR OWN FAMILY OF LANGUAGES

Henry M. Hoenigswald

The previous chapter was concerned with the origins of language, a fascinating question which has challenged many minds at different times — not only linguists, but other scientists as well: psychologists, students of animal behavior, paleontologists. By necessity, the discussion has remained somewhat speculative, perhaps with a touch of phantasy, in the constructive, creative sense of the word.

There is another context in which the factor *time* is encountered in a less ambitious and more technical way, within the confines of linguistics proper. No claim is made here to discovering matters of importance to the past of the human species as such; the time depths involved are much too shallow for that, amounting as they do to rarely more than a few thousand years. I am speaking of the study of linguistic *change*. All language changes constantly. An understanding of change-processes is therefore central to an understanding of language; and if generalizations are possible it is likely that these generalizations will have some importance for the understanding of other human activities.

In many ways phenomena of change are interwoven with the phenomenon of diversity, and it is no accident that we speak of historical and comparative linguistics as one twin discipline within the field. Not only is it trivially true that diversity in time (for instance the difference between Ancient Greek and Modern Greek) is a special case of diversity in general, but it is almost a matter of direct observation that many innovations in speech consist in importing a trait (for instance a word or a construction) from another language or from another variety of the same language, and also, conversely, that, of two persons or groups of persons speaking the "same" language (whatever this may mean), only one may carry out a given innovation, thereby breaking up the speech community. In other words, diversity may lead to change, and change may lead to diversity.

It would be good to be able to deal wsth language diversity as such, but this is not easy. The difficulty of finding a natural classification or typology of languages is familiar from other fields of learning: different criteria will yield different and often unrelated classifications. The late Benjamin Lee Whorf, who did so much to popularize the importance of deep-seated grammatical differences among the languages of the world, thought that most of the languages of Europe form one group (which he called Standard Average European) significantly different from, say, Hopi (the American Indian language in which he had a special interest). One could indeed name many properties which these languages share, perhaps exclusively, and yet it would also be possible to name other properties which some, but not all, of these same languages share with third groups outside the SAE area. It is interesting to note how an appeal to geography always suggests itself in this matter; our intersecting and overlapping groups of languages have a tendency to cover intersecting and overlapping bits of contiguous territory, although the fit is far from perfect.

There is, however, one rather specialized approach which has the unique virtue of proceeding by subsequent subdivision or branching, and hence gives us the well-known tree-shaped model showing stocks, families, subfamilies, languages, and dialects of languages. Each tree represents a history in the sense that we wish to say that we know, either by observation or by inference, that certain recurrent regularities which are discovered in a matching of, say, French, Italian, and Rumanian are the effects of different innovations undergone by one and the same ancestor language in different localities (in this case, different parts of the Roman empire). That the inferences are fairly reliable appears from the fact that the reconstructed ancestor language is in most respects like the Latin which we read in the written records of Latin that have come down to us; this gives us faith in reconstructions which we cannot confirm because no written records exist. Family trees depict the proliferation and extinction of speech communities. They aim at assigning unambiguous locations in time to known languages, thus defining the degree of their "relationship" in the technical meaning of the word. Note that "relationship" does not primarily mean mutual intelligibility, parallelism of structure, or some other kind of descriptive resemblance, although it is quite true that closely related languages may still be mutually intelligible, and it is also true that some innovations lead to important changes in grammatical build, whereas others, just as extensive by some agreed-upon standard, do not.

Our knowledge of the many thousand languages spoken in the world is disastrously uneven. Consequently we cannot even begin to organize all the languages of the world, present and past, into genealogical trees. Some language families are far better understood than others. Among the better-known ones are the Semitic languages (Arabic, Hebrew, Ethiopic), the Finno-Ugric languages (Finnish, Hungarian, Lapp) the Turkic languages of southeastern Europe and central Asia, the Bantu languages of southern Africa, the Algonquian languages (especially those of the Great Lakes region), the Dravidian languages of south India, the Malayo-Polynesian languages (stretching from Madagascar off Africa to Easter Island), and of course the Indo-European languages, of which English, Hindi–Urdu (spoken in parts of India), Spanish, and Russian are at the present time extremely important in numerical strength. Apart from colonial expansion since the Renaissance, the Indo-European languages are widespread and cover a near-continuous territory extending from Ceylon in the east to Iceland, Ireland, and the Spanish-Portuguese peninsula in the west. They are greatly diversified. Some of them are known to us from literary texts that go back to antiquity. Thus the documents written in Hittite (since extinct) and those in Mycenaean Greek (which has a nearly linear descendant still spoken in southeastern Europe) were executed in the second millennium B.C., and a good many features contained in the oral tradition which is characteristic of the Vedas of India must be of even greater antiquity. For these and other reasons our picture of our own family of languages is rather full and concrete; in sketching it, we have the further advantage of being able to build on something like one hundred fifty years of concerted scholarly effort.

The major subfamilies within Indo-European are the following: Indic (or Indo-Aryan), Iranian, Armenian in Asia; Slavic, Baltic, and Albanian in the continental mass of eastern Europe; Greek and Italic (including Latin and its descendants, the Romance languages) in the Mediterranean basin; Germanic in central and northern Europe, and Celtic, once widely spread over the European continent though now pushed back to parts of the Atlantic rim. Hittite and Tokharian (in Asia Minor, and in an area in central Asia, respectively) are now extinct; there are other splinters, barely known to us, of which the same is true, and we may conjecture, though with meager profit, that there were many additional groups, now lost without a trace.

For various reasons it is believed that the ancestor language common to the subfamilies just listed was spoken, in a reasonably but by no means absolutely unified form, at some time before the end of the Neolithic period somewhere on the land mass of Europe and western Asia — perhaps north of the Black Sea, or, as some scholars prefer, closer to the Baltic Sea. It is interesting to note that some of the argument is itself linguistic in nature. Since it is possible to study the nature of the reconstructed vocabulary (and that includes the meanings attached to words), something can be known about the kinship system, the religion, and the political organization of the speakers of the "Proto Indo-European" language, as the ancestral language is called. Likewise, we may, with all due caution, form an idea about the natural setting by which those speakers were surrounded. There is a powerful enough consensus in the evidence taken from terms having to do with climate, topographic features, fauna, and flora to exclude almost all of the locations outside of the area just indicated, although some of these locations were, in later historical times, inhabited by speakers of descendant Indo-European languages. In part this is, to be sure, merely in agreement with what archeology or history tell us anyhow; the advent of the Indo-Aryans in India, the invasion of the Mediterranean shores by the Greeks and Romans (or their linguistic forebears) needs no indirect semantic reasoning to be accepted as part of history.

The ancestor language must have resembled some of its more archaic descendants, such as Sanskrit and Greek, rather closely. The phonemic system stands out as well defined in our reconstruction. It included a fairly symmetrical array of stops (voiceless, voiced, and "voiced aspirated") for at least four positions, the *p*, *t*, *k*, and *qu* types. In addition, it had a series of "semivowels" (in a wide, somewhat unusual sense of the term) including not only *w* and *y* but also *m*, *n*, *r*, and *l*, as well as a small number of so-called laryngeals; all these semivowels occurred as consonants (that is, in competition with the stops) but also as vowels: *w* as *u*, *y* as *i*, *r* as a syllabic *r* (a phenomenon which is familiar to those who know or speak certain Slavic languages like Czech or Serbo-Croatian). Then, thirdly, there was a class, possibly very small, of phonemes which occurred as vowels only; and, finally, in very striking isolation, one and only one *s*-like consonant which in some ways behaved like the stops. There was a phonemic word accent. There were certain highly systematic rules governing the compatibility of consonants with each other in a given word or word core; but these rules did not lead to alternations between consonant phonemes; the "roots" (as word cores are traditionally called) were characterized by a remarkably stable consonant or semivowel skeleton. Vowels, on the other hand, were not only few in number; they were also subject to a complex system of grammatically determined alternations. In a changed form this alternation lives on in the Germanic languages: an irregular English verb like *sing sung* is a typical instance.

Word order must have been quite free, that is, very much unlike English, in which the position of a word in the sentence is one of the fundamental signals. This freedom went hand in hand, as it often does, with another feature which is not characteristic of English or of a good many other descendant languages of the present time, but which is well preserved in some of the older descendants: elaborate inflection. Inflection was typically by endings rather than by prefix. The endings set nouns off from verbs in a rather clear fashion. Nouns could be compounded together to form other nouns; noun stems could also be suffixed to form, in turn, longer noun-stems that were then subject to inflection for case and number. It was a peculiar characteristic of these two derivational processes (that is, compounding, and derivation by suffix) that they were exocentric. This means that the addition of a first member of a compound or of a word-forming suffix did not merely narrow down the meaning of the second member or that of the stem, but radically changed the total meaning. This is worth mentioning because many of the separate Indo-European languages have lost this restriction; in English (which is an Indo-European language) a schoolboy is a kind of boy, and a leaflet is (or at least was at one time) a kind of leaf. In, say, Ancient Greek, which was more like the ancestor language, such examples are almost nonexistent: *eu* means "good" and *pater*, "father," but *eupator* (with a characteristic change in the vowel) is not a "good father," but someone who comes from a good (noble) father or ancestor. There are innumerable instances, like this, in which many or all descendants have changed from the archaic ancestral type in one and the same general direction. This can play havoc with the task of reconstruction; in fact we are sure to miss features which the protolanguage must have had, simply because a common trend has overtaken the descendants even after they were in other respects quite independent.

The Indo-European verb did not have a complete and filled-out "conjugation." It had a system of "stems" built around a "root" by various devices (reduplication of the initial sound, accent shifts, vowel gradation, suffixation), but not really in such a way as to make predictable the number or particular choice of stems in existence for a given root. One of the central notions that served to classify both the roots and the derivative devices (sometimes in a mutual, circular fashion) was that of "aspect," that is, the punctual as against the durative mode of verbal action.

When we try to picture the course of history between the protolanguage and the age of written texts and direct observation we encounter our greatest difficulties. In fact everybody is agreed that the so-called comparative method, with its tree-model, however modified and perfected, is not always applicable. This is so because it rests on an oversimplification. Speech communities do not always break up in such a way that all communication suddenly ceases.

There may also be transitional periods during which some innovations are general while others pertain to certain districts only (quite aside from the possibility, already mentioned, that identical or parallel events occur even after fairly complete separation). A great deal of sagacity has been expended on efforts to organize the twelve or so major subgroups of Indo-European into a scheme of successive bifurcations and thus to fill in the space between the "root" of the tree and its main branches. But the results have been satisfactory in part only. Much importance used to be attached to a number of connected changes which jointly characterize Indo-Aryan, Iranian, Armenian, Slavic, and Baltic — that is, a fairly coherent area which at the time when the observation was formulated constituted the eastern half of the Indo-European world. This is the celebrated *centum-satem* division: the word for "100" in one of the Iranian languages begins with an *s* rather than with the *k*-like sound of the Latin *centum*. The two languages were of course chosen arbitrarily as examples of East and West; so was the word for "100." The correspondence between *k* and *s* recurs in many words in a way which is defined as "regular," and hence as the effect of what is technically called "sound change" rather than as a mere episode in the history of a particular word. (It is of course precisely the recognition of such regularities which furnishes us with the major tool for reconstruction.) The English form of the word for "100" exemplifies another famous sound correspondence: an English *h* matches the *k* of the other *centum* languages, just as the *f* in *father* and the *th* ($/\theta/$) in *three* match the *p* and the *t* in the corresponding words in virtually all the Indo-European sister languages. This correspondence forms part of "Grimm's law," formulated in the early 1800s; it is an exclusive characteristic of Germanic and thus does not contribute to the problem of special relationships among the major subgroups.

To return to that problem: the fact is that other groupings like that of the *satem* innovation exist, but, again, they overlap and intersect. For instance, a strong bond exists between the Indo-Aryan and the Iranian languages — a bond so strong that it is common to speak of Indo-Iranian; yet Iranian also shares innovations with its Slavic neighbor to the west that exclude its Indo-Aryan partner to the east. Through the Italic languages there runs a division which

65

may not be so old as to destroy the concept of a proto-Italic sub-ancestor; on one side of the division we have Latin and its medieval and modern descendants, the Romance languages, on the other a group of dialects spoken and, luckily, written down, in parts of Italy before the spread of Roman Latin over the peninsula. There is evidence of closeness (but not enough to justify the reconstruction of a common intermediate ancestor) between these "Italic" languages and the Celtic subgroup. A recent discussion of this topic and its implication for prehistory and archeology can be found in *Ancient Indo-European Dialects*.[1] One fact of some importance is that there are no examples of innovations shared by subgroups which, in historical times, are geographically separated by other subgroups. Other language families behave differently, apparently because the patterns of expansion and migration which lie behind all innovations were not the same. It seems that the speakers of Indo-European had a way of moving out radially from a center, with little durable displacement of their relative locations in later times.

As we have already said, the actual daughter languages which we know appear at very different points in history and show very different degrees of diversification. Tokharian is known to us only from the sixth or seventh century A.D. in texts found in Chinese Turkestan; the texts show two rather different varieties of the language. Indo-Aryan enters history early in the form of Sanskrit; the hymns of the Rigveda are of great though undated antiquity; their transmission being essentially oral, the time at which they came into textual existence does not matter much. A tremendous variety of more or less literary forms of Indo-Aryan occurs in written form. Today, Indo-Aryan languages like Hindi–Urdu, Bengali, Gujerati, and Marathi are spoken in north and central India (Sinhalese in Ceylon), by many millions of people. The Iranian languages are similarly diverse; their oldest known forms are the Old Persian of the royal Persian inscriptions, and the Avestan of the canonic scriptures of the Parsis (most of whom have migrated to India). Persian and Pashto (in Afghanistan) are among the most

[1]Henrik Birnbaum and J. Puhvel. *Ancient Indo-European Dialects*. University of California Press, 1965.

important modern forms of Iranian. Hittite, along with a group of very imperfectly known close cognates, appears in the cuneiform texts of Anatolia in the second millennium B.C. and then disappears. Armenian, on the other hand, emerges in consequence of its rather early Christianization, in texts which seem to go back to the fifth century after Christ, in the country south of the Caucasus. At the present there are two main forms of the language: eastern (in the Soviet Union) and western (in the Anatolian peninsula and in the wider secondary diaspora). The Slavic languages, now divided into East Slavic (Russian, Ukrainian, etc.), West Slavic (Polish, Czech), and South Slavic (Bulgarian, Macedonian, Serbo-Croatian, Slovene), are first known to us in a southern variety (labeled Old Church Slavonic) from the ninth Christian century. The Baltic languages are mainly equivalent to Lithuanian and Lettish, which are spoken by roughly four million individuals in an area on the Baltic Sea; the earliest texts come from the sixteenth century. (Some scholars have seen special subfamilial ties between Baltic and Slavic; others differ emphatically.) The Albanians, at the eastern entrance to the Adriatic and in small scatterings in Italy and Greece, may or may not be the linguistic heirs of the Illyrians known to antiquity. Albanian writings first appear in the fifteenth century after Christ.

Greek is one of the most fully known branches of Indo-European. It first appears on clay tablets from Mycenaean times, and a little later (after the so-called dark centuries) in an abundance of local and literary varieties. In Hellenistic times these varieties give way to a more or less uniform standard — in which the New Testament, among other works, is written. The spoken forms of Modern Greek are the result of renewed differentiation; they bear only an occasional relationship to anciently attested localisms. To Latin, its ("Osco-Umbrian") sister dialects, and its Romance offshoots, we have already referred. The major Romance languages are of course Portuguese, Spanish, Catalan, Provençal, French, Rhaeto-Romance (in certain Alpine valleys), Sardinian, and Italian, with its dialectal foundations north and south; then, moving east and crossing a gap (which was once partially filled by a now extinct language), Rumanian. The Celts, too, once inhabited a much larger stretch of territory than they do now. The Romanization of Gaul is a historic fact, and a good many names for rivers and other natural features testify to earlier Celtic occupation of many parts of continental Europe in a way that recalls the Indian names still borne by many American rivers, lakes, and mountains. Since antiquity, Celtic speech has been pushed back westward, to Wales and to Ireland. The Gaelic of Scotland is the result of migration from Ireland, and the Celtic Breton of France was likewise brought across the sea, in this instance from Britain. A few generations ago, British Celtic was still spoken in Cornwall, and Gaelic Celtic on the Isle of Man. There are a few Gaulish inscriptions dating back to the third century B.C. Writing in the extant Celtic languages begins on a precarious scale in the fifth century after Christ, and, on a more regular basis, after the eighth century.

As readers of Caesar's *Gallic Wars* know, Celts had close contact with their Germanic-speaking neighbors. Frequently Germanic speech replaced Celtic, as it did in large parts of Britain. When Germanic languages first emerge into light, they are not overly differentiated from each other, though a threefold division into East, North, and West Germanic stands out. In the East Germanic there is Gothic (the language of the Visigothic Bible of the fourth century); traces survived in the Crimea into the sixteenth century. North Germanic, in the Scandinavian territories, includes Icelandic (dating from the tenth century) and the Continental type, on which the various standard languages with their complicated histories are based. West Germanic appears as High (southern) German, dating from the eighth century, and, in a rather different form, as Low (northern) German a little later. Both the literary German standard and the Yiddish of eastern European Jews are specializations of High German; Dutch-Flemish-Afrikaans, of Low German. A still further variety of West Germanic is represented by Frisian and English.

It is impossible not to speculate a little on the factors which may have brought about all this diversification. Some of it may be viewed as surface variety in the manner in which a common underlying structure reacted to fairly uniform trends as it expanded. In fact much that happened to Indo-European contributed to a remarkably well-defined general effect. The consonant systems have tended to become more symmetrical by integrating the lone s-sound; they have also done away with the laryngeal consonants, such as the entity assumed to have occurred after vocalic */r̥/ in IE (written usually */r̥X/) by dropping them from the flow of speech or by transforming them into mere lengtheners, as when the entity just mentioned became a long syllabic r. The vowel systems have been filled out in various ways, although in this respect the differences remain great. Inflections and derivative processes have become more "regular" in two ways: the extent of vowel alternation has been greatly reduced, and fully implemented verbal paradigms of an increasingly uniform nature have grown up into such well-ordered "conjugations" as those of Latin. At the same time, sound changes have tended to mutilate the end of words to the extent that inherited inflectional endings are obscured or lost. At any rate, whatever may be cause and whatever effect, there has been a large-scale replacement of old inflectional endings dy new, and looser, "analytical" devices of a syntactic nature; prepositions take the place of case endings, compound verb-forms take over from suffixed verb-forms, and so on. Not all descendant languages obey these pressures to the same degree, and no two do so in exactly the same detailed manner, but certain general lines are recognizable.

Important deviations, on the other hand, occur also; sometimes unaccountably, but sometimes precisely where one would expect them, namely, on the rim of the over-all area, where an Indo-European dialect may be exposed to the possibility of being attracted into another typological area. Murray Emeneau has shown that some of the more outlandish developments that characterize Indo-Aryan (that is, the Indo-European spoken in India) were such as to bring it closer to membership in an Indian structure-type to which some non-Indo-European languages also belong. A good case can also be made for Armenian with respect to its neighbors in the Caucasus (a region of enormous typological interest and variety); the changes that are characteristic of Armenian are frequently not at all in line with the trends that seem to govern the more centrally

69

located Indo-European languages. Celtic, too, has developed in somewhat special ways which would accord well with the extreme geographic location which the Celts have come to occupy. There are many unanswered questions here, and much to challenge the student.

7 SOME ASPECTS OF THE HISTORY OF THE ENGLISH LANGUAGE

Hans Kurath

Fifteen hundred years have elapsed since a number of Germanic tribal organizations — Angles, Saxons, and Jutes — invaded the British Isles from the east and the south and pushed the Celtic inhabitants and their languages back in a westerly and northerly direction in what is now England and Scotland. Crossing the Irish Sea in the Middle Ages, English gradually replaced Irish, which is now spoken only by country folk in the northwestern counties of Ireland. In Scotland, Gaelic survives only in the Highlands. The Cornish of Cornwall died out in the seventeenth century, but Welsh survives in full vigor to our day. Throughout the British Isles, English is now the regular means of communication, though Welsh, Irish, or Gaelic may be spoken in the home.

Three major dialects were current in England and southern Scotland during the early Middle Ages: Saxon in the greater part of the south and southwest of England, Anglian from East Anglia northward to Scotland, and Jutish in Kent and on the Isle of Wight. Of these dialects of Old English, West Saxon is well known to us through an extensive literature, including alliterative verse, literary prose, chronicles, translations of the Bible, and treatises on law and folk medicine. As the standard literary language of the Anglo-Saxons from the ninth century onward, it was in use until the Norman conquest. Literary Anglian, though influenced by West Saxon, is represented in *Beowulf*, the great Old English epic, and in extensive interlineary glosses of parts of the Bible. The phonological characteristics of Old Jutish can be gleaned from Middle Kentish texts.

American scholars, notably F. Klaeber, G. P. Krapp, K. Malone, and E. V. K. Dobbie, have made significant contributions to our knowledge of the language and the literature of the Anglo-Saxons.

The Norman conquest of England in the eleventh century marks a sharp turning point in the history of the English people and their language. For three centuries French became the language of all national affairs, whether political, social, or cultural. The West Saxon literary language was soon abandoned, but regional varieties of English continued in use in the homes, in Christian worship, and in the transaction of provincial and local affairs. Beginning in the thirteenth century, regional literary languages based upon the spoken word came into being, first in the southwest (Layamon's *Brut*, saints' lives), later in the north, last in the London area, the chief seat of the French-speaking aristocracy. In Chaucer's time the language of the London and Westminster focal area came to be established as the standard literary language of England. The return to English as the national language reflects the rise of the middle class to power in national and cultural affairs.

During three hundred years of socially graded bilingualism, vast numbers of French words came to be incorporated into the English vocabulary, not only terms for political, social, and cultural matters — *country, city, real, royal, value, money, society* — but also "homely" words, such as *change, move, use, cover, very*. During this period many Latin words were also adopted, especially in translations of learned works, such as treatises on law, theology, philosophy, and medicine. A considerable segment of the vocabulary in these fields dates from this period, as the *Middle English Dictionary* now being published by the University of Michigan amply demonstrates.

The large-scale adoption of foreign words did not materially change the structure of English. Syntax and word inflection remained essentially English. The considerable simplification of Old English noun, adjective, and verb forms exhibited in Chaucer's English is strictly an indigenous development. Though the phonemic system sustained radical changes between 1100 and 1500, the changes cannot be attributed to French or Latin influence. Only one foreign vowel sound was adopted, the *oi* of *point* and *joy* — and it has remained a stranger in the vowel system of Modern English; English folk speech has largely merged it with a native phonemic entity, so that *point* rimes with *pint*. Contrastive voiced and voiceless fricatives developed at this time; in the native word stock the contrast developed in the medial and final positions, as in *offer* vs. *oven*, *bath* vs. *bathe*, *glass* vs. *glaze*. Only in the initial position is this contrast largely due to French influence, as in *fine* vs. *vine*, *seal* vs. *zeal*.

Not only the French sounds but also the inflections and the stress patterns of the adopted words were fitted into the native English system. With certain exceptions, the characteristic end-stress of French words was replaced by fore-stress, as in *cóunty*, *prófit*, *énvoy*, *líberty*. The same adaptation of the foreign stress-patterns took place in words introduced from Latin, as in *návigate*, *régal*, *sécretary*. The persistence of the English system of phonemes, grammatical forms, stress-patterns, and syntactic constructions is by no means unique. The systematic features of the receiving language are generally imposed upon words taken from a foreign language, no matter how numerous.

It is also worth noting that in a running text, as for example in a novel, native English words outnumber adopted foreign words about four to one. Despite English hospitality to words from other languages, it cannot be said that the English lexicon has been overwhelmed by the foreign element.

During the two centuries that separate Chaucer (1400) from Shakespeare (1600), the literary language of England became highly standardized, owing in large measure to Caxton's introduction of printing from the Continent shortly before 1500. The pronunciation of English, to be sure, was far from uniform, even among the social elite and the cultured. In this aspect of English usage, uniformity could be achieved only through intimate and frequent personal contact and by schooling. From the sixteenth century onward, schoolmasters did their best to prescribe "proper" pronunciations; but their conflicting prescriptions themselves show that considerable diversity in usage still existed.

The substantial standardization of cultivated English by the end of

73

the sixteenth century — before English settlements were established overseas — has had tremendous consequences for the history of the language in all parts of the world. It accounts for the ease with which an educated Englishman can communicate with an educated American from any section of the United States or Canada despite the formidable physical barrier that separates the North American continent from the British Isles and despite nearly two centuries of independence of the United States. In later settlements and in countries that came under British political and cultural domination in the eighteenth and nineteenth centuries, Standard English inevitably became the medium of communication in public affairs and the instrument of instruction in the schools. In all parts of the world, speakers of English read the same literary and learned publications and listen to much the same talks on radio and television. This world-wide essential uniformity of literary and of cultivated spoken English is a powerful factor in maintaining cultural ties between continents and in facilitating concerted action in times of crises.

Although relative uniformity prevails on the cultural level in all parts of the world where English is spoken, especially in morphology and syntax, there are nevertheless observable differences in usage from country to country, and within the several countries from region to region. In the British Isles some cultured Scots and Irishmen take pride in their own adaptation of the Received Standard of England. In England itself, the west and the north show the influence of popular speech upon the Standard. Unfortunately we do not have much detailed information about these differences in upper-class speech within the British Isles, except for Scots. Much important work remains to be done in this field, both for scientific and for practical reasons.

In the United States regional differences in pronunciation and in word usage among well-educated speakers are rather marked along the Atlantic coast from Maine to Florida. The systematic survey of this extensive area by the staff of the *Linguistic Atlas* — a project initiated by the American Council of Learned Societies — leaves no doubt about it. The historical reasons for this situation are perfectly clear. Geographically separated from each other for a century or more, and without political, economic, or cultural ties between them before the War for Independence, each of the colonies that were strung out for more than a thousand miles along the Atlantic developed its own regional variety of English under the guidance of Standard British English. Eastern and western New England, the Hudson valley from New York to Albany, eastern Pennsylvania centering on Philadelphia, eastern Virginia to the Blue Ridge, and South Carolina have preserved to this day distinctive configurations of phonological and lexical features that characterize the speech of Bostonians, New Yorkers, Philadelphians, Virginians, and South Carolinians. In the westward movement of the American people, these varieties of English were carried all the way to the Pacific coast in hardly more than half a century: the western New England type via the Great Lakes, the southern plantation type along the Gulf of Mexico, and the Pennsylvania type through the central area.

These three nineteenth-century settlement belts are not as clearly delimited linguistically as the old settlement areas on the Atlantic slope: the farther west, the wider the transition zones reflecting the merging and the crossing of the migration paths.

Some features current on the Atlantic slope did not spread westward, as for example "short" or "checked" vowels in *room* and *whole* and the past-tense form *et* of the verb *eat* of eastern New England. The loss of [r] after vowels, as in *fear, fair, far, four, poor*, has remained confined to the coastal plain along the Atlantic and the Gulf of Mexico. Here the loss of the postvocalic [r] has introduced a new low vowel in such words as *heart, lark* to contrast with that of *hot, lock*. This phonological innovation did not take place in Standard British English until the latter part of the eighteenth century, long after the English colonies had been planted in America. In all probability, it was adopted from England shortly before the Revolution in the major seaports, where the most intimate contacts with the mother country had been maintained throughout the colonial period.

The speech of the vast American middle class and of the folk is naturally much more diversified regionally than cultivated speech. Even so, it exhibits none of the sharp differences that characterize the rural folk speech of the British Isles and of continental Europe. Nor are the social levels of speech anywhere near as clear-cut as in most parts of Europe. The Old World exhibits the linguistic effects of the provincialism and the formidable social barriers of early days. In the New World political boundaries have rarely obstructed communication between political domains, the easy rise of the common man to positions of influence has prevented the development of marked social castes, and relatively early schooling at public expense has created a predominantly middle-class society of well-informed citizens. Hence the relative uniformity of speech from region to region and from one social group to another.

With the expansion from the British Isles to other parts of the world, speakers of English met with many new phenomena, both natural and cultural, and with speakers of various languages. Plants and animals unknown to them in their homeland had to be given names, and the peculiar institutions and practices of the indigenous populations called for new expressions. These needs could be met by adopting the terms used by the earlier inhabitants, such as *wigwam*, *moccasin*; by coining descriptive phrases like *Indian corn*, *ground squirrel*; or by extending the range of application of English words, as in the case of *robin*.

The enrichment of the English vocabulary owing to contacts with speakers of other languages and to living in a new environment can be conveniently illustrated by the vocabulary of American English as recorded and discussed in the four volumes of *A Dictionary of American English* by W. A. Craigie and J. R. Hulbert (1938–1944), in *A Dictionary of Americanisms* by M. M. Mathews (1951) based upon it, and in *The American Language* by H. L. Mencken (1919–1948), revised and brought up to date by R. I. McDavid, Jr. (1963).

Early contact with the Indians, chiefly tribes speaking in Algonkian languages, furnished the settlers with names for new foodstuffs, such as *pone*, *hominy*, *squash*; for animals of the New World, such as *chipmunk*, *moose*, *opossum*, *raccoon*, *skunk*; and for Indian cultural objects and ways, such as *moccasin*, *tomahawk*, *wigwam*, *papoose*, *squaw*, *sachem*, *powwow*, and *totem*.

These Indian words survive to this day, and not only in American English. To be sure, the chipmunk is called a *ground squirrel* in many parts of the United States, and *maize* (an Indian, but not an Algonkian, word) came to be designated by the descriptive English phrase *Indian corn*, soon shortened to *corn*, since it was the chief grain crop of the colonists.

Amerindian place names abound from one end of the North American continent to the other: rivers, such as the *Connecticut, Potomac, Ohio, Mississippi*; lakes, such as *Erie, Huron, Michigan*; mountain ranges, such as the *Alleghenies, Appalachians, Ozarks*; states, such as *Massachusetts, Kentucky, Wisconsin, Oregon, Texas*; and cities, such as *Chattanooga, Chicago, Milwaukee, Omaha*. Some of these toponyms were adopted outright from the Indians, others came to be applied by the English settlers in reference to Indian tribes.

In parts of the present United States and Canada where speakers of other European languages lived in large numbers before the flood of English settlers engulfed them, some everyday non-English words and place names have survived in American English.

In the Hudson Valley, place names like *Brooklyn, Fishkill, Catskills, Amsterdam* and a few homely words like *pot cheese* for "cottage cheese" and *stoop* for a roofed entry to a house come from the Dutch spoken in this area along with English for nearly two centuries.

Place names like *Manheim, Hagerstown*, and *Gettysburg* in eastern Pennsylvania are German in an area that has been bilingual since early colonial days. Only a few simple German words, among them *smearcase* for "cottage cheese" and *dumb* in the sense of "stupid," have more than regional currency in English.

In the basin of the Great Lakes and in the Mississippi Valley such place names as *Detroit, La Crosse, St. Louis, Baton Rouge, New Orleans* dot the vast area in which the French carried on the fur trade and their missionary activities among the Indians before the westward movement from the eastern United States swept into it shortly before 1800. Except for a fair number of French toponyms, the lexical contribution of French to American English is rather slight. In the Midwest we encounter *prairie, portage, butte, cache*, the last for a secret store of provisions or goods (of the far-ranging fur trader); on the lower Mississippi we find *levee* for an embankment and *bayou* (ultimately from Choctaw) for a marshy, sluggish stream.

Spanish place names — *Rio Grande, Colorado, Sierra Nevada, Santa Fe, Los Angeles* among others — characterize the vast Southwest, which did not become a part of the Union until the middle of the nineteenth century. In Texas, New Mexico, Arizona, and southern California, where Spanish is still spoken by sizable elements, numerous Spanish words have limited regional currency in English. Other Spanish terms, especially *ranch*, *corral*, *lasso*, *stampede*, and others connected with the "cattle kingdoms" of the latter part of the nineteenth century, are known wherever English is spoken, owing at least in part to the popular Westerns that glorify the manly virtues of the *vaquero* or cowboy.

Much could be said about the coining of new English words to meet the needs and fads of American life, about scattered transient terms adopted from newcomers like the Germans and the Scandinavians in the Midwest. But I have illustrated some of the ways in which both the British-English and the American-English vocabulary has been enriched through contacts with other peoples.

The spectacular geographical expansion of English, from small beginnings in a part of the British Isles to most of North America and all of Australia and many other areas, exceeds the expansion of Latin under the Romans. Yet this expansion, even though it facilitates communication throughout the world, places a reciprocal burden on native English speakers of learning other tongues in ever increasing numbers.

8 DIALECTS: BRITISH AND AMERICAN STANDARD AND NONSTANDARD

Raven I. McDavid, Jr.

Five or six years ago my younger sister called me on the telephone — long distance, as we put it in America, a "trunk call" in the British Isles — from the same part of South Carolina where we had grown up. When I came to the phone she commented, incredulously, "Brucker, you've been up north so long you talk just like a Yankee!" Although I am sure none of my Chicago neighbors would mistake my way of speaking for that of Paul Douglas or Philip Wrigley, let alone one of the Kennedys, only last month a Texan told me that I had lost all trace of my native accent. Perhaps I have lost some of it; and perhaps the fate of my South Carolina way of speaking during a quarter century of exposure to other parts of the United States is emblematic of the fate of American dialects.

Note that I use the term *dialect* where others might use some other term, such as *accent*. This choice of terms is, basically, the American one. In other parts of the world, scholars would not use *dialect* for the speech of educated men and women; they would restrict it to the speech of the uneducated. They might not use it to describe the speech of a city, but only that of rural areas, usually remote ones. They might not use it to describe the speech of the younger generation, but only that of the older or the old-fashioned. In short, for them *dialect* means a mode of speech quaint and uneducated, found in isolated communities. But we do need a term sufficiently inclusive to describe the fact that educated Britons do not talk the way educated Americans, or Canadians, or Australians, or New Zealanders,

79

or South Africans do — and that even within the same country, as in the United States, there may be sharp regional differences in the speech of the educated. To take five recent presidents, all college graduates: Calvin Coolidge did not talk like Herbert Hoover, and neither of them talked like Franklin D. Roosevelt, John F. Kennedy, or Lyndon Johnson. Rather than attempt to coin a new term, it is best to take a well-known one like *dialect* and define it carefully for our purposes.

As we thus define it, a dialect is simply any habitual variety of a language, regional or social. It may be the variety spoken chiefly by the educated — like Received Standard, which at one time was the mode of speech of those who ran the affairs of the empire and also of those who ministered to the needs of this class, like butlers and club stewards. It may be essentially the speech of the uneducated, as Cockney is the speech of the uneducated Londoner. It may be regional, as the speech of West Riding farmers differs from that of Devonshire farmers. And, particularly in the United States, it may have both regional and social dimensions: educated American speech has many regional varieties — south Texas, Boston, the Hudson Valley, Iowa, Vermont — but in any region, say the Boston area, the speech of the natives will have some common characteristics regardless of social level, though in each region educated speech will differ from the uneducated. Nevertheless, all dialects have this in common: they are absorbed from one's everyday associates in all walks of life. In this respect they differ from varieties of the language picked up through special associations on the job and elsewhere, like most argots and technical jargons, or taken over from the fads of the moment, like most slang.

Dialects seem to be common to all speech communities of any size, though for many of them the precise evidence has been lost. People in different localities use their language somewhat differently; and in any locality the speech of some people or groups of people is considered better than that of others, and hence more worth imitating. The last force — prestige or the lack of it — is the essential cause of the development of social dialects; the development of regional dialects has a somewhat more complex history.

The first explanation of regional differences is the nature of the original settlement. The peculiarities of Kentish speech have long been attributed to the unique settlement of Jutes under Hengist and Horsa; in North America, many features of eastern New England speech — notably the loss of /-r/ in *beard, barn, war* —are explained by the large proportion of East Anglians among the early settlers. Similarly, we may discover the influence of other groups, stubborn Britons or marauding Norsemen, on one side of the Atlantic; French or Spanish-Americans or Germans or Hollanders or Scandinavians on the other. My wife is of Scottish descent but grew up in a Minneapolis neighborhood where Scandinavians were in the majority; today, though she has never learned a Swedish sentence, her intonation shows Scandinavian influence, especially when she is excited, and her use of *bring* and *take* differs from mine in ways not to be explained by the differences in our regional background.

But differences arise in other ways, as from routes of migration and communication. The route favored by wool traders took London speech forms north, toward The Wash; the migrations of Ulster Scots in America took some of their words and phrases from Pennsylvania into the southern uplands, and the Erie Canal and the Great Lakes spread New England words and pronunciations into the northern part of the middle western states.

Political, commercial, and educational forces also influence dialect patterns. We have mentioned the traditional distinctiveness of Kentish and East Anglian speech, though the ancient kingdoms disappeared long before the ultimate consolidation of the heptarchy under Wessex. In the United States, local political boundaries have been less important than in Britain; yet along the Atlantic coast the usage *county site*, "shire town," is practically confined to Georgia, while elsewhere the traditional United States *county seat* alternates with *shire town, county capital*, and *county town*, the last, incidentally, being the prevailing term in Ontario. Pennsylvania is set off from neighboring states — especially West Virginia and Maryland —by the lack of old-fashioned grammatical forms and pronunciations, like *dreen* for *drain*; apparently education in Pennsylvania was both more general and more thorough. It is well known that the limits of many dialect features in England coincide with the old diocesan boundaries — the sea cities also being the principal market towns; similarly, in New England, the term *tonic*, "soda pop" (British *minerals*), is restricted to the wholesale trading area of Boston. On both sides of the Atlantic we find focal and relic areas: in Britain, the principal focus is London; in the United States there are Boston, New York, Philadelphia, Richmond (Virginia), and more recently St. Louis, San Francisco, and Salt Lake City to mention only a few. To the parts of East Anglia that remained linguistic backwaters till the coming of the air bases in World War II, the United States can offer parallels in the Maine coast, the Outer Banks of North Carolina, the Eastern Shore of Chesapeake Bay, and parts of the southern Appalachians.

In Britain, the principal dialect regions seem to have been established rather early: Northumbrian, Mercian, East Anglian, West Saxon, and Kentish. They have largely remained the same, with some new distinctions arising (or at least being deducible from better evidence), and with London developing its own distinctive speech, whose upper-class variety became the prestigious model for most parts of the British Isles and many parts of the commonwealth. Yet some of the old dilaect characteristics are gone: this is particularly true of Kentish, which under the influence of London English has lost one of the most striking features of its medieval dialect, the voicing of initial /f-, s-, θ-/ to /v-, z-, ð-/, as in Medieval Kentish *vot* for "foot" and *zee* for "sea." A trace of this dialectical voicing is found in Standard English *vixen*, female of *fox*, where the Kentish *v* has been borrowed to replace the expected *f* — as also in *vat*, a "tub-like container" — where the expected *f* forms have been found as late as in Shakespeare's time.

In the Uuited States, too, we see regional dialects persisting but many regional features losing ground. The basic regional patterns of speech were established by the end of the eighteenth century. Three major speech regions are to be clearly identified: (1) Northern: New England, the Hudson Valley, and derivative settlements westward; (2) Midland: Pennsylvania and derivative settlements to the west and southwest; (3) Southern: the plantation area of the coastal plain and lower piedmont of the south Atlantic states, and its extensions on the coast of the Gulf of Mexico and in the Mississippi

Valley. Despite subsequent immigration and a variety of social changes, these three major divisions persist, along with many well-defined subdivisions. What is more, it is not difficult to trace the extensions of regional patterns for particular features, even west of the Mississippi.

But the farther west one goes, the less easy it is to recognize clear regions as extensions of the more distinctively marked Atlantic seaboard areas. This fact should not surprise anyone who has tried to trace the British affiliations of even the clearly differentiated American dialects. In both migration from Britain to America and westward migration from the Atlantic seaboard, the new lands were settled by people from all the older regions, though in varying proportions; in both instances, those with the strongest local identity, who most strongly preserved the most characteristically local forms of speech, did not migrate at all but stayed at home. In the United States there has been a rather constant — and large — proportion of the population who change their state of residence between decennial censuses. As the population gets mixed, the sharper regional speech characteristics tend to disappear. As social mobility accompanies regional mobility — Hoovers, Trumans, Eisenhowers, Kennedys, Johnsons rise from humble beginnings to the ranks of the wealthy and powerful — the speech forms of humble life tend to disappear, though the standards of prestigious speech may also be modified in the process. And the blunting of regional dialect differences has been furthered by such powerful and long-persistent forces in American culture as industrialization, urbanization, and mass education. Industrialization replaces home crafts with the technology and specialized terminology of mass production; urbanization accelerates the spread of general commercial terms for items, like foods, that were once produced at home; mass education stigmatizes folk-grammar and folk-pronunciations, replacing them with the standard forms. But regional distinctions persist, not merely along the Atlantic seaboard but farther inland.

The Canadian situation is much the same as that in the United States: local varieties of English are most pronounced in the areas of early settlement — the Atlantic provinces, eastern and southern Ontario, and the coast of British Columbia — and they are weakest in the prairie provinces. For Australia and New Zealand the picture is less clear: on the one hand, many observers say there are *no* regional differences; on the other hand, G. W. Turner (a New Zealander) asserts that regional differences in Australia *and* New Zealand add up to little more than those in the eastern United States; his recent work, *The English Language in Australia and New Zealand*, does not, however, offer evidence of such extensive differences. Of South African English, which has sustained heavy pressure from Afrikaans, we know too little to delineate regional boundaries; of West Indian English, with its heavy African and Latin admixtures, we know enough to assert considerable local variation. Whether such exotica as Tristan da Cunha and Pitcairn-Norfolk are to be considered regional varieties or special creolizations depends on the observer's perspective.

But though regional dialects appear everywhere in the English-speaking world as a result of the same forces, the development of social dialects may take a different direction in one region from what it does in another. We have pointed out that Received Standard has descended and spread from upper-class London speech. But even that upper-class speech has undergone modifications from time to time — most notably during the later Middle Ages when it acquired from northern English speech such everyday words as the plural verb *are* (where many southern British folk dialects still have *be*), the pronouns *she, they, their, them*, and the *-s* inflection for the third-person singular present indicative. Within the British Isles, until the rise of the welfare state, Received Standard — including its pronunciation, RP — has had no serious competitor; Scots and Irish might be tolerated in educated usage — for Scotsmen and Irishmen; all other varieties were linguistically second or third class. In many places overseas Received Standard was the preferred model: in the West Indies, in South Africa, in New Zealand, and Australia. And of course it was the variety of English taught throughout Europe. Lately, to be sure, its prestige has been questioned at home; such new figures of esteem as the Mods and the Beatles on the one hand, and Harold Wilson on the other, share the public eye with the squirearchy and the black-coated gentlemen of the City. Nevertheless, Received Standard — if a Received Standard somewhat altered from that of Bernard Shaw's heyday — is still widely emulated.

On the other side of the Atlantic, however, there was a tradition of autonomy from the beginning. Each colony was a separate foundation, and developed its own elite as time passed. On some of the colonial centers — Boston, Newport, New York, the Virginia ports, and Charleston — the upper-class speech of London exerted some influence through royal governors and their courts, the transient clergy of the Church of England, and some exposure of the sons of planters and merchants to the English universities and the Inns of Court. In such areas there was a loss, as in London, of the /-r/ in *barn* and the like, and an /a/ vowel, of varying quality, in *half, dance,* and similar words. But these influences were lacking in Philadelphia, the most important colonial city, and in 1776 the second most important city under the Crown. There was no royal governor or court; the Church of England was relatively unimportant; the Quakers — the local elite — were excluded from the British universities and the Inns of Court, and had little interest in fashionable British society. After the Revolution the prestige of London English was diminished everywhere in the new nation, and each center developed its own standards, essentially alike in grammar but varying in pronunciation and vocabulary. For a while the literary preeminence of Boston lent special prestige to the speech of eastern New England, but this variety never spread westward. Today Boston is but one of a number of cultural centers. The growing population and wealth of the inland north means that the educated speech of such cities as Cleveland, Detroit, and Chicago becomes increasingly identified as an American standard, with /-r/ preserved in *barn* and /æ/ in *bath* and *dance*. Nevertheless, not only Boston but such southern cities as Atlanta, Nashville, and New Orleans also have their own prestigious speech, and so do San Francisco, Seattle, and other Western cities.

Canada is again very much like the United States in variation of dialects and dialect prestige. Her commonwealth membership means that RP has some prestige, and British immigrants reinforce its tradition; but the new Canadian nationalism is a force for linguistic autonomy. From Toronto to the Rockies, educated

85

Canadian speech is very much like the inland northern speech of the United States in its strong /-r/ in *barn* and *beard* and its /æ/ in *half, dance, command.* But it differs in its centered beginning of /ai/ and /au/ before voiceless consonants, as in *out* and *ice*; and most Canadians do not distinguish such pairs as *cot* and *caught, collar* and *caller.* There is a difference in attitude: the Canadian Broadcasting Corporation recognizes local linguistic standards to the extent that it prefers local announcers to speak the local variety of standard English.

In Australia British speech is still emulated; cultivated Australian is marked by the modification of Australian vowels in the direction of RP. New Zealanders are even more likely to favor British models. For the West Indies, some observers recognize no local varieties of cultivated speech: Received Standard is the model, all else is creole.

With the spread of English as a second language and the vehicle of a great deal of higher education everywhere, there has been an interesting new development: new local varieties of cultivated English, as in India, Pakistan, and the Philippines, are normally modified in the direction of the pronunciation system, including stress and intonation, of the host languages. What will happen to these new varieties of English will depend on a host of political, economic, and social forces; at present, however, they are viable and growing. One condition making for their viability, both on the Indian subcontinent and in the Philippines, is their great usefulness as a general means of communication among populations separated by a myriad of indigenous tongues.

Until recently, there were two typical relationships between standard and nonstandard dialects. In England there was one standard variety, many local nonstandard ones. In the United States, there have been several regional standard varieties, each with corresponding nonstandard ones. Standard and substandard shared the same pronunciation system, the same pronunciation of vowels and consonants, and the typical regional vocabulary; they differed in grammar and in which vowels and consonants occurred in a given word. Educated speakers would say /sofə/ and *I saw*; uneducated ones /sofi/ and *I seen.* Even foreign-language settlements gradually adapted to the local model. But recently the American picture has changed, as Negroes and poor whites have swarmed by the thousands into such northern cities as Cleveland, Detroit, and Chicago. They bring with them a vowel system somewhat different in its systemic aspects from the local norm, sharply different pronunciations of individual vowels, numerous unfamiliar nonstandard grammatical constructions, regional peculiarities in vocabulary, and unfamiliar patterns of stress and pitch. Because Negroes are the most numerous — and certainly the most noticeable — of the new immigrants, all of these strange speech characteristics are identified with "Negro speech." In some northern cities a southern-born college professor may have difficulty getting housing if he telephones a real estate office.

The complex interrelationships of historical, regional, social, and so-called racial forces can be illustrated by a single linguistic feature: the lack of the -*s* form for the third-person singular present indicative, as *he do, she have, it make.* In England this is widely spread in old-fashioned speech, from Norfolk to Somerset; it must have been brought to all the American colonies in the seventeenth and eighteenth centuries. But it survived principally in the south, thanks to a selective cultural differential. Until recently, the south has been the most rural region, least subject to the leveling influence of urban life; it has been the most heavily agricultural, with an emphasis on unskilled labor. It has also been the region whose inhabitants were least given to travel. Its per capita income has been lowest, its average school attendance the least, and its schools poorest in quality. So grammatical forms widely distributed in England became identified in the New World with the south and were used by southerners, both Negro and white. In the south, moreover, the same cultural differentials which operated on the region generally operated to preserve these forms among a greater proportion of Negroes than whites. In the south, Negroes until recently were more predominantly rural than were whites; more of them were in agriculture and in unskilled agricultural labor; they traveled less; their per capita income was less; they had less schooling, and it was poorer in quality. So linguistic features widespread in southern England and identified as southern regional features in the United States have been more strikingly preserved among southern Negroes

87

than among southern whites. And with the migration northward these features have been popularly identified in the north as features of Negro speech.

At one time the student of dialects was tolerated at best as a harmless drudge. Now, on the knowledge that he brings and on the skill with which he can interpret that knowledge to those who make educational policy in the United States, depends — in an awe-inspiring way — the health of the American educational system, and indeed the health of American society. On the one hand, unfilled jobs will not be available to the unemployed 4 per cent until the latter have acquired (among other things) a functioning command of standard English; on the other hand, the dominant culture will not really be able to accept the aspiring minorities until it realizes that all dialects are legitimate forms of the language, arising through normal interactions of human beings in social contexts. As a professional dialectologist I am awed by the responsibility, but inspired by the opportunity.

9 LANGUAGE AND THE TOTAL SYSTEM OF COMMUNICATION

Henry Lee Smith, Jr.

Perhaps it would be best to begin by stating the bias or point of view which will serve as the basis for this chapter. In the first place, I am a linguistic scientist or scientific linguist who is also termed, at times, anthropological linguist or linguistic anthropologist. As an anthropologist, I am primarily concerned with human culture and cultures in the sense in which the anthropologist uses the term: that a culture, or culture in general, is the sum total of the learned, shared and transmitted, patterned and systematized ways man goes about meeting the problems raised by his environment. A culture can thus be thought of as the total way of life of a society or group of people who are seen to be bound together by common experiences and expectancies. Culture is not to be seen as just the things or tools man fashions to make himself more efficient in coping with his day-by-day, year-by-year problems, but as all of his attitudes, assumptions, beliefs, and values — the products of his head and heart as well as of his hands.

Human cultures are all alike in furnishing sets of systematized answers to the universal problems of human existence, but the answers are all different answers, and each culture is therefore unique. Each individual of our species is born into a society that is already a going concern, and since, to all intents and purposes, he is devoid of instincts, he must *learn* to become a human being by internalizing the culture of his group. The kind of learning required to become fully enculturated and socialized is highly exacting, and by far the larger part of this exacting task of learning to become human is handled through the principal modality of human communication — *language*. Language is a learned, shared, and arbitrary *system* of vocal *symbols* through which *human beings* in the same speech community or subculture *interact* and hence *communicate* in terms of their *common cultural experience* and *expectations*.

By far the most important term in this definition is *system*; the systematized and patterned nature of all human culture and of all human behavior cannot be stressed too much. Next in importance are *symbols* and *human beings*. Though it has seemed an oversimplification to many, a real dichotomy can and must be made between the *closed systems* of *signs* or *calls* used by even the most intelligent social animals like the dolphins and the great apes, and the unique, open-ended *symbol* systems which we find universally in the possession of human beings. Whereas animals are triggered off by an immediately perceptible stimulus, like the presence of food or a source of danger, and emit a call heard and recognized by another of the group as a sign of food or danger, man bestows or imparts a meaning to events and artifacts which cannot be directly perceived by the senses. This uniquely human behavior, which Leslie White calls *symboling*, allows us "to comprehend the meaning of *sin* or *Sunday*," something no animal could possibly do. A rat can be conditioned to respond to a red triangle as a sign of food and to react to a yellow circle as a forerunner to an electric shock, but no rat can *warn* another rat of what to expect when neither is in the presence of the experimenter's maze. But man, in quiet retrospect, can talk about things that have happened in the past, things that are happening as he speaks, things that will or may happen, even things that *cannot* happen, and lie about all of them.

Language is seen in our definition as a means through which interaction between human beings takes place, and interaction — *human* interaction — is equated with *communication*. But, further, the communication and interaction goes on only in the matrix of the total *cultural* surroundings of the communicants. Language itself is a system of human culture, in fact the most important system, the system through which the others are principally reflected and transmitted. Once language was in man's possession, culture, his unique adaptive mechanism, became possible. Without language there could be no culture, and man remained homin*oid*; with language and culture, he could and did become homin*ine*.

Throughout this discussion it will have emerged that the anthropological linguist sees language "pulled out," so to speak, of the organisms of the individual human beings who have learned it through interaction with others who have previously learned it or who are still undergoing the enculturation process. The cultural anthropologist, or "culturologist," to use Leslie White's term, is concerned with systematized behavior seen in an *extra-somatic*, or "outside the body," context. In fact, White defines culture as "things and events in the real world dependent upon symboling and seen in an *extra-somatic context*." Thus symbols, culture, and human communication and interaction all become like the warp and woof of an intricately woven and seamless fabric. Some investigators even go so far as to see *all* of culture as communication. Homer Barnett, for example, puts it this way:

> The organization and perpetuation of culture is not dependent upon any person, but upon a complex *interaction* among many. The maintenance mechanisms are not within the individual; they are outside him in society. Consonant with this is a view of the social contract as one whereby men agree to communicate and of *culture* as the *code* by which they communicate.

Whether we choose to go quite so far and see culture as the code by which men communicate, all anthropologists would agree in stressing the group aspects of the process rather than each person's individual handling of the learned and shared modalities. R. L. Birdwhistell, the pioneer in the study of kinesics — the structured use of bodily motion in communication — puts it this way:

> Communication is not a process made up of a total of individual expressions in some action–reaction sequence. It is a system of interaction with a structure independent of the behavior of its individual participants. One person does not "communicate to" another person; he engages in communication with him. A human being does not invent his system of

communication. He may make additions to it, and he may vary the direction of its formulations. However, as a system, it has been in existence for generations. He must learn it in order to be a member of his society.

Communication is multi-functional: it composes not only the primary relations of interaction, but maintains rules for the regulation of these relationships. There are some who would go so far as to make communication co-terminous with culture. I would not. But I would say that communication provides the means of sustaining the patterned interpersonal relationships without which culture would be impossible.

Though this statement might give the impression that Birdwhistell sees communication as a single system, like most anthropologists concerned with human communicative behavior he sees the totality composed of several subsystems. He writes: "Communication is made up of the interdependent activities of a series of abstractable subsystems emergent from the patterning of the several sensory modalities. Kinesics is not the study of communication any more than is linguistics. Both are sciences which investigate subsystems of communication."

Perhaps Birdwhistell goes too far in seeming to imply that language and kinesics are equally important subsystems. Most students of human communication would agree in rating language as by far the most important subsystem, not only of communication but of culture as well. For instance, C. F. Hockett sees language as the only system that shows the "design feature" he calls "duality of patterning." To reiterate terms explained in earlier chapters: language has phonemes — sound types with no intrinsic meaning — which, in a very special way, enter into morphemes — recurring patterned partials that have *grammatical significance*. Thus, though *raft* and *laughed* end in the same sound, or phoneme, the /t/ in *laughed* does something more than simply end the word, which is its function in *raft*. When *laughed* follows the words *he* or *John*, for example, the final /t/ has the grammatical function of indicating what we traditionally call the past tense; it serves as a grammatical ending, or suffix. Language, and only language, has grammar; all the other structured modalities lack this "duality of patterning" which makes language the amazing open-ended system it is. Language, and only language, through itself and by means of itself alone, can relate itself to all of the other systems of culture. For example, using language, we can talk about the intricate structuring of the kinesic system in the minutest detail, and we can do this at high noon or in pitch dark, but we cannot communicate the intricacies of phoneme and morpheme through kinesics.

What we have just said is *not* to be construed as meaning that kinesics is something "not yet fully human" in its structuring, or that gestures and bodily motion are used principally by primitives whose languages are not yet fully developed. Such remarks as the following, by a so-called expert, appeared recently in a local newspaper (and similar statements appear with regrettable frequency in the public press of most western countries): "Some people still make extensive use of gestures and there is a tribe in Africa which cannot communicate much at night because they rely largely on gestures which aren't visible in the dark." Of course there is no such tribe; of course *all* languages are equally complex, and all show duality of patterning. But what is particularly to be deplored is the implication, by the use of the phrase "*still* make extensive use of gestures," that the use of bodily motion for communication is something prehuman or subhuman. Quite the contrary; structured use of bodily motion is *universally* present in human culture and is utilized to about the same extent in all communication systems. To quote Birdwhistell again: "Body motion can be studied as a patterned system which must be learned by every individual if he is to participate fully as a member of his society. Complex and ordered, its internalization is integral to both enculturation and socialization. . . . its patterning is probably every bit as coercive as is that of language."

But kinesics, to which we will return later, is not the only subsystem or group of subsystems intimately bound up with language in forming the totality of the communication "package." A whole spectrum of vocal phenomena, often called "tone of voice" by the nonspecialist, is now referred to as *paralanguage*. These phenomena are — and must be kept — quite distinct from the intonational features of language proper generally referred to as *stress, pitch,* and *juncture* or *transition*. As long ago as 1927, discussing the nonuniversal nature of intonation in language, Edward Sapir wrote: "But . . . there is a second level of socially determined variation in intonation — the musical handling of the voice generally, quite aside from the properly linguistic patterns of intonation." For example, the four relative levels of stress in English (*primary* /´/, *secondary* /^/, *tertiary* /ˋ/, and *weak* /˘/), the four relative pitch heights (numbered 1, 2, 3, 4, in ascending order), and the four *junctures* or *transitions* (*internal open* or "plus" /+/, *pitch sustention* or "single bar" /|/, *terminal fade* or "double cross" /#/, and *terminal rise* or "double bar" /‖/) form three independent but interdependent systems of *prosodic* or *suprasegmental phonemes*. These phonemes enter into suprasegmental morphemes called *superfixes* and *suprafixes*, which serve, among other things, to designate the differences between lexical and tactical phrases; between the principal constituents of a sentence; and between the relationship of clause to clause within a sentence and of various *attachments* to or *insertions* within the main portions of a sentence. In examples 1 and 2 note how stress and pitch serve to furnish a contrast between *lexical phrases*, or "compounds," and *tactical phrases*, in which adjectives modify nouns.

1.*a*	²ă + ³sáfe + jòb¹#	"a burglary"
b	²ă + ²sâfe + ³jób¹#	"a job with security and tenure"
2.*a*	²ă + ³bláck + bòard¹#	"a board to write on"
b	²ă + ³bláck³ bóard¹#	"a board that is black, not green"

In example 3 note how terminal *contours*, which are combinations of pitch phonemes and terminal transition or juncture phonemes, serve to indicate such differing *grammatical functions* as *vocative* and *appositive*.

3.*a*	²Thĕ + ³kíng²#²Jóhn²‖²iš + ³déad¹#
b	²Thĕ + ³kińg²#³Jóhn²#²iš + ³déad¹#

Now notice how the difference between the restrictive (example 4*a*) and nonrestrictive (example 4*b*) clause is signaled by pitch and terminal juncture contrasts:

4.*a* ²Thèy + ²heáled²|²thĕ + ²Ińdians²|²who + wère +
³síck¹#

b ²Thèy + ²heáled²|²thĕ + ³Ińdians²,#²who + wère +
³síck¹#

And, finally, note how a level of pitch only one degree higher can make the difference between asking a simple question of one's mother and asking whether that dear lady is to be the main course in a cannibalistic feast:

5.*a* ²Whât're + wè + ²háving²|²fŏr + ³dínner,²#²Móther?²
b ²Whât're + wè + ²háving²|²for + ³dínner,²#³Móther?³

These examples should illustrate sufficiently the kinds of events Sapir designated as "properly linguistic patterns of intonation."

To turn now to *paralanguage*, Sapir's "second level of socially determined variation in intonation": First, we must consider the physiological, anatomical basis for making these sounds. Just as the physical structure of a musical instrument is a principal determinant of its sound qualities, the physiological structure of the body itself and its actual physical state at any time is a major determinant of *voice set*, or basic voice timbre. As G. L. Trager puts it, voice set "involves the physiological and physical peculiarities resulting in the patterned identification of individuals as members of a societal group," and voice set is consequently affected by body build, state of health, the position within a group, sex, mood, human rhythm phase (such as sleeping or waking), toxic status (including that induced by alcohol or drugs), location in space vis-à-vis others, and perhaps other such states. Voice set can thus be seen as a set of idiosyncratic *preconditionings* forming a background for language itself as well as for the *voice qualities* and *vocalizations* of paralanguage, and thus would be evident throughout the whole of an individual's contribution to the communication and not just in a part. The *voice qualities* of paralanguage are actual and recognizable speech events, phenomena separable and distinct from language proper and from other paralinguistic events. Voice qualities are part of culture, are learned and shared and systematized, and are used by the individual as over-all signals of his perception of the *culturally determined image* of himself in relation to his total environment. Thus he has an *image* of his body, his health, his status, his gender, his mood, his human rhythm, his toxic status, his locale. As R. L. Pittenger states, the difference between [statements about image] really [has] to do with the individual's own perception of the things [described under voice set] rather than the actual physiological, anatomical, chronological state of the organism. Voice qualities are not so much related to the anatomical, physiological status of the individual, but to learned patterns of status and the image within the cultural or interaction setting."

The voice qualities so far abstracted are as follows:

Quality	Description
Pitch range	spread up or down *vs.* narrowed from above or below
Vocal lip-control	heavy rasp *vs.* complete openness
Glottis control	overvoicing and undervoicing *vs.* heavy to slight breathiness
Pitch control	sharp *vs.* smooth transitions
Articulation control	forceful–precise *vs.* relaxed–slurred
Rhythm control	smooth *vs.* jerky
Resonance	booming *vs.* thin
Tempo	increased *vs.* decreased from a norm
Intensity range	increased *vs.* decreased from a norm

Although the descriptions involve pairs of polar opposites, the terms should be thought of as descriptive of extremes between which there are continua of several intermittent degrees. The selection of voice qualities, as we have noted, serves to communicate the image the speaker has of himself as the culture gives him to see himself, and may also project an image quite far removed from reality. A little man may compensate — or overcompensate — by cultivating a voice operating below the norm of his true pitch range and with an increased level of intensity and a booming resonance. On the other hand, a six foot four inch male hypochondriac with an ordinary cold might squeeze his pitch range and decrease his level of intensity to what might be expected in a preadolescent female in order to impress his wife with the seriousness of his condition. A man unused to alcohol might be convinced he is intoxicated after a single weak highball and project the culturally accepted image of the inebriate complex with slurred articulation, slowed tempo, and so on.

The second major area of paralinguistic events is that of *vocalizations*. Three levels have been distinguished — *vocal characterizers, vocal qualifiers*, and *vocal segregates*. All of these events, unlike the voice qualities, are "turned on" and "turned off" at certain perceivable and relatively short intervals, even though the events may be repeated in conjunction with quite a long stretch of language and other communicative behavior. For example, a vocal characterizer like *breaking*, as heard in the "nervous giggle" or in the quite different context of a speech or sermon when the orator uses it to impress us with his sincerity, seldom continues for more than the elapsed time of a single sentence, though the communicator may repeat it a score or more times. Breaking, which Pittenger describes as an "intermittent tenseness and laxness of the vocal musculature creating the tremulousness and the interruption of tone often heard as a signal of great emotion or . . . intense emotional involvement," is to be clearly distinguished from the voice quality *rasp*, which is produced by a *steady* and forceful vocal lip-control and which continues over long stretches of speech. The vocal characterizers *crying* and *laughing* can be heard when one talks through tears or laughter, and vocal characterizers include the phenomena noted when language comes through against *moans, groans, yawns*, or even *belches*.

The second level of vocalizations, the *vocal qualifiers*, are even more restricted in their duration and are even more closely interrelated to the events of language proper. These never seem to continue over more than the space of a single *intonation pattern* of language. The features of *intensity, pitch*, and *duration* form the basis of the three sets of vocal qualifiers, and we can distinguish three levels of *overloudness* set off by three levels of *oversoftness*, three levels of *overhigh pitch* opposed to three levels of *overlow pitch*, and three degrees of *drawl* paired off against three degrees of *clipping* — all relative to a *base line* established for each communicator in each observed communication situation. These events, based on the features of intensity, pitch, and duration, are separate and distinct from the comparable phenomena based on these features and described as voice qualities. That is, the vocal qualifier of overloudness or the vocal qualifier of drawl can be heard in conjunction with relatively short stretches of language as occurring over and above the voice qualities of increased intensity or decreased tempo. Thus the orator, employing the culturally accepted over-all deliberateness of delivery (decreased tempo), can further slow down the articulation rate of certain portions of his speech and at the same time increase the intensity on these same segments or on others.

The *vocal segregates* are the shortest of all, being, in essence, no longer in duration than a single segment, or phone, of language. The segregates are, in fact, a series of noises very similar to phones, and pattern not only terms of oppositions, but also packages which, over-all, are quite similar to words. For example, take the middle-range vocalic segregate or "hesitation noise," usually written *uh* or *er*. It never occurs except with an intonation pattern, usually with a terminal rising pitch, and generally with the vocal qualifier of second-degree drawl. When we isolate the segregate of glottal closure and its "opposite," the full glottal spirant segregate, we find that these, with the hesitation noise we have just described, and with stress and intonation patterns from language proper, make the familiar *uh uh* and *uh huh* which are the segregate packages of dissent and assent. To the first of these we can add the further segregate of open-lip nasalization and get the nasalized *uh uh*, without change of meaning. If we add closed lip nasalization we get a similar variant of the second. We can construct still another variant of the second by adding the low-range vocalic segregate and the vocal qualifier of maximum drawl. This gives an emphasized variant of the assent package.

Typical packages of segregates with no vocalics and, therefore, no stress or intonation patterns are the *dental continuant* accompanied by *expiration* and prolonged by double-plus *drawl*, or the "hiss of derision." This can be compared to the Japanese *palatal continuant* with *inspiration* and *drawl* to give the "honorific hiss," which some scholars have mistakenly taken for a phoneme of the Japanese linguistic system. One man's phoneme *may* be another man's vocal segregate, however, as can be shown by comparing the American (English) *alveolar inspirated click*, sometimes spelled *tut tut*, to the click phone of the same type in Hottentot, where the fly that carries sleeping sickness is the *tsetse* fly.

Thus language and paralanguage are intricately interrelated in each culture's over-all communication system, and kinesics is also closely interconnected with both language and paralanguage. Neither paralanguage nor kinesics shows Hockett's duality of patterning, and there are quite striking analogies between the structuring of the two subsystems. Birdwhistell, though he states that "we have thus far been unable to isolate a grammar or syntax in the kinesic system," draws an analogy between kinesics and language which seems almost to imply that they *are* comparable systems. That is, he finds it useful to distinguish between *microkinesics* and *parakinesics*: microkinesics is seen to be composed of what he calls "kines, kinemorphs and complex kine-morphic constructions (comparable to phonemes, morphemes, and syntactic sentences). "Comparable" hardly seems the term to use here, since what Birdwhistell terms a "full kinemorph" — for example, one consisting of a head-nod kine and kines "including eyebrows and eyes" — seems far more like a packaging of vocal segregates than, say, the putting together of the morphemes resulting in the lexical item *laughed*.

But Birdwhistell's parakinesic events are certainly strikingly analogous to paralinguistic events, since he recognizes a body base directly comparable to voice set and a list of body sets which are abstractable as expressing status, gender, age-grade, health image, rhythm image, territorial status, mode, and toxic image. Further, he sets up paired *action modifiers*, such as graceful–awkward, rhythmic–disrhythmic, fast–slow, unilateral–bilateral, which are directly parallel to the voice qualities of paralanguage. Even more striking is the level of phenomena he terms *motion qualifiers*, which, like the vocal qualifiers of language, can be seen to occur in three major areas — *intensity*, concerned with the degree of muscular tension in production of kine, kinemorph, or kinemorphic construction, which is almost exactly comparable to intensity or loudness in paralanguage; *duration* or *velocity*, the length of time given kine, kinemorph, or construction, and very like the drawl-clipping scale for duration in paralanguage; and *range*, concerned with the extent of movement involved in the production of kine, kinemorph, or construction, quite like the pitch height or pitch range of the vocal qualifiers. However, unlike the case of the vocal qualifiers, for which three levels of phenomena above and below a base line are established, Birdwhistell finds only two levels above and below his "normal" for the qualifier range. Thus, for intensity he establishes *overtense* and *tense* above normal and *lax* and *overlax* below normal.

In addition to these marked parallelisms, Birdwhistell's analysis of *gestures* seems to fit very closely with the analysis of packages of vocal segregates. Birdwhistell, though, makes them more analogous to bound morphemes in the words of language. He writes:

> What we popularly call "gestures" whether of the shape of a "thumbed nose," a "head shake" . . . or a "clenched fist" are revealed by analysis to be specially bound kinemorphs which cannot appear in isolation as a complete action. That is, "gestures" are like the stem forms in language in that they are always bound up in a more complex package, the analysis of which must be completed before the "social meaning" of the complex can be assessed.

Again, this description seems more in consonance with our analysis of the vocal segregate packages *uh uh* and *uh huh*, encased as they always are in a matrix of language and more often than not accompanied by paralinguistic vocal qualifiers. Here, too, the vocal segregates are "bound" and "cannot appear in isolation." Again, the "social meaning" of the package cannot be assessed unless the analysis of the "more complex package" is "completed." To see, as Birdwhistell does, the components of a gesture package as nearer the bound base-morpheme *cept* in "con*cept*" or "pre*cept*" is needlessly ignoring the far closer analogies presented by the nonlinguistic vocal segregates and, furthermore, serves to obscure both the nature of gestures and the true relationship of bound morphemes to other morphemes in language.

More recently, Birdwhistell has remarked on what he calls *suprasegmental kinemorphemes*, which are analogous to the stresses and terminal junctures of language, and which serve to identify phrases, clauses, sentences, "paragraphs," and other major sequences which have special internal connectedness. These entities are distinguished from what he calls *kinesic markers*, which seem to have a special relationship to the behavior of particular classes of lexical and syntactical items of language. Kinesics is thus very closely bound in with language and with paralanguage, although certain kinesic events are more closely bound in with language than others which may be seen to "cross-reference in a variety of ways, the kinesic or linguistic messages emitted or received."

I think the interrelatedness and completely human nature of all of the modalities in the total communication package must be mentioned again. Together these form a package which is perhaps best likened to a coaxial cable carrying many messages at the same time. There is a danger in thinking that language, and language alone, is the only important modality because it is the most highly structured one. There is a danger in thinking that only language displays a cognitive function and that the other modalities are merely modifying the message carried by language or are merely expressive of individual personality differences. (Birdwhistell guesses that no more than 30 to 35 percent of the social meaning of a conversation or an interaction is carried by the words. Finally, there is a danger in thinking that the sole and true purpose of communication is to inject new information into an interaction situation. On the contrary, Birdwhistell makes an eloquent plea for what he calls "the *integrational* aspect of the communicative process," which includes all the behavioral operations that (1) keep the system in operation; (2) regulate the interactional process; (3) cross-reference particular messages to comprehensibility in a particular context; and (4) relate the particular context to the larger contexts of which the particular action is but a special situation.

Of course, new information is important, but it is far more important for people to be constantly assured of the "rightness," or congruence, of the way in which information is added or fed into the interaction or withheld from it. When we say "How are you?" we expect the answer "Fine," or an equivalent, not a long account of aches and pains. We don't want new information in this situation, and the other person knows it. The exchange of stereotyped greeting and response is designed only to reassure each participant that he and his fellow communicant are equally practicing members of the same society and carriers of the same culture. Language, in fact, is far more than words, and communication requires far more than language alone.

BIBLIOGRAPHY

Homer Barnett. *Innovation, the Basis of Cultural Change.* McGraw, 1953.

Ray L. Birdwhistell. *Introduction to Kinesics.* Washington, D. C., Foreign Service Institute, 1952.

Edward T. Hall. *The Silent Language.* Doubleday, 1959.

Robert E. Pittenger, Charles F. Hockett, and John Danehy. *The First Five Minutes.* Martineau, 1960.

George L. Trager and Edward T. Hall. *The Analysis of Culture.* Washington, D. C., Foreign Service Instutute, 1953.

George L. Trager and Henry Lee Smith, Jr. *An Outline of English Structure,* Studies in Linguistics, Occasional Paper 3, 1951.

Leslie A. White. *The Science of Culture.* Grove, 1958.

10 NATIONAL AND INTERNATIONAL LANGUAGES

Einar Haugen

It is one of the features we take more or less for granted about our world that each nation has a language of its own. In France they speak and write French, in Italy Italian, in Germany German, in Russia Russian, and in England English. Yet it takes only a moment's reflection to realize that there are many nations of which this is not true. On the one hand, there are some that have no language of their own, and on the other, those that have more than one. We Americans have no language of our own, in spite of some assertions to the contrary; at most we have an American variety of the English language. We share this language not only with its motherland England but also with England's many former colonies. Belgium and Switzerland are in the same situation: there is no Belgian or Swiss language. Instead each shares two or more languages with its neighbors: Belgium has Dutch and French, while Switzerland has German, French, and Italian. Yugoslavia has three languages of its own: Serbo-Croatian, the most important, and Slovenian, in the north, and Macedonian, in the south. India has fourteen official languages, one of which, Hindi, is scheduled to become the national language; but English, the language of India's former masters, is still the most widely used in official communications.

When we look around the world, we find that in fact very few nations have one and only one language. Even the countries which come closest to this situation have minority populations that speak other languages: in France there are German speakers in Alsace-

Lorraine, Breton speakers in Brittany, and Basque speakers in the Pyrenees, not to speak of the fact that each region of France has its own local dialect; in southern France the dialects are so different from Standard French that they can be regarded as a separate language, which has been written under the name Provençal. Every European country of any size has both of these deviations from its national language: lumps of unassimilated "foreigners" and regional variations in speech which may create an almost total gap in understanding between the users of the national language and the users of the local dialects. In the newly created nations of the world there may be so great a variation in language that there is not even any accepted national standard. It is one of the most acute problems of many newly created African nations that their tribal languages are so diverse and so little cultivated that none of them can be used as a common medium of communication for modern purposes. In such situations their rulers are forced to continue the use of the language of their former masters, usually English or French. They are put into the uncomfortable position of having to use languages that are not the mother tongues of anyone in their own population and that are so remote from their own that years of schooling are required for mastery.

The most impressive thing about the language situation in the world is its tremendous complexity. People who are looking for easy solutions to the world's problems have advocated that everyone should learn English, or if not English, then some artificial and neutral language like Esperanto. But the fact is that there are enormous resistances to both of these solutions, and it is not at all certain that either one would be a good solution. In any case it can be asserted with some confidence that the world is not ready for any such solution and that it would be utopian to try to put it into effect. Instead, we need to understand a little better how the present situation came to pass and how language actually works in the life of the community.

The problem is the extremely unequal distribution of man's languages: of the three thousand or more languages in the world, the vast majority are spoken by tiny groups of people scattered in remote places. Only a few have any great number of followers. In language as among nations there are the haves and the have-nots. We find some areas in which a great variety of languages appear to have been spoken within a very small area over a long time; these are often bordered by other areas in which one language has spread widely at the expense of others. One region of high density is California, where over one hundred languages were spoken by the Indians at the coming of the white man. The Great Plains, on the other hand, were dominated by two or three major languages, such as the Algonkian and the Sioux. Central Africa, a land of dense jungles, has a patchwork-quilt of languages to this day, while South Africa is almost entirely dominated by one language family, the Bantu. New Guinea is crowded with languages, while the islands around, from Indonesia to Hawaii, are dominated by one language family, the Malayo-Polynesian. In Europe the Caucasus is a region of high density of mutually incomprehensible and unrelated languages, while most of Europe to the west of it and a great portion of Asia to the east are dominated by the Indo-European family of languages, which probably spread out over its present area some four thousand years ago.

In each case it is clear that in areas where small populations could easily isolate themselves from each other and live their lives untroubled by their neighbors, they tended also in the course of time to develop their own language. This process of gradual and unconscious differentiation of language over a period of time is one of the most characteristic features of language, one which has been much studied by linguists. It attracted the attention of the ancient Jews, who invented the story of the Tower of Babel to account for it. While the Lord's dramatic intervention made a good story, the facts show that the process itself is usually quite undramatic. People who do not communicate with each other simply drift apart. One reason is that every person has to learn the language anew, and therefore does not learn it quite the same. The cumulative changes of all the new learners in every generation constitute the basis for linguistic change and gradual splitting off. If we could imagine a world in which all human beings were living in small tribal communities, each one completely independent of the other, we would probably find that each such community would in a few thousand years speak its own language, which would be completely incomprehensible to every other community. This certainly is the reason that in Europe practically every town or country parish has its own dialect; these are only a few hundred years old, and yet they often show tremendous differentiation. This kind of gradual and unconscious splitting is often presented in the image of a tree with branches dividing off from the trunk, and twigs from the branches.

In actual fact, however, very few communities are left alone to this extent. In all areas where the possibilities for defense and isolation have been low, populations have been more mobile. They have communicated with their neighbors in daily life; they have conquered or have been conquered by them and have entered into larger communities with a social organization of higher and lower strata. The results have been that language changes have not all been unconscious drifts away from a common source, but have been spread far and wide by the movements of ideas, of goods, and of people. These changes have been like waves, washing away barriers to communication, so that large populations share a language instead of falling apart into dialects. If we wish to continue the image of the tree, we may say that some trees have been pruned so that most of their twigs have been eliminated in favor of a few major branches. In some cases grafts have been performed, so that essentially new languages have been imposed on old trees.

This is the process that underlies the creation of all those languages that we now refer to as national or international languages. They are the result not only of a gradual differentiation, but also of a deliberate unification and cultivation. They are steps on the path toward a universal world language, in contrast to the numerous spoken languages of local tribes and the innumerable local dialects still used in the world. They are everywhere the result of a concentration of political power, which establishes dominion over an area in which it is convenient for that power to have a single language for communicating with its subjects. Over and above the face-to-face communication of the local groups, there are networks of communication among officials and leaders, who adopt a language as a means of maintaining their position and facilitating the business of government.

This was already true in the ancient world. Greek did not become a single language until the time of the conquest of the Greeks by Philip of Macedon and the establishment of his empire. Before that time each city-state had its own dialect of Greek, which it jealously preserved as a symbol of its identity. Similarly, Latin was a creation of the Roman state, originally based on the speech of the tiny area of Latium and developed by the early rulers of Rome as an instrument of government. Throughout its existence as an official language of government and literature it was a highly artificial product of intellectual activity. The Romans spread its use throughout the western part of their empire, so that the Italians, the French, the Spaniards, and the Portuguese today speak varieties of Latin. But the language did not take root in the eastern part of the empire, where Greek remained dominant because of its cultural strength. The Roman intellectuals even learned Greek and imitated its forms in Latin. This increased the gap that had always existed in Rome between the cultivated Latin of writing and the daily speech of the average Roman. We have no direct evidence on the way the Romans spoke, but we can tell by inscriptions written by bad spellers, and by dialogue in plays, as well as by comparing daughter languages. The word for "head" in official Latin was *caput*, but in daily speech it was *testa*, clearly a slang word for the head originally meaning a "pot"; this is the word in modern French, *tête*.

Latin continued to be used as the language of government and culture in Europe long after the fall of the Roman empire. Not only was it used in the countries where a form of Latin was spoken, but also in those countries where the Roman Catholic church established its form of Christianity. Because of this, Latin became to some degree the model of what a language should be if it were to serve as a vehicle of national and international culture. Both Greek and Latin are languages which can be referred to as normalized, or standardized, or, in short, standard languages: They have been codified, or, in other words, have been analyzed in writing and turned into a set of rules which can be taught in school. In the process of codification a number of decisions have been made as to which of various competing forms should be regarded as correct. Wherever there is human speech, there are certain to be differing pronunciations, disagreements on grammatical forms, and different opinions on the names of things. These disagreements are small within a small community, and the standard languages have usually come into being in a small community, often an elite recruited from various parts of the country or the empire. The standard languages have therefore nearly always been clique languages, either grown up in or regulated by the ruling network of a country. Very seldom can one say that the grammarians who wrote the grammars have made the languages: they have only acted as arbiters of taste.

Most of the major European languages were not normalized until the time of the Renaissance. This means that until the sixteenth century they occupied only a secondary position within their countries, since Latin was the universal language of learning. This did not mean that great literature was not written in them: Dante created Italian literature in the first half of the fourteenth century, and Chaucer at least greatly developed English literature in its second half. Both of these writers did an enormous service to their languages when they proved that they could be used as vehicles of great poetry. But they did not create these languages: they only helped to make the selection that eventually became the standard. Dante chose the language of Florence and Chaucer the language of London because these were centers of government and culture. English did not become what it is today until close to the end of the sixteenth century, when men of learning and culture had worked for some centuries on it to make it as useful for all kinds of writing as Latin had been. French came into its own in 1539, when it took the place of Latin in the courts of France. The German we know today was shaped as the government language of Upper Saxony, where the Holy Roman Empire had its seat at one time. When Luther adopted it in the 1540s for his Bible translation, it was carried into areas which had never before used High German.

It was in the Renaissance that the first grammars were written for English, French, and German — an acknowledgment of their importance and a necessary part of their normalization. The close connection between grammar and politics is shown in the fact that the first Spanish grammar appeared in 1492 and was dedicated to Queen Isabella; it was intended to be a companion of the empire, the author wrote, and should spread Spanish along with the rule of the Spaniards. The first language academy was established in Florence in 1582; in 1612 this academy published one of the first one-language dictionaries in the world. This model was followed in France, where Cardinal Richelieu cannily formed an academy in 1635 as part of his plans for unifying the country. It is hard to be sure of just what role the French academy actually has played in the regulation of the French language, but there can be no doubt that French is the most highly regulated and normalized language of Europe. The French take a fierce pride in its correctness, although a famous French linguist, Antoine Meillet, has written that in its fixed form it "has never been the language of any but a few people and is today not the spoken language of anyone." English writers of the seventeenth and eighteenth centuries agitated for the creation of an English academy, but failed to overcome an English distaste for this kind of official regulation. One of those who opposed it was Samuel Johnson, in the name of "the spirit of English liberty"; his own dictionary of 1755, however, had very much the same effect an academy would have had — an irony typical of England, where the regulation has always been informal and based on private enterprise. This tradition was passed on to the United States, where Noah Webster and his successors became the unofficial arbiters of English usage. The feeling is so strong in the United States that when a new edition of Webster's dictionary made some mild changes in its judgments a few years ago there was a tremendous outcry among the literary critics.

One of the major factors in the establishment of standard languages in Europe was the invention of printing, which made it possible to multiply the number of copies of all forms of writing and led to the public school, through which every citizen could learn to read and write and participate in the affairs of state. In Greece and Rome the standard language had been the possession of small ruling cliques; in modern Europe it could spread to an entire population. What had been taught only to the children of the elite could now be taught to everyone. The ideal of democracy could only be realized through an educated citizenry. This became clear in the eighteenth century, which ended with the American and French revolutions. Ideologically, these established the right of each nation to rule its own affairs, including the right of everyone to participate in the common language in which those affairs are conducted. When we add to this notion the fact of enormous mobility of modern man and the wide spread of international means of communication, it is clear that even the nation is not an adequate framework of contact. Many look beyond the borders of their nations to an international brotherhood of man and envisage the time when the national languages will give way to international communication.

The period of history since the French Revolution is a short one, and it is hard to evaluate in terms of the long run. But it has shown two opposing developments, both of which are likely to continue and both of which may bear within themselves the possibilities of a fruitful solution of the language problem of the world.

On the one hand, each political unit has seen a vital part of its national policy to lie in cultivating and strengthening its national language. This means that as the new nations came into being in the nineteenth and twentieth century, each one emphasized its own language. When Greece was liberated from Turkey, it re-established a form of Greek as nearly like that of Ancient Greek as possible. When Norway was liberated from Denmark and Sweden, it bent its best efforts to the development of a Norwegian language which had been lost during its union with these countries. The language map of Europe is today dotted with literary languages never heard of in 1800: Slovak, Ukrainian, Macedonian, Estonian, Faroese, Catalan, Romansch. Outside Europe the most spectacular rise of a new language is the establishment of Modern Hebrew in Israel, truly a new graft on an old stem. Almost as remarkable is the creation of Indonesian, a special form of Malayan which is now the official language of Indonesia. Minority populations, even in long-established countries, are refusing to accept the language of the majority and rebel against notions of the inferiority of local speech habits, notions which have reduced them in the past to second-class status and excluded them from the best jobs. This is conspicuous in the restlessness of the French in Canada, of the Flemish in Belgium, and of the Dravidian and Bengali speakers in India, to mention a few examples.

In each of these countries a language has become part of the struggle for national identity, which means that it is a great deal more than just a practical problem. However convenient a single language may be for rulers, those rulers must also take into account the feelings and attitudes of the peoples who must use the language. If there is a national language with which the citizens of the nation can identify themselves, the rulers are in luck. Then the work of national academies and committees for the cultivation of the language can bear fruit, and the youngsters in school will grow up as loyal supporters and users of that language. Their emotions are involved with the language because it truly gives voice to their inmost experiences and does not reduce them to inferior members of society. The culture of the world and of their own nation comes to them through a single well-developed and consistent medium which is close enough to their mother tongue to feel familiar. But without a prior national language there are inevitable conflicts and problems which can only be solved by intelligent, reasoned, understanding policies of language teaching.

If we transfer this situation to the international scene, we see that the world as a whole is in much the same state as were the nations of Europe at the time of the Renaissance and as are many new nations today. In a period when the masses of Europe were illiterate, it was easy to establish such languages as French or English in the usage of the elites. As the population was gradually educated, the norms that were already established could be passed on to the masses. In the course of time this has led to the weakening and partial disappearance of local dialects, especially in the areas within easy reach of capital cities like London and Paris. Some languages, for example Cornish, have disappeared entirely, and others, for example Scottish Gaelic, are strongly threatened. But a few have managed to survive and create many important cultural values for themselves and others, because of the intense devotion of their supporters to the cause of the language. In such cases the rulers must either face the possibility of a divided nation or else adopt a policy of patience and tolerance toward minorities. If the minority is sufficiently aware of the need for learning the majority language, it will do so for purely practical reasons. The learning of a second language is no calamity; on the contrary, it can be made an experience of great value. It is important that any group have a written, standard language of its own in which it can take pride; this contributes to its dignity and its awareness of self. But if the language has few adherents there is also a need for a second language for wider communication.

It seems to me that the nations of the world today stand in this situation: there are a few languages, like English, French, Russian, and Chinese, and some others, which are rivals for the future standard language of the world. Every standard language of the past has acquired its strength from the power of the nations that used it. The necessity for a single world language does not arise unless and until a single world government is established. Anyone who needs to learn the world languages of today will do so; we need only observe the tremendous increase in the teaching of Russian in American schools since World War II. In the meantime, each national language must strive to make itself as rich and responsive to the culture of our day as possible. The diversity of language is part of the interesting diversity of culture which characterizes man. Any attempt to legislate this diversity out of existence is not only futile, it is also culturally crippling. Any attempt to substitute an artificially created language for these languages is equally futile and dangerous.

In history we have moved from local tribes to regional unions to nation-states, and from the natural diversification of languages to a pruning and grafting which has given us the relatively small number of standard languages that now exist. When the day is ripe, we will move beyond the nation, into world government, and with it we will find our way to a world language.

BIBLIOGRAPHY

Karl W. Deutsch. *Nationalism and Social Communication.* Massachusetts Institute of Technology Press, 1953.
Einar Haugen. *Language Conflict and Language Planning: The Case of Modern Norwegian.* Harvard University Press, 1966.

Heinz Kloss. *Die Entwicklung neuer germanischer Kultursprachen von 1800 bis 1950.* Pohl, 1952.

Stanley Lieberson, ed. *Explorations in Sociolinguistics.* Special issue of *Sociological Inquiry*, XXXVI, No. 2 (Spring 1966), pp. 131–134.

Punya Sloka Ray. *Language Standardization.* Mouton, 1963.

Frank A. Rice. *Study of the Role of Second Languages in Asia, Africa, and Latin America.* Center for Applied Linguistics, 1962.

I I LINGUISTICS AND INSTRUCTION IN THE NATIVE LANGUAGE

Albert H. Marckwardt

In most countries of the world, as children begin their education, approximately half of the entire school day is devoted to instruction in the use of the mother tongue. The schools of the United States, England, and Canada are no exception. In the later school years other subjects in the curriculum take up more time, but some attention to English is required throughout the first eleven years of schooling at the very least.

For several reasons the aims and scope of English as a school subject have remained somewhat vague in the United States. But no matter whether it is limited to the reading of the so-called classics and the writing of essays on the one hand, or if, on the other, it is broadened to include such activities as engaging in telephone conversations, conducting panel discussions, and writing party invitations and business letters, language is central to all of them. It would be strange indeed, therefore, if the concepts, methods of analysis and description, and the factual data about the English language which have resulted from some three decades of systematic inquiry did not have many immediate and practical applications to the teaching of English in the schools.

At the same time we must understand that the general state of the English language in this country has a definite bearing upon our educational program. One aspect of American society which truly sets the United States apart from every other country in the world is the high degree of mobility, both geographic and social.

Our disposition to move about the country has resulted in an almost total disappearance of local dialects to the extent that only a few broad regional types of speech are recognizable, none of which enjoys a commanding prestige. The language of Dean Rusk, Robert McNamara, and Edward Kennedy indicates the general section of the country in which each man spent his youth, but the dialect of no one of them can be considered inferior or superior to the others.

At the same time, it has been possible over the past three centuries for a person of humble origin with very little formal education, by dint of hard work and innate ability, to succeed to a position of influence in our political and economic life. Consequently, the affairs of the country have been carried on at times in a mixture of Standard and non-Standard English. This has, upon occasion, given the lie to the teacher's admonition to Johnny to avoid *ain't* and multiple negatives if he hopes to become president of the local bank or a member of the city council. There have been bank presidents and aldermen who simply murdered the language, but many of them have also been quite aware of their linguistic shortcomings and have been emphatic in their determination that their children should not labor under a similar handicap.

The result has been pressure upon the schools to give every child a command of the language adequate to the position in life which his ability might enable him to attain. Since more than 90 per cent of the youth population of the country is enrolled in our elementary and secondary schools, this amounts in effect to an insistence that the schools provide a command of Standard English to almost fifty million students, many of whom come from homes and neighborhoods where the prestige form of the language is not regularly spoken. It is a charge astounding in its magnitude; no other educational system has as yet attempted anything like it.

Here another complicating factor enters the situation. Because of our vast numbers and territorial spread, any concept of a linguistic standard realistically considered must admit the existence of many variant forms. It must be flexible and not monolithic. We cannot honestly approve *toward* and reject *towards* when the cold hard facts tell us that as many cultivated speakers use one of the forms as use the other. We cannot justifiably condemn, as some textbooks were accustomed to do, the omitted relative construction (*He is the man I saw downtown*) or *none* with a plural verb when they have been in the language for centuries. Thus the determination of the standard becomes a complex and delicate matter. We know that most competent speakers of the language depend upon instinct, upon a "feel" not only for what is acceptable but for what is likely to be most effective in a given situation.

At this point the upward mobility moves in to plague us. Although the culturally assured may be content to depend upon intuition or relatively vague principle in matters of behavior generally, as well as in language, it is notoriously unsatisfactory to the parvenu. When he is confronted by a complicated array of cutlery at a formal dinner, he has no faith in instinct. His fear is that he will arrive at the dessert course with only a soup spoon or a salad fork. He wants instruction with respect to specific items of behavior. He demands simple answers, situations presented in black and white. A range of choices leaves him uncomfortable and unsatisfied.

This is precisely the spirit which has characterized the treatment of language in books written for the general public and in much of the English instruction in our schools. It is a spirit which inevitably runs counter to the complexities inherent in any realistic view of what constitutes the standard language in this country at the present time. It explains in great part the hostile reception accorded in some quarters to *Webster's Third New International Dictionary* upon its appearance in 1961. Thus the first responsibility of the English teacher is to go beyond his textbooks, to prepare himself to use and to understand the factual sources of information about Standard English which the scholarship of the past decades and centuries has made available. On the surface this seems simple enough, but in fact it requires of him a degree of sophistication in the interpretation and evaluation of evidence and the courage to form and maintain his own conclusions.

But the collection of data, no matter how delicate and refined the process may be, is no more than the first step in any science. Far more important is the organization of pertinent fact into an orderly and comprehensive system. This is what linguistics seeks to do with respect to each of the world's languages. What, then, is the connection between such a body of organized and systematic knowledge about the English language and the way in which a teacher proceeds to develop in his students a degree of competence in the use of it?

From one point of view this is an instance of the relationship between pure and applied science, a relationship which prevails in any number of fields of knowledge. Physics and chemistry, for example, find their application in various types of engineering. Along with geology they constitute the basis of metallurgy. The farmer makes practical use of botany and chemistry.

It is a fact of human history that the application of scientific knowledge often lags considerably behind its development or discovery. Charles C. Fries has pointed out a number of times that although William Harvey discovered the circulation of blood in 1628, George Washington was bled for pneumonia in 1798, almost two centuries later. It has taken decades to translate what we know of the chemistry of soils into farm practices the world over. Just so, in many areas of instruction, the gap between new developments in content and theory as derived from research and their application in the classroom is painfully apparent. The teaching of the English language is no exception.

The principal question, of course, is how such an application is to be made and what it may best consist of. Despite the fact that we now have available linguistically oriented English-language teaching materials on many levels, where ten years ago there were virtually none, I still believe that the most important contribution that linguistics can make to the classroom English teacher is in reshaping his view of language and of language learning. These are matters of attitude and concept rather than of one grammatical analysis as compared with another or of a series of judgments about the acceptability of any number of specific forms and expressions. Linguistically sound teaching materials can be expected to produce satisfactory results only when they are used by linguistically knowledgeable and sophisticated teachers. Such a sophistication rests upon an understanding of certain principles.

The first of these concerns the relationship between the language as spoken and as written. Unfortunately linguists have seldom dealt with this matter clearly and satisfactorily. They often use the phrase "primacy of the spoken language" in a way that suggests the written form is somewhat inferior and devoid of interest. Statements of this kind frequently fail of their purpose. They succeed only in shocking the English teacher who places a high value upon written works of literature and who looks upon spoken English as a somewhat disorganized and corrupted version of writing, inferior in its adherence to what he considers to be valid logical and grammatical principle.

For his part, the linguist views language as patterned behavior. He conceives of grammar as a series of carefully constructed statements describing the nature of these patterns and applicable to the total system of the language. Experience has taught him that upon occasion the written form of the language either fails completely to disclose the pattern of a linguistic structure or may reveal it only in part. He knows, for example, that for most speakers of English the definite article *the* has two pronunciations, one of which employs the initial vowel of *about*, the other the final vowel of *very*. He knows also that the first of these occurs before consonant sounds (*the book*) and the second before vowels (*the apple*), a distribution identical to that of the forms *a* and *an* of the definite article. Our writing system shows this distribution for the indefinite article but not for the definite.

In approximately one hundred English words the position of the stress is a major clue to the part-of-speech function they perform. Thus *subjéct* and *convért*, with primary stress on the second syllable, are immediately recognized as verbs, whereas in *súbject* and *cónvert* the stress on the first syllable marks them as nouns. The presence or absence of secondary stress on the final syllables of *separate* and *intimate* identifies them as verbs or adjectives (*sépăràte* verb; *sépărăte* adjective). Since our writing system indicates the stress only very clumsily and usually not at all, stress is another structural feature detectable only in the spoken language.

Admittedly, these are perhaps not matters of great moment to the classroom English teacher, for they involve features of the grammar which most children master internally before they begin their schooling. But to the linguist, whose aim is to comprehend all of the structural patterns of the language, they are important, and they help to explain his initial and continuing concern with speech.

There are some other ways of considering the relationship between the spoken language and the writing system which the teacher should take into account. Every person knows how to speak for some years before he is able to read or write. Collectively, mankind has been speaking for possibly more than fifty or a hundred thousand years. At most, writing is not more than six thousand years old. Even in this literate age, each one of us speaks far more than he writes. And, finally, of the more than three thousand languages in the world, there are hundreds which are spoken but for which no writing system has been devised. There are no written languages that are not spoken or have not been spoken at some time. All these factors enter into the linguist's concept of the primary nature of speech.

This is not to suggest that the written language is unimportant or that it should not be carefully studied. Certainly, the greatest monuments of our culture appear in written form. Over the centuries, writing has made it possible for us to communicate independently of human presence or human memory. Yet we must realize that writing is a limited, not a full presentation of the stream of speech. It reveals very little of intonation, stress, and juncture, all of which function as part of the system of the language. The speaker can, moreover, adjust and correct his language as he goes along; writing is committed to a single and purely linear presentation. For this reason the necessity for greater tightness of logical structure in writing becomes understandable. Stress and intonation will properly and adequately signal whether the word *only* modifies subject or object in "He only had five dollars." In writing the potential ambiguity must be resolved by distinguishing between *He only* and *only five dollars*. This does not make of writing a superior instrument, merely a somewhat different one. But such differences and the reasons for them should be explored much more fully than they have been in the past. If they are understood by the teacher, they can be used effectively in the improvement of student composition.

For many years scholars have realized that the traditional method of grammatical analysis is not always the most suitable instrument for describing the structure of English. There are historical reasons for this. The grammar of the Western world developed originally as a device for describing the structure of written Greek — the etymon *gramma* itself meant "letter." It performed its task effectively. It was somewhat less efficient but nevertheless quite serviceable in describing Latin. Both of these classical languages were primarily inflectional. They signaled most noun relationships, the time and nature of actions, and the degree or comparison of qualities almost entirely by means of the inflections that were added to words. In turn, the inflections figured heavily as a means of identifying parts of speech and classifying their various functions.

Modern English operates quite differently. It has inflections, but not many. Word order has become an important device for signaling relationships — we distinguish, for example, between a *house-boat* and a *boat-house* — and so have prepositions, auxiliary verbs, and other groups of what have come to be called function words.

As a consequence, if our grammar is to fit the language, the use of word order and function words must be duly recognized in it. It is not often that one finds in a description of English a careful account of those situations in which either the inflected genitive or the periphrastic construction with *of* is permissible (*the dog's tail, the tail of the dog*), those in which only the inflected form may be used (*world's fair, stone's throw*), and those in which only the *of* phrases occur (*crown of thorns, three of them*).

Our school grammars concentrate, often in a quite unrealistic fashion, upon the relative suitability of *shall* and *will* as future auxiliaries, but ignore the situations where such other constructions as *going to* or the simple present tense are obligatory or may serve as alternate forms. They seldom explain the distinction between the use of *he eats* to indicate habitual or customary action and *he is eating* for an actual ongoing activity, and they almost always neglect to point out how often *he used to eat* functions as a past tense of *he eats*. Rarely do they take the trouble to describe the ordering of modifying elements before a substantive, as they occur in the sequence *all the six ugly new red brick apartments*. Nor are they likely to include within an account of English verb-structures such combinations as *keep working* and *get moving*, which are as much a part of the English verb system as combinations like *must say* or *should go*.

There are values for both teacher and student in recognizing that the proper function of grammar is to account for the total structure of the language, no matter how much it may transcend the limits of the conventional, logical, and neatly conceived categories. Such a recognition will serve as a corrective to the piecemeal approach that forms the basis of what has often been called "functional grammar," a concentration upon the few specific rules which are directed toward the most common and serious infelicities of language. As H. A. Gleason has commented, "Grammar becomes trivial when its systematic organization is destroyed."

Moreover, the various approaches to grammar which are employed by linguists today — the structural, the tagmemic, the transformational, the stratificational — serve to alert the teacher that, to use the words of Browning, the business of *hoti* is not likely to be settled in this generation or the next, any more than are the current issues in physics or psychology. Language is human behavior, a highly complex form of it, just as literature comprises a number of intricate and complicated linguistic activities. Just as there will continue to be any number of critical approaches to poetry, the drama, and the novel, so may we expect from the linguistic scientists a considerable variety in their ways of looking at, describing, and accounting for the language we use. We may confidently expect in the future not one grammar but many. It is the responsibility of the classroom teacher to accept this, to be prepared to discriminate among them, and to make his own evaluations. In addition, he must be willing to learn far more about language behavior and ways of describing it than he is ever likely to teach.

The preoccupation of the linguists with language as pattern and system has also led them to give much attention to the way in which the individual acquires the system, the way in which he learns to use the language. They have made a significant point of how early in life this acquisition takes place. The following quotation from Charles F. Hockett[1] is typical of their point of view: "By the age of

[1]Charles F. Hockett. *A Course in Modern Linguistics.* Macmillan, 1959, p. 360.

four to six, the normal child is a linguistic adult. He controls, with marginal exceptions if any, the phonemic system of the language; he handles effortlessly the grammatical core; he knows and uses the basic contentive vocabulary of the language."

This observation is important in that it places the language activities of the child during his early school years in a proper focus. While Hockett may have overstated the case as far as the more complex sentence patterns are concerned, certainly the child of six does know how to use the regular inflectional patterns in pluralizing nouns and forming the past tense of verbs. Moreover, we can assume that the subject–verb–object and adjective–noun sequences are established. This means, contrary to the supposition of many teachers, that when the pupil learns to read he is not learning language — he is learning to master the writing system, at a level far below the language that he already knows and uses. It will probably be some three years before reading becomes for him a means of extending his experience with and control of the language. In the meantime, his oral language activities during the school day, if properly directed, can serve as a means of expanding not only his vocabulary but also the basic patterns which he already employs, and of developing a flexibility in their use. For a while, at least, he will write much as he speaks, but the time will come when he is ready to give conscious attention to the structural differences between spoken and written English. What is significant for the teacher is the realization that these various language activities are not all of one piece, that each has its peculiar problems and requires a somewhat different instructional approach.

This leads one to ask about the usefulness of linguistics in connection with the developing language competence of children. At the outset a fundamental distinction must be drawn between what is taught directly in the classroom and what the teacher should know as background and context for his teaching activities. This distinction seems simple enough, but it is often overlooked in discussions of "the new" English. What the teacher should know of linguistics is far more important — and extensive — than whatever he may teach about it. And again this matter must be considered in relation to each of the aspects of the language which figure in the school program.

Recently linguists have been asked to help with the preparation of all kinds of English-language textbooks: reading materials, spelling texts, manuals for the improvement of writing. They have attempted to apply the results of their discipline to these various ends. In some instances the teaching materials they have developed differ radically from the textbooks previously in use. In order to use these new materials effectively, teachers must know why they are as they are, must be aware of the ideas and assumptions about language upon which they rest. And if, through force of circumstances, a teacher must use textbooks which do not reflect current advances in language study, a familiarity with the present state of linguistic knowledge will be helpful in detecting and coping with their inadequacies.

With respect to reading and spelling, the linguists have looked to the correspondences between phonemes and their graphic representation and also to the technique of minimal differentiation in developing teaching procedures. Their materials focus upon the simplest and more regular spellings at the beginning, usually the single-letter spellings for the so-called short vowels, and go on gradually to the more complex and less regular. To develop the child's ability to make the split-second conversion of a series of symbols to their spoken equivalent, they depend upon the repetitive impact of words which are alike except for a single minimal feature: *pat, rat, cat, mat*. This approach has both its strong and weak points. Its strength lies in the emphasis upon the fundamental regularity which underlies the English spelling system. Our orthography is not wholly chaotic. There is a gradation in the fit between sound and spelling. The linguists have devised the strategy of moving from the highly regular, through those situations in which the irregularities fall into patterned sets, to the few really anomalous occurrences. Thus pattern rather than word frequency becomes the key to a linguistically oriented approach to reading and spelling. But a too strict adherence to it can lead to materials with little intrinsic interest. There have been occasions when this approach left children with an ability but not a desire to read. Without question the contribution of the linguist is more effective when his talents are employed in conjunction with experts in other areas.

A century ago it was assumed that if the principal rules and definitions of grammar were thoroughly committed to memory, the pupil would then be able to apply them, and his speech and writing would benefit thereby. This seems to have been a mistaken theory founded upon a vain hope. It produced students able to parse with virtuosity, but whose language seemed singularly unaffected by the process, leading many educators to the conclusion that there was simply no transfer from a knowledge of grammar to the practical use of the language.

Many linguists today are less willing to concede the point. They are more likely to place the blame upon the grammar itself as an ill-fitting and at best a partial description of the language and to contend that a more accurate and comprehensive account of the structure may well lead to a more dextrous and effective employment of the language. This remains to be proved, if indeed it can be, but at any rate it has served as a working hypothesis for many of the language textbooks being prepared at the various English curriculum study centers. Since this is the case, it is reasonable to ask where the potential applications of linguistic knowledge may lie.

First of all, there are millions of children whose only contact with Standard English is the classroom; the language of the home and of the streets or playground is substandard. If they are to acquire Standard English, it will be by dint of repetitive drill and systematic reinforcement, concentrating upon a small number of items at a time, for the purpose of developing the correct form as a habitual and instantaneous response. Such teaching must be well planned; one cannot afford to waste time on what the student already commands. An effective program, therefore, must be based upon a contrastive study of Standard English and the substandard dialect prevalent in the community in order to identify what must be emphasized and what can be safely ignored. This has given a new practical and pedagogical importance to the study of social dialects, especially those characteristic of our large urban centers. Several extensive projects are currently under way, notably in New York, Chicago, and Washington, D.C.

But it is in the expansion as well as the fixation of language patterns that linguistic knowledge may be put to advantageous use, both in warning the student of the pitfalls involved in inadequately controlled expression and in making him aware of the resources of the language. In short, there is both a negative and a positive role for a soundly based knowledge of language structure.

The negative role consists chiefly in the avoidance of structural ambiguity. Quite regularly, throughout his *Structure of English*, Charles C. Fries points to syntactic situations where the grammatical meaning is vague because of the lack of unambiguous formal markers. Noam Chomsky has employed transformational techniques as a means of identifying and accounting for structurally ambiguous situations. Norman C. Stageberg has recognized some twenty constructions or construction types which are responsible for most of the ambiguity in student writing. At the very least, recognition of these can serve as a series of warnings and help the student to understand the source and nature of his difficulty.

As for the positive role: Most teachers would like to see their students achieve a greater degree of dexterity in the manipulation of the structural patterns of the language than is usual with them. To accomplish this we must teach them the patterns as patterns first of all, and then the ways in which they may be expanded. A number of textbooks now do this to a considerable extent, employing diagrams and formulas effectively to this end. Recently, as a consequence of a number of studies on what has been called generative rhetoric, the technique has been applied to the paragraph and the entire theme as well.

Linguistics, of course, has a potential application to the highly selective use of language which we call literature — also a concern of the English classroom — but that is a topic in itself (see Chapter 16).

A concluding note of caution is in order. Children learned to read long before the development of linguistics as a systematic study. They learned to express themselves, both in speech and in writing. The history of education is replete with methods and approaches which their proponents hoped, and too often claimed, might perform miracles. There will be no miracles in native language instruction, if for no other reason than that most of the child's language activities are carried on outside of the classroom, where teachers, approaches, and methods have no part. The knowledge of language which linguistics provides can, however, aid the teacher in coping with many of the language problems that arise. It will not furnish the sole answer, but it can be a significant help in many instances — if, and only if, the teacher is equipped to make an intelligent and sophisticated use of it.

12 DICTIONARIES AND USAGE

Thomas Pyles

In a society which, theoretically at least, is classless, it is obviously important that everyone should have the opportunity to learn to speak and write well, whatever "well" may happen to mean. America has no courtly social caste upon which to model its manners in speech, only a school tradition — which is nonetheless potent. This tradition dates back to the days when, in colonial New England, a schoolhouse stood beside every church (almost every church). By the latter half of the seventeenth century, these church schools passed into the jurisdiction of the state and became district schools. In the south and in the middle states, attitudes toward learning were somewhat less zealous than among the Puritans.

The New England tradition, which was ultimately to become the American tradition, gave rise to Noah Webster, the most important single figure in American lexicography. Webster was, unlike his English predecessor Samuel Johnson, primarily a pedant. Johnson tried schoolmastering, true, but he was above all a gifted man of letters who wrote a great dictionary; Webster tried many things other than schoolmastering, but all his long life — he belonged to a Revolutionary War regiment which never heard the crack of rifle fire, and lived into the reign of Queen Victoria — he was by temperament and inclination a schoolmaster. And, with all his quirks and crotchets, coupled with an arrogance which makes it difficult for us to regard him with any degree of warmth, he may be said to have started a distinguished tradition in American lexicography.

Webster was quite fanciful in many of his etymologies for he did not have a really expert knowledge of all the languages with which he claimed familiarity; the fact is that his knowledge of language in general was weak even for his day. He was sufficiently dogmatic to declare that it was better to be unfashionably right — remember, he was essentially a Puritan — than fashionably wrong, whatever in the world that could possibly mean. But he was a man of really tremendous energy and industry, and, in the opinion of Sir James Murray, the great first editor of the *Oxford English Dictionary*, "a born definer of words."

Beginning with the revision, after his death in 1843, of his *American Dictionary of the English Language* (1828), there have been many excellent American dictionaries for general use. There are more than a half dozen in circulation today, three of which bear Webster's name, and others are in preparation — not to mention such specialized works as the *Dictionary of American English* (the principal editor of which was a Scotsman, Sir William Craigie), the *Dictionary of Americanisms*, the *Dictionary of American Regional English*, now in preparation, and the various dictionaries of slang, argot, and vernacular.

Though "Old Noah" — one always thinks of him thus, for he seems never to have had any youth — has, of course, had nothing to do with these current dictionaries, not even those which bear his name. Naive people may still say "according to Webster" when they want to settle an argument about what a word is supposed to mean. They may even proceed to cite some work which they refer to as "the dictionary," whether or not it happens to bear his name — to such an extent is Noah Webster associated with lexicography in the popular mind. Of course any definition cited today is unlikely to stem from any dictionary actually prepared by him; but his name confers a sort of authority to the notions regarding the inflexibility of language dear to the heart of the average man. Webster must in large part be credited with the veneration in which dictionaries are held.

But another force, growing out of the same tradition that gave us Webster, helps to account for American linguistic attitudes (though it must be stated emphatically that most of the attitudes to be discussed in this chapter are by no means exclusively American). This force is a widespread, though only partial literacy which is equatable with *education* in the older sense of that word only by a tremendous stretch of the imagination; it is a result of the public school system — public school, of course, in the American sense. The American desire for schooling, if not indeed for learning, which is rather more difficult to come by, is evidenced in the early township schools and in the "little red schoolhouses," the rural schools of the nineteenth and early twentieth centuries. I cannot testify that all these were painted red, but it would seem from the American proverbial expression that most of them were.

These are supposed to have imparted a particularly sound, "no-nonsense" education in such fundamentals as "readin', writin', and 'rithmetic" — sometimes affectionately referred to as "the three *r*'s." Even highly cultivated Americans see these rural schools — which in fact must have been rather dismal institutions, as often as not presided over, in H. L. Mencken's phrase, by milkmaids armed with hickory sticks and yokels in frock coats — through the nostalgic shimmer of romance and patriotism. To question the sources of their authority is still to bring down coals of fire upon the linguist's head. It can be said for them, however, that they did try, by means of constant drill and that good old American institution, the spelling bee — a contest in which sides were chosen and each side attempted to "spell down" the other — to combat the troublesome and inconsistent matter of English spelling. Time-wasting perhaps it was; effective it may have been, though every generation tends to think that the succeeding generation is made up of miserable spellers. The bad spelling of the young is almost invariably attributed — and with some justice — to deficiencies in the educational system: "Schools aren't what they were in my day." Inasmuch as the layman usually confuses writing with language, this is taken as evidence of the deterioration of English. The spelling text used throughout the nineteenth century (still in use in a few private schools, I am told) was Noah Webster's *Spelling Book*, the "blue-back speller," first published in 1783. It must be one of the best-selling books of all times.

In view of the fact that litterateurs supply most of the data on which the scholar bases his conclusions concerning the nature of Standard English, one would expect literary men to be more or less self-assured about their usage — to assume, as English writers did for the better part of a thousand years, that what they write is indeed "good English." On the contrary, many seem to regard hoary old precepts as the *summum bonum* of what they have been trained to think of as grammar. Thus, a well-known and highly successful American writer has stated that consulting H. W. Fowler's *Modern English Usage* — which is actually somewhat more "liberal" than many an American school text — made him realize how bad a writer he was and encouraged him to do better, just as if one ever "did better" merely by following handbook precepts. A few are, in fact, considerably more puristic in their attitudes, if not actually in their practice, than most teachers nowadays; for even the most benighted teacher must by now have felt some slight impact of the scholarly study of language as it is used — or, as some would put it, have to some extent been corrupted by the National Council of Teachers of English. Note, however, this statement by an American writer and critic, himself a teacher of English for a single year (1913–1914 — long before the rise of enlightened attitudes toward usage in this country, and only a few years after the first meeting of the National Council of Teachers of English, which has long fostered such enlightened attitudes): "Some of the editors in our leading publishing houses are apparently as ignorant of the fundamentals of good English as the writers over whose copy they labor," going on to say that many of the books being printed nowadays "would not have passed muster by the nineteenth-century schoolmarm of the little red schoolhouse enshrined in American memory." I really do not know what the gentleman has in mind. The books that I read which are published even by disreputable American publishers contain few if any of the purist's supposed errors in grammar, though their style may frequently be halting and dull and their choice of words not precisely what mine might have been. But that is another matter entirely.

There can be little doubt that the inadequately educated, unsophisticated teacher of the near past — the schoolmarm dedicated to her little red schoolhouse, and her metropolitan counterpart — has to a large extent fostered the layman's confused notions about English usage, his belief that there are many rules governing English which must not be broken by those who aspire to write and speak well, despite the fact that great writers and speakers have in fact broken them without compunction, often without even any awareness that such rules existed. Because of the general belief that these rules are the stock-in-trade of the teacher of English, teachers are often expected to make decisions about such unimportant matters of English usage as the *it's I, it's me* alternative.

It is a popular assumption that, as in morals, so in language there is invariably a sharp line of demarcation between "right" and "wrong." (Whether this is altogether true in the moral sphere need not concern us.) It follows from this assumption that there must be no schisms in language. It is generally supposed to be the scholar's business to determine, by some appeal to logic, analogy, Latin grammar, or historical development, or simply by afflatus, what choice between alternative constructions one *ought* to make. Consequently he is often consulted respectfully by business and professional men whose attitude toward him in other circumstances might well be somewhat condescending. He is, moreover, thought incompetent, or at the least disobliging, if he refuses to falsify the facts of usage as he knows them from firsthand observation. As for the construction *it's me, it's I*, for instance, he will be aware that educated speakers might use either form: the valet Jeeves would be more apt to choose the less natural *I* than his master Bertie Wooster. The plain fact is, however, that the occasion for either rarely arises. In answer to some such question as "Who's there?" one would, for instance, ordinarily merely announce one's name.

A caste dialect in the European sense is largely a matter of pronunciation and intonation, though word choice is often quite important. Because of the size, the settlement history, and the cultural history of the United States, no single type of pronunciation has ever been able to establish itself as a standard comparable to what is known as Received Pronunciation recorded principally by H. C. Wyld and Daniel Jones and referred to as *U* (for upper-class) by A. S. C. Ross and subsequently by The Hon. Nancy Mitford, in her widely publicized article "The English Aristocracy," in *Encounter*.

The American uses the pronunciation of the region in which he has in his early childhood acquired his speech habits; thus, the Chicagoan speaks in one way, the Bostonian of the same status in another, the Virginian in another, and the Texan in yet another; yet the differences are not very great, for American English has always been noted for its uniformity. With the exception of Gullah, spoken by Negroes living along the coastal region of South Carolina and Georgia, both on the Sea Islands and on the mainland, there are no types of American English which are not readily understandable in all parts of the country, though a certain tolerance is sometimes necessary. To the layman's ear many of the differences, at least away from the Atlantic coast, are so subtle as to be practically indiscernible, though everyone can tell a speaker from the deep south from one from the middle west. There are, of course, types of American pronunciation which are regarded as substandard; but these are more noticeable in the metropolitan than in the rural areas and are due to a number of factors which it would be irrelevant to discuss here.

There is thus a good deal of truth in the statement of an English journalist that "in America, where it is grammar, not accent, that places you, anyone can learn the grammar." Consequently, much of the teaching in the lower schools has been largely concerned with the inculcation of grammatical precepts calculated to imbue the pupil with what is nowadays referred to as status, to put him into possession of what is assumed to be the prestige dialect. *Status* is perhaps only another word for *class*, but in this case it is class based upon the mastery of a fairly simple set of precepts — nothing so difficult as the acquisition of a caste "accent" — rather than upon birth and breeding.

The linguist's main contention about prescriptive teaching, which in itself he has not the slightest objection to, is that its precepts should be properly based — that is, based on the *actual* usage of reputable speakers and writers rather than notions of what *should* be or arbitrary appeals to such extralinguistic factors as logic, analogy, the historical development of the language, and the like. From appeals of this sort have come taboos, some of them more or less confined to the classroom, against such usages as these:

he don't (now old fashioned in cultivated speech, but frequent a generation ago until a schoolteachers' crusade blacklisted it)

ain't I (a variant of British *aren't I*)

reference by the plural pronoun to the indefinite pronouns *everyone, someone,* and the like (as in *Everyone cheered the returning hero, and he waved his hand to them* — just try substituting the prescribed *him* for *them* in that sentence)

due to as a compound preposition (as in *Due to his lack of foresight, the battle was lost*)

the so-called split infinitive (that is, the insertion of a word, usually an adverb, or a phrase between *to* and the verb form)

the omission of *shall-will* distinction (artificial for Americans)

the terminal preposition (as in *What is the world coming to?*)

these (or *those*) *kind* (or *sort*)

the reason is because

like introducing a clause

different than (or *to*)

supposedly misplaced *only* (as in *He only arrived a few minutes ago*, purists preferring us to say *He arrived only a few minutes ago*)

supposed misuse of *who* for *whom* in such a sentence as *Who are you waiting for?* (which also offends by its terminal preposition)

All these locutions actually occur, some perhaps infrequently, in the discourse of educated speakers, British as well as American, when they are not thinking of the schoolmaster's ruler hovering over their knuckles. Some occur as well in the works of highly respectable authors. My files, necessarily somewhat more limited than those of the editors of the *Oxford English Dictionary* and *Webster's Third*, abound in illustrative citations. But there are many circles — not very interesting or lively circles, it is true — in which the breaking of such taboos might cause eyebrows to lift. The ambitious young person not yet established in his career had best watch his words;

they need not be interesting words, stylishly put together, but they must be correct ones, as correctness is conceived in such circles.

The old teaching — the "old purist junk," as the late Sterling Andrus Leonard once called it — lingers on, despite enlightened dictionaries and the efforts of such objective students of usage as Leonard himself, the late George Philip Krapp, the late Porter Perrin, Albert H. Marckwardt, Robert Pooley, Kemp Malone, Charles Carpenter Fries, Margaret Bryant, and a good many others whose findings have fallen upon deaf ears in many pedagogical circles. The usual reaction to any studies which demonstrate the great discrepancy between textbook rules and the actual usage of recognized speakers and writers is abusive attack upon those who have made such studies — an attack often fortified by newspaper editorials pointing out that the English language is going to the dogs. A frequent assertion is that such scholars, who have merely examined the same evidence that is there for all to examine, are "permissive" — a voguish adjective nowadays, with pejorative connotations; with them, it is said, "anything goes." Nothing could be further from the truth.

The critical reception of *Webster's Third* when it first appeared in 1961 — a work based on sound editorial principles which do not actually depart much from those of the great *Oxford English Dictionary* — indicates that many of our most eminent critics believe that a dictionary ought to be a law book, and moreover one which incorporates all their own crotchets, prejudices, and misconceptions rather than a record of the usage of writers and speakers of the language who are persons of some prominence in modern life, though not necessarily concerned with the arts and sciences. Despite the considerably greater enlightenment shown by the English critics, the fact remains that many persons on both sides of the Atlantic still conceive of some *ideal* English language, its rules embalmed forever in moldy textbooks, whose standards everyone should continually aspire to speak up to and to write up to. The distinguished efforts of a generation of scholars who have devoted themselves to the study of English usage have as yet made little impact on the public mind — and I refer here to the educated public, of course, for no one else cares much one way or the other. Perhaps it will require yet another generation to take heed of what has already been done. By then, other changes will have occurred in the language, though fortunately they will be comparatively slight.

When, a number of years ago, an American cigarette adopted the advertising slogan *it tastes good like a cigarette should*, there were storms of protest from the purists, who had been taught to believe that, according to some God-given law, *like* could not be thus used as a conjunction — though it had been so used many times before by not contemptible writers, among them Robert Southey, Charles Darwin, Cardinal Newman, William Morris, and George Bernard Shaw. Fowler, usually regarded as a custodian of the purity of the English language, says of the construction in his *Modern English Usage*: "It is the established way of putting the thing among all who have not been taught to avoid it. . . . But in good writing this particular *like* is very rare, and even those writers with whom sound English is a matter of care and study rather than of right instinct, and to whom *like* was once the natural word, usually weed it out." One wonders just what is gained by so doing.

And so it goes. Students have made great progress in establishing what *is* good English, assuming that we accept as a definition of good English the usage of those whom we should expect to speak and write good English — and I know of no better definition. In any case, this usage is amply recorded in the myriad pages of the *Oxford English Dictionary*, in Otto Jespersen's *Modern English Grammar*, in the works of other great Continental Anglicists, in the works of many English and American scholars, in the valuable materials of the *Linguistic Atlas* of the United States and Canada, in scores of learned articles and notes in such American journals as *American Speech*, the *English Journal*, and *College English*, and in our on-the-whole excellent dictionaries.

It is ironic that, in a period which has produced the liveliest linguistic research since the nineteenth-century work of Rasmus Rask, Jacob Grimm, and Franz Bopp, popular attitudes should lag so far behind. Arbitrary notions about English usage which date from the eighteenth century should, one would suppose, have been dissipated by now. But, on the contrary, they have retained so much of their original potency that any questioning of their validity for all sorts and conditions of men is regarded as a linguistic heresy. But what the social scientists have called "cultural lag" is in no sense peculiar to America, nor to linguistic attitudes.

13 LINGUISTICS AND TEACHING FOREIGN LANGUAGES

David DeCamp

The linguistic approach to teaching foreign languages can best be described by contrasting it with two other approaches which preceded it: the translation method and the direct method. Let me explain by use of analogy. Suppose you wish to play the piano. Someone recommends to you a teacher with a considerable reputation as a concert pianist, and you arrive at his studio eager for your first lesson. Instead of letting you sit down at the piano, however, your teacher insists on lecturing you about the history and construction of pianos, the theory of harmony, and the great piano music of the past. Throughout the lesson, you do not touch the piano, and your teacher plays no more than half a dozen notes as an illustration for his lecture. If your teacher continues with this method in subsequent lessons, you are a fool if you do not abandon him and seek a better teacher.

The hopelessness of trying to learn to play the piano without ever playing it has always been obvious. Yet until very recently, this was the only common method for teaching a language. In the translation method, the teacher lectures his students in their native language on the grammar of the target language, allows his students little or no opportunity to use the language, and seldom uses it himself. As the student "progresses," he may be required to recite conjugations of irregular verbs, but he seldom hears or speaks any real sentences in the language other than the examples provided as illustrations of grammatical points. A good deal of class time is taken up by translating the daily lesson into the student's native language, but he is never asked whether he really understands the passage which he is translating.

To return to our analogy, suppose you change piano teachers, and your new teacher immediately seats you at the piano and puts a Beethoven sonata on the music rack. "But," you protest, "I can't play this. I've never touched a piano before." "Never mind," your teacher assures you. "I'll play the first few bars, and then you imitate me and try to go on from there. Don't worry if you make a lot of mistakes." By the end of a few lessons and a few weeks of practice, perhaps you can indeed hit the right notes for the first few bars. If you continue long enough, you may even learn to play the entire sonata. I suppose one could learn to play the piano by this method, and I once knew a piano teacher who defended it. I believe, however, that we would all recognize that this method of sudden and total immersion into all the complexities of a difficult piano work is not the most efficient way to learn piano playing.

In the 1920s and 1930s, language teachers practicing the direct method did indeed practice such a policy of total immersion. Especially at commercial language schools, such as Berlitz, both teacher and student were strictly forbidden to use anything but the target language. The teacher tried to engage the student in free conversation, illustrating the meaning by means of gestures, pantomime, and stage props. Although the subject matter of these conversations was planned in advance in order to concentrate on certain types of vocabulary in each lesson, there was little or no control of the sentence patterns, and the student was immediately exposed to the entire bewildering range of the syntax of the language. The emphasis was on the natural functional use of the target language from the very beginning, and both grammatical explanations and grammatical drills were avoided. People could and indeed did learn foreign languages by the direct method, which is more than can be said for the translation method, and the commercial schools using this method certainly did a better job than the public schools, most of which were still stumbling along with the translation method.

If you are wise, however, you will also abandon your second piano teacher and look for a third, one who will indeed require you to practice the piano from the very beginning, but who will not hesitate to give you an explanation as well as a demonstration if he believes that it will help you, and, most important of all, one who will carefully control the musical patterns which you are to learn. This teacher will ask you to practice scales and finger exercises so that you attain proficiency in the fundamentals. He will start you off with simple one-line melodies in the key of C, with simple, straightforward rhythms. He will introduce the complexities of music one at a time: playing chords, sharps and flats, and more complicated rhythms. You will progress through carefully graded stages until you arrive at a level of proficiency high enough for you to try the Beethoven sonata.

These principles have long been recognized in music teaching, but few language teachers practiced them before World War II. Of course there were a few forward-looking pioneers in language teaching who had long required their students to make active use of the target language without making a fetish of it and who carefully graded and controlled the sentence patterns which their students were practicing. The rank and file of language teachers, however, practiced the translation method or the direct method, as many of them, unfortunately, still do today.

The linguistic method was not invented during World War II, but it received its greatest impetus from that war. All the major nations were faced with the urgent need for teaching foreign languages to large numbers of students at a vastly accelerated pace. Some of these languages, especially those of Asia, had seldom been taught in Europe or America, so that there was no tradition of teaching these languages to depend upon, in some cases no textbooks, grammars, or dictionaries. Sometimes the teacher was faced with the threefold task of learning the language himself, writing the textbook, and teaching the language to others, simultaneously.

Despite these apparent handicaps, the accelerated wartime language programs were highly successful. People learned languages much more rapidly than had been believed possible and with a degree of accuracy, especially in pronunciation, higher than previously attained. Before the war, many language teachers insisted that no one but a child could ever learn a foreign language without a strong foreign accent and that no one could become fluent in a foreign language without living for years in the country where it was spoken. Most of us no longer believe that this is true.

Until now I have been speaking of the linguistic method as if it were a single invariable technique. Actually there are many different schools of thought on language teaching today, all of which may properly claim to be linguistically oriented. Furthermore, teaching methodology has continued to evolve and develop since the war, so that we now look at the wartime courses as rather naive and crude. All linguistic methods of language teaching, however, have shared the same fundamental principles: active practice in the language and careful control and grading of the grammatical patterns.

The wartime courses consisted primarily of dialogues for the student to memorize and of drills in which the student merely imitated the teacher. It was for this reason that many people called this approach the mim-mem method (*mim*icry and *mem*orization). More modern techniques still involve a great deal of mim-mem practice, but they require the student to do much more than merely mimic and memorize.

For one thing we now place a much greater emphasis on recognition or discrimination drills. The linguistic contrast between the English words *beat* and *bit* is not normally perceived by a speaker of Spanish, for example, and merely imitating the pronunciation of the words *beat* and *bit*, even when presented together as a minimal pair, will not necessarily succeed in teaching the Spanish student of English to perceive this contrast. Therefore, special recognition drills are provided. The simplest of these is a "same-different" drill, in which the student is taught to recognize that the pair of sentences *He beat his wife* and *He beat his wife* are the same, but that *He beat his wife* and *He bit his wife* are different. More sophisticated recognition drills require the student to identify which of a pair of minimal utterances has been spoken even though he is given only one member of the pair. Minimal-pair recognition drills are best known in teaching pronunciation, but the same principle is applied in teaching grammatical contrasts (*He eats roast beef* and *He is eating roast beef*) and in teaching vocabulary (*The teacher was wise, The teacher was intelligent*).

Today we not only require the student to discriminate between utterances which he has never heard, we also require him to go beyond the pattern which he has memorized, to vary the pattern and create new sentences of his own. The development of production drills, in which the student is required to formulate and produce sentences in a controlled pattern instead of merely imitating them, parallels and perhaps results from the increasing interest which theoretical linguists have taken in a speaker's ability to produce new sentences which he has never heard before. Two decades ago, American linguists were primarily concerned with the linguistic analysis of utterances already spoken, that is, the analysis of a corpus or text. We are now much more interested in determining the potential sentences which a speaker of the language might utter, a virtually unlimited set of possible sentences. This concern with describing potential utterances is by no means limited to the generative-transformational school but is shared by a great many linguists who do not agree with Noam Chomsky and his followers.

Anyone learning a language hears only a few thousand sentences of that language during the time the learning process is going on. Yet he can afterward speak or understand any of an almost infinite number of sentences which he has never heard before. There is nothing mysterious about this. Let me use another analogy, this time with arithmetic. If you start out counting 1, 2, 3, 4 . . . . , how far can you count? The only limitation is the amount of time you have. You could start right now and keep on counting until the day of your death, but you would never run out of numbers. In the process you would speak many numbers which you had never heard or even thought of before, yet these would seem perfectly normal to you. For example, take the number 73,451,866,635,926. It has probably never before been spoken in all history, never before been written down or even thought of. Yet you recognize it as a perfectly normal — that is, "grammatical" — number. You not only understand it, but you can manipulate it; I could ask you to multiply it by 7 or to subtract 35 from it. You could do this because you once learned the ten numbers 1, 2, 3, 4, 5, 6, 7, 8, 9, and 0 and a set of rules for combining them, so that you now can "recognize" numbers you have never seen before.

It is easy to think of sentences which have never before been spoken. They occur frequently in every normal conversation. Take the following sentence: *Pointing out the limitations of the old translation and direct methods, the bearded linguist explained the advantages of the linguistic approach to language teaching.* I am reasonably sure that this sentence has never before been spoken. Yet you can understand it. Furthermore, you can manipulate it, just as you did the number. I could ask you to make the sentence negative or to turn it into a question. You could do this because you once learned all the words in that sentence and a set of rules for combining them. Perhaps at the time you were learning these rules, especially if you are a native speaker of English, you did not think of them as rules, for they were not stated formally like the rules in a grammar book, but you somehow did get into your head a system of operations, one which at least *could* be stated as a set of rules, and which now enables you to deal with sentences which you have never heard before.

The best modern language courses still must include a great deal of mimicry and memorization. There is no substitute for them in language learning. But the best language teachers now know that mimicry and memorization by themselves are inadequate. The student must go beyond the pattern which he has imitated and memorized and must create new sentences of his own. Otherwise he will learn only what a parrot can learn: to repeat sentences he has heard other people say. Apparently neither the parrot nor any animal other than man has the human mental ability to break down sentences and then rebuild the same elements into new and meaningful sentences. It is this ability which distinguishes human speech from animal imitations of it. It is perhaps the ability which most sharply distinguishes the human race from other animals.

The current emphasis on active production in language learning results not only from developments in modern theoretical linguistics but also from developments in psychology, especially in the theory of learning. The classical behaviorist theories of the conditioned response might have been adequate to explain the simple language learning of the parrot, but not that of humans. Perhaps the parrot learns to "speak" in the same way Pavlov's dog learned to salivate whenever it heard a bell ring. But Pavlov's dog did not become actively conscious of the conditioning process, nor did it become actively cooperative and independently begin initiating new responses of its own. The human language student plays a much more active role in the learning process than does the parrot or dog. The relations between human stimulus and response are so complex that we must also consider the nature of the organism which receives the stimulus, moderates it, and produces the response. We must consider what the active mind of the student contributes. Classical behaviorism is still not dead, and of course it contributed a great deal in its time. The simple stimulus–response model of language behavior which Leonard Bloomfield described in 1933 was a great improvement over the fuzzy thinking which had preceded it — a sort of mystic mentalism — but today his formula strikes both linguists and psychologists as naive. Though Bloomfield's ideas were the basis of the successful wartime language courses, we find them inadequate for the even more successful language courses of the 1960s.

This does not mean that we have now gone back to the old memorization of grammatical rules. The core of all good language teaching is still active pattern drill. It is just that we now try harder to make the student aware of what is happening during the pattern drill, to enlist his active cooperation, and to take advantage of his human ability to do what Pavlov's dog could not do. We now teach each aspect of the language (each grammatical pattern, each vocabulary group, each set of sounds) in five stages, which have been called (1) recognition, (2) imitation, (3) repetition, (4) variation, and (5) selection.

The recognition stage does not include learning the meaning of a new word or pattern. Meaning is a matter of context and may be taught simultaneously with all five stages; it cannot be fully mastered until the selection stage. By recognition we mean the ability to discriminate between two different utterances and to recognize that a given word or sentence is a repetition of one which the speaker has already spoken, or that it is a new and different word or sentence. Until the learner can discriminate between the English words *beat* and *bit*, until he realizes that they are indeed two different words, he can make very little use of the information that one word means something you do with your teeth and the other means something you do with a stick. He must recognize that the sentence *He is eating roast beef* is different from *He eats roast beef* before he can associate one with continuative present action and the other with habitual activity. The beginning student of a language does not hear sounds and words and sentences in the language he is studying. He hears only a continuous smear of garbled sound. As he progresses, he is amazed that the speakers of that language seem to be improving in articulation. Even if he does not understand what they are saying, it sounds to him as if they are speaking more clearly.

The recognition stage is taught by means of recognition drills of the type I have already described, drills which require the student to determine whether a pair of utterances are the same or different and to identify which of a possible pair of utterances is the one he actually hears spoken. Then comes stage 2, the imitation stage, in which the student must himself produce the same utterances he has been learning to hear. Sometimes the teacher may ask the student to imitate a single word, but it is always better to have the word in the context of a sentence. Even a simple sentence like *This is a book* is better than the word *book* in isolation, first because it is easier to learn a new word in a familiar context than in isolation, second because the pronunciation will be more normal and natural if imitated in context, and third because essential grammatical information will be learned at the same time. The student who begins by imitating *This is a book* and *This is water*, rather than the words *book* and *water* in isolation, will later have no difficulty in remembering that *book* is a countable noun in English whereas *water* is a mass abstract noun which cannot be counted without naming the counting unit, as in *two cups of water, two liters of water*. Ideally the sentences imitated should themselves not be in isolation but should be in the context of a dialogue, which should in turn represent a natural social context, for example a conversation between friends or between shopkeeper and shopper.

The teacher strives for perfection in the imitation stage, including accurate mimicry of the appropriate gestures and facial expressions. We now know that a so-called foreign accent is nothing but the combination of many small errors, each of which may be so small as to be barely perceptible when considered separately but which become very noticeable in combination. In practice, however, the teacher usually must settle for less than perfect imitation. The time is limited and there are many things which the student must accomplish besides a "good accent." The mimicry–memorization process must go on, however, until the student's response is fluent and reasonably accurate, and — most important — until it is largely reduced to physical motor habit. This is stage 3, repetition, and its function is to relieve the student's mind of the burden of consciously controlling all the details of the sentence. As long as the student has to think about where to put his tongue to articulate the vowel of the word *beat*, as long as he has to remember consciously that the plural of *man* is *men*, not *mans*, he will not be fluent and will not be ready to proceed to the fourth stage. If we had to think consciously about all the muscular movements involved in walking, we couldn't walk very well either. Fortunately, a great deal of what we do when we walk or talk becomes controlled by habit after a period of practice, thus freeing our attention for other matters.

As I stated earlier, some of the wartime language courses emphasized only the first three stages, recognition, imitation, and repetition. Modern courses devote a great amount of time to stage 4, variation. If the student is to go beyond the learning capacity of the parrot, which can only imitate what its master has said, he must learn to vary the patterns he has learned. The dialogues a student memorizes should be as practical and useful as possible, but they cannot anticipate every use the student will want to make of the language. He may have memorized the sentences necessary for buying a pair of shoes, for example, but what if he wants to buy a hat instead of shoes? He must then adapt the dialogue to make it apply to a new situation.

Rather than leave this adaptation entirely up to the student to learn for himself, the modern teacher conducts three kinds of variation drill: substitution drills, transformation drills, and combinatory drills. All three types may take a dialogue the student has memorized or some other form of mim-mem drill as their point of departure, but they go beyond the stage of mimicry and memorization. In a substitution drill, the student is required to hold constant the basic structure of the sentence and to substitute new vocabulary, one word at a time. If the student has already learned the English sentence *George eats roast beef*, the teacher might give as a cue the single word *lamb*. The student would then respond with the sentence *George eats roast lamb*, even though he might never have heard that sentence before. Notice that in a substitution drill, the teacher must give only the cues for substitution. If the teacher himself speaks the sentence *George eats roast lamb*, then it is he who has done the substitution, and to the student this is nothing but another mim-mem drill. *George eats roast beef, George eats roast lamb*, is a simple substitution drill in which the student need only substitute one word and then reproduce the sentence. More advanced substitution drills require the student to make changes elsewhere in the sentence in order to make other words agree grammatically with the word he has substituted. For example, the teacher might require the student to substitute the word *children* for the word *boy* in the sentence *The boy brought his books with him*. The proper response, of course, would be *The children brought their books with them*. When substituting *children* for *boy*, the student must also change *his* to *their* and *him* to *them*.

A transformation drill is just the converse of a substitution drill. Instead of holding the sentence pattern constant and substituting new vocabulary into the pattern, the transformation drill holds the vocabulary constant — at least the principal content vocabulary — and changes the sentence to a different but related pattern. For example, the student might be given the sentence *George ate the roast beef* and then be asked to produce the sentence *Did George eat the roast beef?* or *What did George eat?* or *George didn't eat the roast beef, did he?*

In a combinatory drill, the student is given two simple sentences and is asked to combine them into a more complex pattern. The easiest of these drills involves simple conjunction. Given the two sentences *We sat under a tree* and *We ate our lunch*, the student must produce the sentence *We sat under a tree and ate our lunch*. More advanced combinatory drills might require the student to take the same two sentences and combine them into more sophisticated combinations, like *We sat under a tree to eat our lunch* and *We sat under a tree eating our lunch*.

Finally, there is selection, stage 5. The student has learned to recognize and imitate a construction in the language. He has practiced it until he produces it promptly, correctly, and automatically, and he has learned to vary the construction in order to produce new sentences. Now he must know *when* he should use it. This includes understanding the meaning and also the social implications of a statement. Is it casual and slangy, suitable only for use among personal friends of equal status, like the American greeting *Hi!*, or is it courteous and formal, suitable for use in situations requiring respect? Putting the selection stage last does not mean we want to keep the student ignorant of the meaning and have him practice meaningless gibberish. By this stage he probably has a rough idea of the meaning just from the way the drills have been presented. But we do believe that a precise sense of meaning, especially subtle distinctions, can be obtained only from within the language, not through translation. Consequently the selection stage must wait until the student is actually able to use the constructions whose meanings he then needs to understand. I have seen English teachers waste hours of valuable class time vainly trying to explain (in the students' native language, of course) the subtle distinctions between English words like *tall* and *high* or *wise* and *intelligent*, and between grammatical constructions like *He eats roast beef* and *He is eating roast beef*. All the abstract explanations in the world are not as effective as a few minutes of selection drill, practice drills which place the newly learned constructions in meaningful and contrastive contexts. For example, the teacher may ask a series of questions to be answered by the students, the correct answers depending on what the teacher is doing at the moment. *Do I teach English? Yes, you do. Am I teaching English? Yes, you are. Do I drink coffee? Yes, you do. Am I drinking coffee? No, you aren't.* Such a drill can be used, however, only after the student is able to use the forms and so match up answers like *Yes, you are* and *No, you aren't* with questions like *Am I combing my hair?*

Most American linguists agree on these five stages of language learning as I have described them. On some points, however, there is disagreement. For example, when and how should reading and writing be introduced? Many eminent linguists believe that reading and writing should be delayed until the student has gained considerable proficiency in the spoken language, and that it should then be taught as a visible, written representation of the spoken language, almost as if it were a phonetic transcription. They advocate a great deal of attention to the correspondences between the spoken sounds and the written letters. They require their students to read out loud and to listen to the spoken language while following the written text. Together with other American linguists, however, I advocate that the student learn to read and write each new sentence pattern as soon as possible after he has learned to speak it. I would keep reading aloud to a minimum. I believe that the teaching of reading and writing should follow the same five stages as the teaching of the spoken language; that a great deal of controlled and graded written drill should also be provided, so that the student learns to recognize and distinguish written signals, to imitate them, to vary the written patterns by substitution, transformation, and combination, and to select the appropriate written expression without having to speak it first and then write it down like a secretary taking dictation.

American linguists also disagree on the teaching of pronunciation, and again methods reflect general linguistic theories. Those who still believe in a simplistic phonemic theory tend to teach sounds as segmental units: the English /p/, /t/, and /k/ sounds, for example. Those who believe in the feature analysis of phonology, however, tend to drill students on phonetic features such as voicing, aspiration, or nasality, features shared by several sounds of the language.

Yet we linguists agree far more than we disagree on language teaching. And when we do disagree, our different approaches provide an excellent opportunity for testing our different theories. If a linguistic theory is valid, it will be applicable. Theoretical and applied linguistics have developed side by side, and each has drawn upon the other. Problems encountered in teaching languages have revealed gaps in our knowledge of their structure and inadequacies in our general theories of language.

14 LINGUISTICS AND ANTHROPOLOGY

Norman A. McQuown

The subject matter of linguistics is language, man's prime means of communication. Language is the chief instrument through which man thinks and with which he integrates himself, both internally and externally, both as a functioning individual and as an active participant in a human group, a member of human society. Language is the principal tool through which one man passes on his personal and social integration, his cultivated ways of behaving, to his offspring, and through which he induces his peers to share his culture and, with him, to form a larger social group.

The subject matter of anthropology is man. Anthropology studies man's body, as it is today and as it was in the past. It studies the behavior of man's body, and through the external manifestations of that behavior, its effects on other men and on man's physical surroundings. Among the external manifestations of man's behavior are the stance and motion of his body, the reflection of these in the behavior of other men, and their permanent effect on the materials and the objects in the world about him. The most highly specialized aspect of man's externally manifest behavior is his vocal activity. Such activity involves his diaphragm, his lungs, his voice-box, and his nose and mouth. Since the most active organ in man's mouth is his tongue, such vocal activity came to be called *lingua*, from the word for tongue, by the Romans — in English, *language*, the subject matter of linguistics.

From the point of view of the anthropologist, then, the scientific

149

field of linguistics is a subfield of anthropology, and a most important one, whose successful pursuit is a prerequisite to effective work in certain other anthropological subfields. Preliminary spadework by the anthropologist who studies man's language prepares the ground for the anthropologist who would study man's cultivated ways of behaving and the internal patterns which lie behind them, for these constitute his culture and are largely manifest in his language. The anthropologist who studies man's language also provides his colleague who would study man's relations with other men, largely made possible by language, with an indispensable tool. Man's ways of behaving and of relating are mediated by his language, and both are characterized and categorized by internal characteristics and categories of the language through which they operate.

Man is an internally complex animal. So great is his inner complexity, and so potentially large the number and varied the character of the elements through which that internal complexity may be externally manifest, that every human group behaves in ways peculiar to it alone and every human individual possesses certain elements of behavior or certain characteristics of such elements which are, for the moment at least, unique to him as an individual. Among human activities language is probably the most complex and the most varied. Man speaks many tongues. It is not surprising, then, that language, properly broken up into its component elements and properly characterized with respect to the larger structures within which these elements function, can serve as a sensitive index to other human activity: to the culture and the social organization of human groups, and to the private cultures and the social placement of individual men.

The variety and complexity of human languages have placed a considerable analytic burden on the linguist–anthropologist who would break them down into their elements and who would describe the larger linguistic structures in which such elements figure. The techniques devised for confronting the linguist–analyst with the object of his analysis, for initial segmentation of the linguistic stream into discrete units, for discovery of structures or patterns employing the segments that lie within and behind the stream, for placing the segments within the structures, and for interrelating structures (and their internal segments) within one linguistic subsystem with those within another, have served as a model to other anthropologists for the analysis of other aspects of man's culture and social relations. The recent successes of these techniques in the analysis of language have nourished the hope that the linguistic analogy might help other anthropologists to solve the analytic problems with which they struggle.

The anthropologist characterizes and places one human group with respect to another, and one human language with respect to another, and seeks to generalize such characterization and such placement.

All human beings possess two legs, and two arms, two feet and two hands, and five digits on each foot and on each hand. On each hand one of the digits is opposable to the other four. All human groups possess individuals of two different sexes, male and female, and characteristic roles for adult individuals of each sex, those of father and mother. One of the smallest social groups among all human beings is the nuclear family, made up of one individual of each sex, and their common progeny.

All human languages characteristically manifest themselves externally via sound waves in the surrounding atmosphere, waves which result from the impingement of moving vocal organs on the air in that atmosphere. The movement of the organs and the internal organization of the manifesting sound waves are in all human languages describable as a limited number of features of sound and a limited number of units in a system of sounds. The inventory of features in all languages is the same: "compact," "diffuse," "flat," "sharp," "lax," "tense"; vowel-like, consonant-like.

All languages possess both vowels and consonants, occurring in strings which enter into or represent larger units (syllables, words, phrases, sentences), and such larger units typically are joined one with another in still larger structures (words, phrases, sentences, texts) whose internal members belong to a limited number of large linguistic categories.

All languages have subjects and predicates, and in most languages subjects are typically manifested by nouns, predicates by verbs. In all languages, some of the larger structures are typically bound up with others in a conversion relationship. One structure presupposes or is necessarily thought of as a transformation of another. Many languages possess a structure labeled "active" in which a subject is linked with a predicate consisting of a verb and an object. Many, but not all, of these same languages possess a structure labeled "passive" in which a subject is linked with a predicate consisting of a verb and an agent. In such languages *John hit Bill* is indissolubly bound up with *Bill was hit by John*, and the subject of the first is the agent of the second; the object of the first, the subject of the second.

Although the inventory of physiological attributes of all human beings is the same, their social and cultural utilization is extremely diverse. The "lily-feet" of Old China's concubines were found only there and are, fortunately, no longer found in any group. The legs-akimbo, foot-on-opposite-knee stance characteristic of Masai herdsmen is not widespread; and the flat-footed full-squat posture of Singhalese tradesmen is characteristic of a limited number of groups in the Orient.

Although the potential inventory of human sounds and the higher structures manifest in strings of such sounds is the same in all languages, the actual selection of sounds and higher structures, as well as their internal characteristics, is different in each group, and in some respect unique in each individual. Although all languages possess vowels and consonants, their absolute number and their proportions to each other are extremely varied. Some languages possess 3 vowels (Arabic in the Middle East, Totonac in Middle America), some 5 (Old and New World Spanish, Middle American Maya), some 7 (Italian, Portuguese), some 9 (English, Estonian), some 12 (Danish, Haitian Creole). Some languages possess 8 consonants (Hawaiian), or 12 (Arapaho); some 24 (English, Persian); some 36 (Navaho or Tibetan); some 48 (the Kabardian of the Caucasus, the Zulu of South Africa). Some languages possess only 15 sounds in all (Hawaiian, Arapaho), some possess as many as 50 (Navaho, Scottish Gaelic) or even 75 (the Abkhaz of the Caucasus). All languages possess sentences consisting of a subject and a predicate. But not all languages possess interrelated active and passive subject-predicate constructions. In some languages one cannot match *John hit Bill* with *Bill was hit by John*, but only with *Bill was the object of a blow from John*. All languages possess parts of speech. But some languages possess only "full" or "core" words and peripheral particles. Although many possess categories which we can call nouns and verbs, few distinguish substantives from adjectives or adjectives from adverbs. In Latin, both nouns and adjectives are kinds of substantives, and in Japanese both action words and quality words are kinds of verbs.

Although this complexity and variety is characteristic of all human groups and individuals, it is by no means to be taken for granted as equally true of all other sentient species or even of all other mammals (porpoises) or mammalian species closely related to human beings (orangutans, chimpanzees, gorillas). Although human beings make use of diaphragm, lungs, voice-box, nose, and mouth to effect vibrations in the air surrounding them and to make possible communication with their fellows (and with themselves), it is by no means to be taken for granted that other species, even closely related ones, will use the same means or the same medium for similar purposes. Porpoises do use a voice-box and do use a vibrating medium, but the medium is typically water, not air. Gorillas do use a vocal apparatus much like that of human beings, but the percussive effect of blows with their fists on their chests is an important ingredient of some of their communication, which is otherwise purely vocal. Even human beings do not communicate merely by means of sounds produced by their vocal apparatus: a typical accompaniment of this highly specialized body movement is more generalized movement of other parts of the body, some of it with a specificity approaching that of spoken language. The relative importance, furthermore, of different mechanisms (speech and other body motion) and of different media (sound and light, the auditory and the visual) varies from situation to situation, from human group to human group, and from one species of mammal to another.

Anthropologists, therefore, have been interested not merely in human beings, and linguistic anthropologists not merely in human speech. They have also investigated communicative behavior in other species closely and not so closely related to man, and communicative activity other than speech, human and nonhuman. In recent times, anthropologists who have studied man and have been exposed to linguistic method and weaned on linguistic problems have turned their attention to the communicational behavior and social organization of the nonhuman higher primates (gibbons, baboons, chimpanzees). Anthropologists have even become involved in studying such behavior in other mammals (the porpoises or dolphins) and in other nonmammalian species (the bees). Such research activity is an indispensable prelude to a fuller understanding of the communicational behavior of man himself as well as that of other terrestrial species, and a prelude, likewise, to first contact with nonterrestrial sentient beings and the solution of the problems of extraterrestrial communication.

The range of research activity of the linguist–anthropologist, therefore, is broad. Linguistic anthropologists have in the past typically studied the languages of primitive or preliterate human groups in the world's underdeveloped areas: they have investigated the languages of the Eskimo and of hundreds of American Indian groups, from the Athabascans of northern Canada and Alaska through the Algonkians of the American Great Lakes; from the Sioux and the Cheyenne, the Kiowa and the Apache, of the Great Plains and the Southwest, to the Aztecs and the Maya of Mexico and Guatemala, the Quechua-speaking descendants of the Incas in the South American Andes, the primitive Indians of the Amazon basin in Brazil, and the Patagonians of the Argentine and Tierra del Fuego. They have studied the languages of Negro Africa, of New Guinea, Australia, and the islands of the Pacific, of the Islamic world from Morocco to the Philippines, and the mountain tribes of south and southeast Asia.

In recent times linguistic anthropologists have also been turning their attention to the pidginized and Creolized languages around the world, to North Africa and the African coast from Tangiers to the Cape of Good Hope, to coastal India, the East Indies, and China, and to the islands and shores of the Caribbean in the New World. Such languages developed as European traders carried on business with the local primitives; they are for the most part "simplified" versions of the European tongues spoken by the great colonizing nations (Portugal, Spain, England, and France).

Some linguistic anthropologists have turned their attention to the socially distinct varieties of the languages of the great civilized nations of Europe, the Near East, and south and east Asia. They are investigating the local varieties of the languages of the New World, and of the former colonies in the Old World, both established in new homes by emigrants from nations of great civilization.

In the 1960s, then, the discovery is being made that the primitives and the exotics have no monopoly on socially significant linguistic variation; and, just as one great social anthropologist shifted his attention some thirty years ago from the Australian primitives to the not-so-primitives of New England and the middle west in the United States so are some linguistic anthropologists shifting their attention from social dialects in India or North Africa to social dialects in the great urban centers of New York, Washington, and Chicago or the Ibero-American urban centers of Mexico City, Rio de Janeiro, and Buenos Aires.

The enormous structural variety of human languages, on the one hand, and the minutiae of social dialect variation, on the other, have forced the development of more sophisticated methods of linguistic analysis and of more adequate means of processing large quantities of linguistic data. The contributions of nonanthropological linguists to the first and of computer technology to the second have paced each other in rapid development since the 1950s. Logicians and mathematicians have contributed to the development of a more adequate model of linguistic structure, computer technicians and programmers have devised mechanico-electronic routines for analyzing linguistic texts and for preparing dictionaries from the results of such analysis, and some progress has been made toward machine translation of text materials from one language into another. These developments toward more satisfactory linguistic analysis and toward more efficient handling of large quantities of linguistic data have been of great value not only to the linguist–anthropologist. They have also stimulated the anthropologist interested in a more effective extraction of the cultural content of linguistic texts, and in a more satisfactory description of other patterns of sociocultural behavior, as these are reflected in such texts or in other media, to attempt to use linguistic analytic method and linguistically based computer-routines to discover, for example, what culturally significant distinctions the Philippine Subanun make in categories of disease, or the Maya-Tzeltal make in selecting firewood; what socially significant distinctions are reflected in the choice of verb forms by the Japanese or Koreans, or in the selection of pronouns by the Russians or the Maya-Quiché.

Linguistic anthropologists have in recent times also developed an interest in microanalysis of the significant patterns of speech and body motion as these are evidenced in films and videotape recordings of typical interviews. Such interviews, between psychoneurotic patient and his psychiatrist, between job-seeker and his potential employer, between penitent and his confessor, or between anthropological fieldworker and his informant, are subjected to microanalysis by the linguist–anthropologist in order to detect significant clues in speech or in body motion — clues indicative of psychoneurosis and the progress of its therapy; of the personal and sociocultural characteristics of the job applicant and the task his future employer wishes him to perform; of the state of a penitent's soul and the status of the cathartic activity of his confessor; of the analytic frame employed by the anthropologist and the specific import of his informant's responses for particular aspects of the systematic description he is constructing of a society and culture. Such clues are invaluable leads, therefore, to the patterns of cultural behavior and of social relations.

In the course of the linguist–anthropologist's microanalytic activity new areas of communicative behavior have been brought into focus. Parallel to the language, the vowels and consonants, the words and phrases normally rendered in our alphabetic writing by letters and spaces on the printed page, every speaker employs another system of signals, his paralanguage. This paralanguage, weakly represented on the printed page by marks of punctuation, consists of variations in intensity and in speed, of variable collocations of diaphragm and inter-rib muscles, of larynx and pharynx, and even of specific dispositions of the speaker's tongue and uvula;

it runs parallel to his language (which makes use of these same or-gans), interpenetrates with it, supplements it, and even, on occasion, supplants it. It often is not *what* an intercommunicant says, but *how* he says it, that makes up the principal message being conveyed in an interview. Likewise supplementary, or even substitute, are the signals carried in another system of kinetic activity, that expressed in the movement of an intercommunicant's body, where discriminations and counterdiscriminations make up a system of interchanging stance and gesture in an ongoing dance in which leader and partner continually shift roles. Parallel to the field of linguistics, then, the new fields of paralinguistics and kinesics have had to be created to make possible a precise and specific taking into account of all the communicative ingredients in the heard and seen behavior of the participants in an interview.

The difficulties of bringing bits of such behavior into focus and freezing them for analysis are leading to the creation of a whole new panoply of mechanical and electronic aids to linguistic, para-linguistic, and kinesic analysis. Sound-film projectors which allow the speed of the film to be controlled, single frames to be stopped, and reverse and forward sweeps to be run on a succession of frames are being developed to bring into analytic focus body motions otherwise too multifaceted or too fleeting for easy observation. Magnetic-tape recording-and-playback apparatus has been de-veloped to perform a similar function for the linguistic and para-linguistic activity of speech. The two devices have been combined in the film with a magnetic sound-stripe; the most recent develop-ment is a single-medium, broad-band magnetic tape, the videotape recorder.

None of this mechanico-electronic apparatus as yet performs the tasks required of it with ease, with dispatch, and with accuracy, and the progress of scientific investigation in the new field of micro-analysis of communicative behavior is being held up for want of proper machinery. The interpretation of the many-staved symphonic scores which result from the recording of the element into which microanalysis breaks up the stream of speech and body motion is likewise seriously impeded for a different reason: the sociocultural contexts, both for groups and for individuals among intercommunicants, of the linguistic, paralinguistic, and kinesic elements are unknown. Current sociological and social-psychological investigation has not as yet adequately identified the groups, nor have the subvarieties of the English or of any other language as yet been adequately investigated by the linguists whose task it is to describe them.

The import — psychiatric, public relations, religious, or sociocultural — of bits or constellations of intercommunicative behavior will remain obscure, therefore, even after they have been isolated, until the level of development of sociology, social psychology, and sociolinguistics is such as to provide the microanalyst with the necessary tools for their interpretation. When such tools are made available, small samples of such behavior will yield very precise indications of the psychic, social-psychologic, spiritual, and sociocultural state of individuals in their relations with the society and the world which surround them, and will make possible accurate diagnosis of psychic and spiritual ills and effective monitoring of the progress of the therapy which remedies them. In an inescapable dialectic, the process of description itself, carried on by sociologist and by linguist, will be considerably advanced by skillful application of the new microanalytic tools.

Since the range of the research activity of the linguist–anthropologist is broad, practical applications of its results are many and varied.

The preparer of foreign-language textbooks and the teacher of foreign languages, using the detailed structural descriptions and linguistic inventories the linguist–anthropologist provides for the speech of a primitive tribe or for the verbalizations of his social-anthropologist client, may work up practical teaching materials for acquainting the social anthropologist with the speech of the community he would investigate or for familiarizing his informant with the speech of the community to which the social anthropologist belongs. Such practical teaching materials constitute an indispensable entree into an alien society and culture. The combined practical and theoretical command of the language which they facilitate provides a day-to-day tool for the controlled investigation of the functioning of that society and culture. Reverse application of the tool is indispensable to effective acquisition by members of the alien society and culture of an understanding of, a tolerance for, and smoothly operating relations with the society and culture of which the social anthropologist is a member. The initial entree, then, for raising the level of underdeveloped nations to that of more developed ones, and the operating tool for carrying on subsequent relations among them, is the language. The linguist–anthropologist, in providing the entree, and the social anthropologist, in making full analytic use of it, endow the practical politician with the means for coping with the evolving problems of such underdeveloped nations. And their number has swelled in recent years. At the risk of possibly excessive repetition, we can say nearly all the same things about dealing with subgroups in our own culture.

The preparer of school grammars and the teacher of rhetoric, using the detailed structural descriptions and linguistic inventories which the linguist–anthropologist (or his colleague the linguist–sociologist) provides for the speech of minority groups within a nation, or for the speech of his sociologist client, may elaborate practical teaching materials for acquainting the sociologist with the speech of the minority community he would investigate, or for familiarizing his informants within that minority community with the speech of the majority community to which the sociologist belongs. Such practical teaching materials, here too, constitute an indispensable entree into the minority society and culture. The combined theoretical and practical command of the language which they make available provides a day-to-day tool for the controlled investigation of the functioning of that minority society and culture. Reverse application of the tool is indispensable to effective acquisition by members of the minority society and culture of an understanding of, a tolerance for, and smoothly operating relations with the majority society and culture of which the sociologist is a member. The initial entree, then, for achieving an understanding of and for raising the level of an underprivileged minority to that of a more privileged majority, and the operating tool for carrying on subsequent relations between minority and majority is the language, or, more precisely in this case, the social dialect. The linguist–sociologist, in providing the entree, and the sociologist, in making

159

full analytic use of it, endow the practical politician with the means for coping with the developmental problems of such underprivileged minorities. And their needs have become even more evident in recent months.

The preparer of role-training manuals and the teacher of styles of speech and body motion appropriate to such roles, using the detailed structural descriptions and linguistic, paralinguistic, and kinesic inventories which the anthropologist–sociologist–linguist–paralinguist–kinesicist provides for the speech and body motion of lay participants in personal and social interaction, or for that of their psychiatrist, social psychologist, cleric, or social-anthropologist client, may put together practical teaching materials for acquainting the psychiatrist, social psychologist, cleric, or social anthropologist with the speech and body motion of the individuals or small groups whose social behavior he would investigate. Such materials may serve as well to familiarize the patient, the client, the parishioner, or the informant, as the case may be, with the speech and body motion of the small group to which his therapist, his clinician, his confessor, or his scientist-communicant belongs. Such practical training materials, similarly, constitute an indispensable entree into an interlocutor's society and culture, and into his personal integration of societal and cultural norms. They likewise make possible that combined practical and theoretical command of the interlocutor's speech and body motion which provides, in turn, a day-to-day tool for the controlled investigation of their functioning in the interlocutor's personal and social relations. Reverse application of the tool is indispensable to effective acquisition by an interlocutor of an understanding of, a tolerance for, and smoothly operating relations with the subsociety and subculture of which his co-interlocutor is a member. The initial entree, then, for bringing about mutual tolerance, and smoothly operating personal and social relations among interlocutors is their language, or, more specifically here, their speech and body motion. The linguist–paralinguist–kinesicist–sociologist–anthropologist, in providing the entree, and the psychiatrist, the social psychologist, the cleric, or the social anthropologist, in making full analytic use of it, endow the clinical psychologist, the social worker, the lay cleric, or the practical politician with the means for coping with the developmental problems of individuals in a hostile society. And as modern society and culture increases the number and the complexity of the demands it makes upon such individuals, their needs are becoming ever more apparent.

Linguistics in anthropology, then, with its more recently developed and more recently recognized allies, paralinguistics and kinesics, on the one hand, and sociology, on the other, will play an increasingly important role in resolving problems of human relations, whether such problems are evident between different nations, between different groups within nations, or between individual human beings in their more personal contacts.

15 LANGUAGE AND PSYCHOLOGY

John B. Carroll

The language I use in writing is English. A reader who is a native speaker will have little trouble in understanding what I write, nor would he have difficulty in understanding my speech if he were listening to this chapter delivered as a lecture. If the reader has learned English as a foreign language, he might have more difficulty in understanding and might even find himself making quick mental translation into his native tongue. Let us suppose that such a student were listening to me reading this paragraph aloud. Both he and I would be using a language. I have used the language as the medium in which I have encoded my message and if I were reading it aloud, I would be using my vocal apparatus — my lungs, my larynx, and the various parts of my mouth to create a physical sound which could be recorded mechanically on tape or disc, and transmitted by radio. Were he listening to me, the hearer would be engaged in the truly remarkable feat of hearing this physical sound not as a jumble of noises, but as a sequence of speech sound which he recognized as words and sentences in the English language. And he would be engaged in the even more remarkable feat of understanding the concepts and thoughts conveyed in these words, these sentences.

Most of the chapters in this book are concerned only with language, considered as a system of symbols for communicating meanings. The English language is just one of many such systems, and it can be studied in the abstract, by studying the various kinds of units that are involved in a language system — units such as phonemes, words, and sentence structures — with little reference to how the speakers of that language actually use the system in creating and understanding sentences. Study of language systems in the abstract is the province of the science of linguistics. But the study of how people *use* a language system, and how they learn to use it, is the province of psychology, or more specifically, the province of a specialty which has come to be called *psycholinguistics*. For there is a peculiarly intimate relation between linguistics and psychology when we consider language. Developing a theory of language systems in the abstract means developing at the same time a theory of the "competence" of users of the language. That is, a description of a language system states, in effect, what a person must have learned in order to use that language either as a speaker or as a hearer. Since language systems turn out to be remarkably rich and complicated, it follows that a speaker of a language has learned something that is remarkably rich and complicated.

One of the first tasks of the psychology of language is to account for how a child learns this system as his mother tongue. It would appear that one must have a powerful theory of learning to do so; some linguistic theorists have been of the opinion that no currently available theory of learning is sufficiently powerful to do this, but there are eminent psychologists who claim that their theories of learning *can* handle the problem — that, although a language system is complex, the child's learning of that system can be accounted for by appeal to what they consider to be relatively well-established principles of learning, applied in various combinations. The intellectual battle has been joined, but there is no victory in sight for either side. Only in very recent years has the child's learning of language been looked at. Currently the problem is to collect enough data from enough children to enable one to draw some conclusions. For it is not merely a matter of enumerating the words that the child uses or measuring the lengths of his sentences; one must examine in great depth how the various grammatical structures of the child's language change and unfold as they converge toward the grammatical structures of the adult language. At the same time, it is up to the psychologist to re-examine his theories of learning and if necessary to develop new theories. A theory of learning that may be adequate to account for the behavior of a rat in a maze *may* not be adequate to account for a child's learning of, say, grammatical agreement between noun and verb, although some psychologists would argue that there is nothing different in principle between these behaviors. Obviously this is a tremendously complex and theoretical issue; as a psychologist, my sympathies are with those who claim that no totally new learning theory is required to account for the child's learning of language, but rather that our theories of learning only need certain revisions and extensions. But in this I may be totally wrong, and I must admit that there is something unsatisfying about the principles of learning that we have. For example, one of the currently most favored principles of learning, at least among many psychologists, is the principle of reinforcement: briefly, that we tend to learn whatever responses get reinforced or rewarded, that is, whatever responses have satisfying consequences. This principle may indeed explain how learning is *motivated*, but it does not explain how the learning itself takes place or how the individual creates new responses.

Although the learning of complex grammatical rules is difficult to explain, how children learn the meanings of language symbols is not. There is at least a considerable number of language symbols — words like *banana*, *telephone*, *drop*, *yellow*, *swift* — that correspond to the concepts the child derives from ordinary experience. There is good reason to believe that fairly simple principles of "conditioning" can explain the child's learning of these symbols. Some experimental psychologists have shown how classical Pavlovian conditioning can be used to manipulate the child's use and interpretation of such language symbols. And what is called operant conditioning — as discussed by the American psychologist B. F. Skinner — can be used to teach a child to use a given word to denote a given concept.

Psycholinguistics has also been concerned with the way people learn foreign languages. The debate as to whether the learning of a foreign language by an adult, say, is qualitatively different from a child's acquisition of his native language remains unsolved. Perhaps some of the same learning principles can be invoked in either case, but most of the evidence supports the view that these two forms of learning are different. In learning his native language, a child is at the same time learning new concepts. A person learning a foreign language has already learned these concepts; and he has already learned names for them in his native language. Furthermore, while all normal children learn their native language at about the same pace, people who learn a foreign language after childhood learn at different rates. In fact, some people seem to have considerable difficulty in learning foreign languages, and it is possible to measure various aspects of this aptitude. For example, some people seem to have special difficulties in learning to remember the sounds and words of a foreign language; some people (not always the same ones) have special difficulties in learning the grammatical features. Further, it is possible that people learn foreign languages in different ways. Some learn a foreign language with relatively little reference to their native language system; this seems to happen most frequently when the individual is transferred into the environment of the foreign language and is forced to speak it to communicate. Others learn a foreign language largely as a translation, so to speak, of their native language; this seems to happen frequently when a foreign language is learned from books.

Thus far the learning of linguistic systems — either the native language or a foreign language — has been in question. But the psychology of language is also concerned with how people *use* the language systems they have acquired, that is, with what has been called *performance*, as distinguished from *competence*.

A complete scientific explanation of how people use language is at present far out of reach. Because the use of language is involved in so much of human behavior, the psychology of language ultimately has to explain a large part of human behavior. To progress toward this goal, the psycholinguist, like his colleagues in other fields of science, must often content himself with small steps. Psychology is a field in which there have thus far been very few great discoveries, very few breakthroughs, but over the past fifty years a good deal of progress has been made.

There are different levels on which explanations can be made. The layman who wonders about the workings of the mind probably demands, first of all, an explanation on the neurological level. But there has been little success in explaining language behavior neurologically. To be sure, one can trace back into the brain the nerves that carry auditory messages from the ear, or the nerves that control the various parts of the speech musculature; but next to nothing is known about how language knowledge is stored in the brain or about how the brain works as sentences are formulated. One of the few things that neurologists can agree upon is that in most persons the control center for speech is located in only one hemisphere, usually the left. Postmortem studies of aphasics — persons who have lost the power to speak — show that lesions can occur in various areas of the cortex, and there is some evidence that the location of the lesion is correlated with the type of speech loss. But even this evidence has not helped much in explaining speech behavior.

It is far better to keep to a behavioral level of explanation, relying on careful observation of normal speech behavior and also on carefully designed experiments specifying special conditions and tasks for the language user to reveal some of the relationships between stimulus conditions and speech behavior and — eventually — inferences about the processes that govern these relationships.

In fact, one can derive considerable information from observations of ordinary speech behavior — for example, some idea of what the speaker has learned, and the relative strengths of these learnings. We can count all the words an individual uses in a number of situations and observe which words are used most frequently. Recent studies show that a mathematical theory of word frequency can be developed in such a way as to predict, from the distribution of word frequencies in a fair-sized sample, the size of the vocabulary of the speaker. The resulting sizes of vocabularies are staggering; educated speakers of normal intelligence have vocabularies that extend at least to 100,000 words — though interpretation of such figures depends partly on how the word-unit is defined (for example, are *go*, *goes*, *gone*, and *went* different words or variants of the single morpheme *go*?). However words are counted, it is evident that vocabularies are larger than one might expect. Linguistic units constitute what is probably the largest single class of knowledges possessed by the individual. Even words that occur less than once in one million words, like *nepotism*, *sextant*, *numismatics*, *convene*, are immediately recognized and understood by the educated adult. In fact, adult speakers can make fairly accurate judgments of the relative frequency of words, and when these judgments are pooled they show quite a high correspondence to actual word counts. And when adults have to learn to associate arbitrary pairs of words, they are better able to learn pairs consisting of frequently used words than pairs of rare words. Word frequency is a powerful variable, then, in various kinds of speech behavior.

Ordinary observation of speech behavior can also suggest something about the processes of sentence formulation. The normal flow of speech is often interrupted by various kinds of hesitations. In the spoken sentence "The *ah* first thing I want to do is *ah* locate my *ah* suitcase," some of the hesitations may represent periods in which the speaker is actually deciding what he wants to do but they may also represent periods in which he searches for words or grammatical patterns that express his thoughts. Studies of speech hesitation show that they are more likely to occur directly before points of high selectivity — points at which it would be possible to insert any one of a number of words. Hesitations are not likely to occur in the middle of highly automatized sequences, in the middle, for example, of *as a matter of fact.* One theory that arises out of such observations is that the formulation of sentences takes place in two levels or stages: (a) grammatical selection, in which the speaker selects the over-all grammatical frame for the sentence or a part of it (is it to be declarative, or a question?), and (b) word selection, in which particular words are fitted into particular "slots" in the sentence. The theory does not state which of these kinds of selection takes place first; actually they may take place in any order, for in the formulation of a complex sentence there is undoubtedly a succession of various kinds of selections. Although speech must necessarily come out in a temporal order (or, if it is English, "from left to right"), there is evidence to suggest that the speaker formulates large chunks of his sentences all at once. For example, in the question "Who did you come home with?" the last word, *with*, must have been formulated even at the beginning, because it is closely associated with the first word, *who*, as evidenced in another possible form of the question: "With whom did you come home?" One grammatical theory asserts, in fact, that such a question is actually formulated as a derivation of some underlying structure that can be represented as "You come *past tense* home with somebody *question*." This poses the problem of how a speaker learns to make the complicated series of transformations involved. A simpler explanation is that the learning of the framework of a question like "Who did you come home with?" is quite separate from the learning of the declarative form, "I came home with my sister," say, and that this in turn is quite separate from the learning of the framework of the imperative form, "Come home with my sister."

Ordinary observation also tells something about the kinds of stimulus situations that give rise to various kinds of sentences. In general, declarative sentence structures, for example, are used, when the speaker perceives that he has information to transmit to the hearer; question structures, when he needs some kind of information or action from the hearer.

But ordinary observation has its limitations, for one cannot control conditions as well as one can in a formal experiment. A simple experiment that suggests interesting ideas about how words are stored in memory has been made by Roger Brown at Harvard. This experiment concerned the TOT, or "tip-of-the-tongue," phenomenon: that experience of searching for some word or name that is "on the tip of the tongue" but cannot be recalled. For example, recently I was trying to recall the word *contagious*, but I could only remember *incongruous*, *contextual*, and *infectious* — all of them similar to the word I sought, in general length (number of syllables), stress pattern, and certain combinations of sounds (*con*, *-ous*), and one of them, *infectious*, overlapping semantically with the target word (both referred to disease). Brown sought to generate TOT phenomena wholesale. To a group of 56 college students, Brown read definitions of relatively rare words, asking them to write the word referred to if they could recall it. In about 13 per cent of all possible instances, subjects reported a TOT phenomenon — they intuitively felt they knew the word referred to but could not recall it. The subjects were asked to give as much information as they could about each such case; they were asked to report, or guess, the number of syllables, the first letter, words of similar sound, and words of similar meaning.

Brown found statistically significant evidence that in the TOT phenomenon the subjects' guesses of the initial letter and the number of syllables of the target word bear a positive relation to the actual characteristics of the target word. In other words, storage of words in memory includes something about their abstract form. It is as if all the words in our memory are stored like cards in a keysort file. The definition causes the subject to select cards that are edge-punched for certain semantic features. For example, what word is referred to by the definition "a navigational instrument used in measuring angular distances, especially the altitude of sun, moon, and stars at sea"? The key semantic features are "navigation," "instrument," and "geometry," and with these you might think of a group of words including *astrolabe*, *compass*, *protractor*. Although you can't think of *sextant*, which is the correct word, something you fish up from your memory makes you think of *secant*, *sextet*, and *sexton*. To continue the analogy to cards in a keysort file: it is as if the card with the word *sextant* in your mental dictionary has that word so faintly written on it that all you can make out is that it has two syllables and the first syllable is something like *sec-* or *sex-*. So you think of words like that, and perhaps you eventually recognize *sextant*.

Of course, most of the time we can instantaneously recall the words we want. The experimental study of the TOT phenomenon slows down the process of word recall so that it can be examined in detail.

Another kind of experiment that has been a favorite of psycholinguists is the free-association experiment, first developed by psychiatrists to study mental inhibitions in psychopathology. The procedure is to announce or expose a word to a subject and ask him to report the first word that comes to mind other than the stimulus word. For example, to the stimulus *light* many persons will respond with *dark*; others will give *lamp*, *bright*, *sun*, *bulb*, *heavy*, *day*, and so on. Note that all these words have a *semantic* relation to the stimulus word; only rarely will a subject give a "clang" association based solely on phonetic similarity (*delight*, *fight*). Of course, if he is asked to give a rhyme, he can usually do so quite easily. Children, even without special instructions, are somewhat more likely than adults to give "clang" associations. Adults usually give words that are the same part of speech as the stimulus word, but children are more likely to give a word that could be used in sequence with the stimulus word in a sentence — to *light*, for example, they tend to respond with *bulb* or *dress*. This difference in the responses of children and adults has been interpreted to mean that as a person grows older, he is more and more likely to organize his memory traces for words into sets of grammatical equivalence classes. James Deese of Johns Hopkins University has analyzed the structure of the associations revealed in the free-association experiment. He shows that these associations are organized in a number of semantic dimensions or categories. He finds that most of the adjectival concepts of our language can be reduced to about forty bipolar concepts — pairs like *Above–Below*, *Alone–Together*, *Active–Passive*, *Alive–Dead*. The free-association technique, therefore, has yielded information on the structure of thought.

In fact, the psychology of language can hardly be studied without at least some reference to the psychology of thinking and concept formation. A large number of words in any language can be regarded as names of concepts. In order to use a word properly, one must have acquired the underlying concepts. Dictionary definitions are frequently attempts to describe the criterial attributes of concepts. The question has often been asked, To what extent does a language direct the course of thought? Evidence from the psychology of the deaf before they have acquired language suggests that they can indeed think without using the *names* of concepts that language offers, but they *must* think with something like concepts. For a person who has learned a language, thinking can certainly be much faster and smoother. Language undoubtedly influences thinking in the way it names and defines concepts. If someone should tell me that there is something called *thrizymia* (which there is not, so far as I know) I would be immediately curious about what it is; the mere existence of a word invites us to inquire into its meaning, or rather, into the nature of the concept that lies behind it. Moreover, we are tempted to conclude that no two words can have exactly the same meaning, even though they may actually refer to the same thing. Jessica Mitford, in *The American Way of Death*, has pointed out that undertakers have tried to veil the meanings of certain words by substituting certain other words with different connotations. For example, in the undertaking world, one does not dig a grave and then fill it; rather, one *opens* and *closes* it. A cemetery is not a cemetery but a *memorial park*. The language psychologist studies the connotations of words as well as the concepts they represent. For example, what is the difference between *nice* and *good*? Both are adjectives expressing favorable evaluation. One psychologist, Charles Osgood of the University of Illinois, has developed a technique, the *semantic differential*, for measuring subtle differences in connotation. *Nice* is found to connote something mildly feminine, *good* is neutral in connotation. Osgood finds three major dimensions inherent in connotative meaning: the "evaluative" dimension — how good or bad the concept is; the "potency" dimension — how big and powerful the concept is; and the "activity" dimension — to what degree the concept suggests active, fast, and perhaps unexpected action. In studies using the semantic-differential technique in different languages, he has found these three dimensions to be universal.

The hypothesis of "linguistic relativity" — the hypothesis that the thinking of the speakers of a given language is affected by the structure of that language — was advanced by the American linguist Benjamin L. Whorf in a famous series of papers published around 1940, just before his death.[1] As a former student of Whorf's I led a series of investigations to try to confirm this hypothesis. We explored whether there were any major ways in which the thinking of certain groups of southwestern American Indians when using their own language differed from the thinking of speakers of English. By and large it was extremely difficult to discover any such differences. The differences we did find were trivial and were certainly unrelated to ability to solve problems or to philosophies. In fact, we were impressed again with that marvelous characteristic of language, its power to express any thought and any conception. All languages contain a well-nigh universal set of categories. To be sure, languages differ in the ways they apply and combine these categories, and it is

[1]The writings of Whorf are most readily available in John B. Carroll, ed., *Language, Thought, and Reality; Selected Writings of Benjamin Lee Whorf*. Massachusetts Institute of Technology Press, 1956.

important to observe these differences in making a translation from one language to another. But, if there are differences in the thought processes of speakers of different languages, it is most probable that they are attributable to differences in culture and education and not to differences in language.

16 LINGUISTICS AND LITERATURE: PROSE AND POETRY

Curtis W. Hayes

As a science, linguistics is relatively new. Modern structural linguistics, for instance, is generally dated as beginning in 1933 with the publication of Leonard Bloomfield's now-classic *Language*. And the origin of the even newer school of the science that is called by its adherents transformational-generative linguistics may be dated from 1957, the year that Noam Chomsky revolutionized the linguistic world with his now-famous monograph *Syntactic Structures*. It is a truism to say that these two schools of thought have had a great impact: Their development, and their elaboration of the theoretical nature of the activity of describing and analyzing languages, caused a greatly increased interest in applied, practical linguistics — there is, for example, the great leap forward in the teaching of foreign languages, a leap clearly derived from linguists who were using the new methods of exact description of languages.

Another practical use of these methods is in the explication and analysis of literature. Here we have one of the most recent applications of the tools of linguistic science; as Roman Jakobson observed in his remarks concluding the Ninth International Congress of Linguists, "For the first time a special section of a linguistic congress has dealt with stylistics and poetics: the study of poetry has been conceived as inseparable from linguistics and as its pertinent task."[1]

[1]In Horace G. Lunt, ed., *Proceedings of the Ninth International Congress of Linguists*. Mouton, 1964, pp. 1135 ff.

Some literary critics have been disturbed by the application of recent linguistic techniques to the study of literature, and it is true that some linguists appear to have believed that the age-old problems of literary criticism could be solved in summary fashion by the application of these methods. It is clear today, however, that the apparent conflict between the critic and the linguist is almost always the result of misunderstanding: The critic ignores the findings of the linguist, and the linguist ignores the perceptive observations of the critic; the linguist is eager to point out that the critic's pronouncements are too vague and too imprecise to be of much value, and the critic assumes that strict linguistic analysis of a text will destroy or seriously impair its beauty. Such a contretemps should be intolerable. Ideally both critic and linguist are sensitive and perceptive readers; and both can and should contribute to literary analysis and criticism. For example, Nils Erik Enkvist and his coauthors argue in their study *Linguistics and Style*,[2] that a detailed analysis of a text should not destroy the "wonder" of that text but rather should enhance it.

A number of students have attempted to explain the reason for the gulf that appears to separate the linguist from the literary critic. David Lodge, for example, suggests in his study *The Language of Fiction*[3] that part of the difficulty lies in a misinterpretation of the roles of linguist and critic. He says, for instance, "The discipline of linguistics will never *replace* literary criticism, or radically change the basis of its claims to be a useful and meaningful form of human inquiry. It is the essential characteristic of modern linguistics that it claims to be a science. It is the essential characteristic of literature that it concerns values. And values are not amenable to scientific method."

The distinction Lodge suggests, that there is indeed a difference between literary analysis and literary criticism, is perhaps a useful one. The linguist is primarily interested in objective, verifiable data, and thus he is more concerned with analysis. The literary student, in

[2]Nils Erik Enkvist, John Spencer, and Michael J. Gregory. *Linguistics and Style*. Oxford University Press, 1964.
[3]David Lodge. *The Language of Fiction*. Columbia University Press, 1966.

contrast, is primarily interested in value and thus more interested in criticism.

This is not to say that never the twain shall meet. A few scholars have successfully combined the two disciplines, and some have suggested that criticism depends first upon detailed analysis. Archibald A. Hill has been one of the more successful in combining the two. Take, for example, the way in which he moves from linguistic analysis to literary value in his now-famous "Analysis of *The Windhover:* An Experiment in Structural Method"[4] and in "Some Points in the Analysis of Keats' *Grecian Urn*."[5] Hill does not, in these articles, overtly make the distinction between analysis and criticism, however. He has said, in commenting upon one of his studies, "I do not know, and do not much care, whether the method I have followed is linguistic or literary. There is a reason for my indifference. I think of the two disciplines as one, and I do not believe that it is impossible to carry on both, either successively or at the same time."

As in the eighteenth century rhetoric and poetics were combined into one discipline, so today a rapprochement of linguistic analysis and literary criticism is needed. John Spencer remarks, "Few literary scholars would suggest that literature can be satisfactorily studied without due attention to its medium, language. Nor would many linguists justify the investigation of literary language without guidance from those who devote themselves to the study of literature. There would, moreover, be a measure of agreement on both sides that the student of literature, whatever his particular interest, ought to be trained in the study of both language and literature."[6]

Still other scholars have been concerned with the linguist's right to make analyses of literary texts. For example, Charles T. Scott, a student of literature as well as a linguist, argues in his monograph "Persian and Arabic Riddles: A Language-Centered Approach to Genre Definition"[7] that because language is the "vehicle" of literature, the linguist has the right to make literary judgments:

[4]*PMLA*, LXX, No. 5 (December 1955), 968–978.
[5]Forthcoming, in a volume of studies for Rudolph Willord, University of Texas.
[6]Enkvist, Spencer, and Gregory. *Op. cit.* vii.
[7]*International Journal of American Linguistics*, XXI, Pt. 2 (October 1965).

It can be said safely that literary texts are utterance-tokens of given languages, constructed of, and presented through, available linguistic structures. Therefore, since the linguist must necessarily operate within the domain of his discipline — the study and analysis of the structure of language and their interrelated subsystems — it is but an easy step to a position which holds that the linguist, in dealing with literary utterances, is at the same time dealing with phenomena proper to this discipline, and is consequently justified in engaging in analyses of literary texts.

I take as one premise that literature is language, and is thus amenable to linguistic analysis. I also believe that incorporating some of the techniques of linguistic analysis into the description of literary utterances will enhance the description of those texts. I think it will be useful to survey a few specific proposals for the application of these techniques, concentrating on the application of the relatively new model of linguistic description, generative-transformational (TG) grammar, to the analysis of literary utterances. Although I confine myself to this limited area of linguistic science, I do not wish it to be inferred that earlier attempts in the linguistic analysis of literary texts have been unsuccessful. On the contrary, the structural school, as well as other schools of linguistic science, have contributed immensely valuable observations about literature and its relationship to language.

Samuel Levin and James P. Thorne have incorporated the TG model of grammatical relationships in their analysis of poetic texts, and Richard Ohmann and I have used the model in the explication of the characteristics of prose style. Robert Stockwell explains the philosophical justification for generative grammars in Chapter 24 of this book, here I point out two principles of TG grammar which have an important, though an indirect, bearing on the analysis of literature.

First, a TG grammar will generate (enumerate or specify) all the grammatical sentences of a language and none of the ungrammatical ones. The grammar, in a very strict sense, characterizes the notion of the sentence. To put it simply and briefly, a TG grammar will allow a sentence such as *John admires sincerity*, but it will block an obvious ungrammatical sequence such as *Boy the ball the kick*. And it will, through the system of its rules governing co-occurrences, block a slightly deviant sentence such as *Sincerity loves John*. That is, the grammatical rules will not allow an abstract noun (*sincerity*) to be the subject of a sentence with an animate verb — in this case *loves*.

Second, a TG grammar is inherently capable of accounting for deep syntactical relationships. That is, TG grammar can explain the constituent framework of all sentences (it provides a structural description for each), whether the sentence happens to be simple, compound, complex, or compound-complex. And, in addition, the grammar is able to do this within a framework which uses a finite set of rules to characterize each sentence. The importance of these generalizations will become obvious.

One of the first students of literature to incorporate TG grammar as an aid in literary analysis was Samuel Levin. He has dealt with various aspects of the explanatory power of TG grammar. In two articles, "On Automatic Production of Poetic Sequences"[8] and "Internal and External Deviation in Poetry,"[9] Levin effectively uses the framework provided by TG grammar to account for certain deviant utterances found in poetry. In "On Automatic Production" he explains how utterances such as *It is a hungry dance* (Wallace Stevens), *Her hair's warm sibilance* (Hart Crane), and *Behind a face of hands* (Dylan Thomas), which are characteristically poetic, would be enumerated by a generative grammar. Basing his analysis on the premise that TG grammar may be used to represent a norm of the language (that is, it specifies only grammatical utterances — ungrammatical utterances lie outside the norm), he argues that the three poetic sequences are deviations from that norm. "We are only interested," he says, "in trying to show that certain sequences, which one would characterize in some presystematic way as being poetic, can be rationalized as violators of grammatical rules." His principal point is that the restrictions which would disallow a sequence such as *It is a hungry dance* have been relaxed, and this is what one would and could expect in poetry. "In effect, then," he observes, "what the poets have done in producing these sentences has been to suspend the grammatical restriction on co-occurrence possibilities."

[8] *Texas Studies in Literature and Language*, V, No. 1 (Spring 1963), 138–146.
[9] *Word*, XXI (August 1965), 225–237.

In a more recent paper, Levin concerns himself with two utterances, clearly deviant, from poems by e. e. cummings and Dylan Thomas.[10] The utterances are *He danced his did* and *a grief ago*. Levin's purpose is "to deal with sequences which, presumably, a grammar of English would not generate, sequences thus that are either ungrammatical or semigrammatical." In the matter of grammaticality and semigrammaticality Levin follows Chomsky, who has discussed the notion of degrees of grammaticalness elsewhere. At the risk of oversimplification, the essence of the argument is that there is an area, not clearly defined, between a sentence which is unequivocally grammatical (*The man hit the ball*) and a sentence which is clearly ungrammatical (*Man the ball the hit*). The gray area in between may be represented by the sentence *Sincerity loves John* or the utterances which Levin deals with, *He danced his did* and *a grief ago*. In analyzing the two semigrammatical utterances from poetry, it is Levin's aim to "discuss the grammaticalness of such sequences, and . . . [to] introduce a procedure which, though different in operations, yields results which are consistent with the results given by Chomsky's formulation."

In attempting to determine the degree of grammaticalness associated with cummings' utterances, Levin first assumes that the utterances are ungrammatical, or (following his observations in "On Automatic Production) that the utterances are in some manner deviations from the norm. He next takes into account the general nature of TG rules and hypothesizes about how these rules could be "fixed" to allow for the deviant utterances. He treats, finally, the consequences of procedure two, in that he discusses the general nature of other sequences which would be generated as a consequence of such "fixing."

The last procedure allows Levin to measure the degree of grammaticalness associated with each of the two utterances: it "is then a function of the number of unwanted consequences (i.e. those sentences beyond the one in question) that the revised rule generates: the greater the number of such unwanted consequences entrained, the less grammatical is the sentence in question; the fewer such

[10]Samuel Levin. "Poetry and Grammaticalness," in S. Levin and S. Chatman, eds. *Essay on the Language of Literature*. Boston (1967), pp. 224–230.

unwanted consequences the revised rule generates, the more grammatical is the sentence in question."

In order to "fix" a grammar (that is, to revise the normal rules so that the grammar will generate the deviant utterance) there are two methods which may be used. On the one hand, the grammar may incorporate a new rule; on the other, certain co-occurrence restrictions may be relaxed. For the sequence *He danced his did*, using the first method, this would involve specifying the new rule $NP \rightarrow Verb$ (noun phrase may consist of verb), which would break a general grammatical rule which specifies that only N and not V may be the result of the rewriting of NP; in technical terms, NP dominates N, never V. The consequences of this new rule would be a large, perhaps infinite, number of unwanted sequences, any verb having the privilege of occurring after T (determiner). The revised grammar would then allow such unwanted sequences as *my went* and *the had*.

If the co-occurrence rules were relaxed to permit *did* to become a noun, the result would be identical to the results of the first method of generation, described above, in terms of the generation of a large number of unwanted sentences. If $N \rightarrow did$, eventually the sequence $T + Adj + N$ would obtain — generating, in one instance, *the beautiful did*.

The utterance *a grief ago* is different from the utterance *He danced his did* in a number of ways. For instance, there is a rule in the normal English grammar which specifies sequences such as *some time ago*, *a while back*, *a year ago*, all of which are in some way related in form, if not in content, to the sequence *a grief ago*.

Using the formula T_x (*determiner*) N_y (*noun*) D_z (*adverb*) to represent the sequence *a while back*, Levin points out that N_y also represents, more generally, a subclass of nouns semantically defined as temporal nouns.

To permit the generation of a *grief ago*, the co-occurrence restrictions (which allow only N_y to be rewritten as a temporal noun) would have to be relaxed to include nouns which indicate states of mind. Therefore, the revised rule would read

$$N_y \rightarrow \begin{Bmatrix} N_{temp} \\ N_{state\ of\ mind} \end{Bmatrix}$$

By incorporating this new rule into the grammar, Levin says, the grammar will generate sequences like *a happiness ago*, *some sorrow back*, *a disappointment ago*.

Why is it readily perceivable to the sensitive reader, Levin asks, that the sequence *a grief ago* appears more grammatical than *He danced his did*? It must be that the two sequences differ in degree of grammaticality, and indeed they do, because the sequence *He danced his did* breaks a more general rule than the sequence *a grief ago*. That is, for the grammar to permit the occurrence of *He danced his did* would require the additional rule $NP \rightarrow V$, and since V is any *verb*, the addition of this rule would break the restriction that previously disallowed any V to be an N. The rule which distinguished the class N from the class V is, moreover, a more general rule than the rule which distinguished one subclass of nouns from another. To put it another way, the sequence *a grief ago* violates a more specific rule (a lower-order rule) and as a consequence, the new rule would permit a smaller number of ungrammatical sequences.

The important thing, in short, is that the consequence of manipulating the rules of the grammar to include sequences analogous to *a grief ago* is much less extreme, in terms of unwanted sentences, than if the grammar were revised to generate sequences analogous to *He danced his did*.

The degree of grammaticalness associated with these sequences has an important consideration for the analysis of literary texts. Since there are no sentences paralleling the more ungrammatical *He danced his did*, the reader cannot extract meaning (as Levin uses the term) from the new sequence. By way of contrast, the sequence *a grief ago*, which is less ungrammatical, has many analogies in a normal grammar, for example *a while back* and *some time ago*; and as a result of these analogies the reader can impose a semantic interpretation on *grief*. Since *grief* is substituted for a temporal noun, the reader will perhaps think of *grief* as implying time.

To summarize Levin's valuable contribution to the analysis of literary texts, we can say that TG grammar is a useful tool in characterizing the deviation from the norm in poetic utterances. It is also useful, though more indirectly so, in assigning semantic interpretations to those sequences which are semigrammatical but have analogical counterparts in a normal grammar of English. Levin's work, because it is new and experimental, has not yet been fully accepted. But it has given insight into the complex relationships that we so often admire in poetry.

Richard Ohmann was probably the first scholar to suggest the feasibility of using TG grammar as a model in the analysis of prose style. In his paper "Generative Grammars and the Concept of Literary Style,"[11] he points out that an idiosyncratic prose style represents a "characteristic use of language" as reflected by the "habitual and recurrent" use of certain specified grammatical patterns of the language. It is Ohmann's contention that "recent developments in generative grammar, particularly on the transformational model, promise first, to clear away a good deal of the mist from stylistic theory, and, second, to make possible a corresponding refinement in the practice of stylistic analysis."

Sensitive readers of literature are gifted with certain insights, which Ohmann calls stylistic intuitions. These intuitions, says Ohmann, make it possible for sensitive readers, first, to identify certain passages as having been written by familiar authors and, second, to make parodies of the prose style of these writers that are recognizable as such. Ohmann posits from these facts that style must exist apart from content. That is, style consists not of the message associated with the discourse but of the grammatical patterns, or "transformations," writers employ in expressing that message. His thesis is, briefly, that the transformations which a writer uses significantly reflect what a sensitive reader perceives as literary style. He says, moreover, that "there is at least some reason, then, to hold that a style is in part a characteristic way of deploying the transformational apparatus of a language, and to expect that transformational analysis will be a valuable aid to the description of actual style."

Ohmann bases his analysis of literary style on the earlier model of TG grammar. He uses the TG framework to explain the differences intuitively felt to exist among writers and takes as models Ernest Hemingway, D. H. Lawrence, Henry James, and William Faulkner.

[11] *Word*, XX (December 1964), 423–439.

He observes that each author favors certain "habitual and recurrent" grammatical transformations: Faulkner, for example, the relative-clause transformation, the conjunction transformation, and the comparison transformation.

Ohmann's procedure may be made clear by looking at his analysis of Ernest Hemingway's prose style, impressionistically described by certain critics, Ohmann says, as the *style indirect libre*. The selection Ohmann examines is from Hemingway's "Soldier's Home," and the passage reflects the characteristics of Hemingway's style:

> So his mother prayed for him and then they stood up and Krebs kissed his mother and went out of the house. He had tried so to keep his life from being complicated. Still, none of it had touched him. He felt sorry for his mother and she had made him lie. He would go to Kansas City and get a job and she would feel all right about it. There would be one more scene maybe before he got away. He would not go down to his father's office. He would miss that one. He wanted his life to go smoothly. It had just gotten going that way. Well, that was all over now, anyway. He would go over to the schoolyard and watch Helen play indoor baseball.*

The passage reflects the "recurrent and habitual use" of the following transformations:

1. The quotation, or reported-thought, transformation:

    $\left.\begin{array}{l}He\ thought\ NP_{abst}\\ She\ had\ made\ me\ lie\end{array}\right\}$ → *He thought, "She has made me lie."*

2. Indirect-discourse transformation (change of pronouns and verb tense):

    He thought, "She had made me lie" → *He thought that she had made him lie.*

3. Deletion transformation:

    He thought that she had made him lie → *She had made him lie.*

Hemingway's dependence upon these transformations is not altogether apparent until these transformations are reversed and the prose passage is written without their use:

> So his mother prayed for him and they stood up and Krebs kissed his mother and went out of the house. He thought this: I have tried so to keep my life from being complicated. Still, none of it has touched me. I have felt sorry for my mother and she has made me lie. I will go to Kansas City and get a job and she will feel all right about it. There will be one more scene maybe before I get away. I will not go down to my father's office. I will miss that one. I want my life to go smoothly. It has just gotten going that way. Well, that is all over now, anyway. I will go over to the schoolyard and watch Helen play indoor baseball.

Reversal of these transformations, as above, produces a style without the idiosyncratic patterns which we have commonly associated with Hemingway's writing.

Ohmann's employment of TG grammar as an aid in characterizing the notion of literary style and in capturing the differences which exist among the diverse prose styles of Hemingway, Faulkner, James, and Lawrence has been both perceptive and illuminating. In a manner of speaking, Ohmann's analysis is dependent upon establishing *qualitative* differences among these authors. Each author characteristically employs certain transformations, to the virtual exclusion of all others. Given the repertoire of transformations in the language, no writer uses all, but only a small number, of the grammatical possibilities available to him.

I have also used the transformational model to indicate syntactical relationships in an attempt to explain intuitive responses to certain writers. Although I have used TG grammar as an experiment in establishing certain measurable correlates between the prose styles of two diverse authors (Edward Gibbon and Ernest Hemingway), I have been more interested in the larger problem of establishing more general attributes of eighteenth-century prose style. The eighteenth century has long been noted for a characteristic prose style, and it is generally held today that certain eighteenth-century authors exhibit a remarkable similarity of style. There is a great deal of similarity, for instance, between the prose styles of Edward

Gibbon and Samuel Johnson; and it would appear upon first impression that the prose of these authors does not reflect *qualitative* differences. If we intuitively distinguish between Johnson and Gibbon, then this difference must be *quantitative*. The bases, that is, for this distinction may lie in the varying numbers and types of transformations used. In other words, Johnson may be "habitual and recurrent" in his use of some transformations, Gibbon in others.

The study of eighteenth-century prose style is important in another respect, for in the prose style of no other period do we find so many impressionistic labels. The prose of Edward Gibbon, for example, is almost always described as being "grand," "complex," and "ornate." There is a measure of truth associated with these labels, and I am sure that Gibbon's style exhibits degrees of complexity, grandness, and ornateness. The linguist's task, however, is to determine if there are attributes in Gibbon's prose which might account for these impressions. It has been my thesis that syntactical patterns or transformations can in great measure account for them.

My method of analysis can be viewed largely as the procedure of taking a textual sentence and "rewriting" it into a series of simple source sentences. These sentences may or may not be kernel or minimal sentences. In the nomenclature of the traditional grammarian, complex and compound sentences are the results of bringing together two or more sentences into a more complicated or complex sentence. And, in general, the number of transformations employed and the types of transformations used to build the textual sentence reflect syntactical style. Analysis of a textual sentence should make this procedure clear. The sentence from Gibbon's *Decline and Fall of the Roman Empire*

> Their discontents were secretly fomented by Laetus, their praefect, who found, when it was too late, that his new emperor would reward a servant, but would not be ruled by a favourite.

can be analyzed into the *source sentences*

1. Laetus secretly fomented their discontents.
2. Laetus was their praefect.
3. Laetus found NP^2-Adv T.

4. It was too late then.
5. His new emperor would reward a servant.
6. A favourite would not rule his new emperor.

The transformations are manipulations which ultimately lead to the textual sentence. The source sentences can be thought of as the input sentences:

1. Passive transformation (of source sentence 1): Their discontents were secretly fomented by Laetus.
2a. Relative-clause transformation (of source sentence 2): who was their praefect.
2b. Deletion (ellipsis) of relative (who) and "be" (of source sentence 3): their praefect.
3. Relative-clause transformation (of source sentence 3): who found $NP^2 — AdvT$.
   Adverb-shift transformation: who found, $AdvT, NP^2$
4. WH transformation (adverbial) (of source sentence 4): when it was too late.
5. Factive (that) transformation (of source sentence 5): that his new emperor would reward a servant.
6a. Negative transformation (of source sentence 6): A favourite would not rule his new emperor.
6b. Passive transformation: His new emperor would not be ruled by a favourite.
6c. Conjunctive transformation for 5 and 6: source sentence 5 and source sentence 6, with deletion equals textual sentence.

From the results of this sketchy analysis we tentatively posit that intuitive impressions reflect various degrees of grammatical or transformational processes. For example, "ornateness," traditionally employed to describe styles which exhibit the schemes of balance and antithesis, is reflected by Gibbon's use of a specific transformation, exemplified in 6c. A larger sample would undoubtedly reinforce our impression that this grammatical pattern is indeed "habitual and recurrent" in Gibbon's prose style. "Grandness" and "complexity" may in this limited analysis be represented by instances of embedding (relative-clause, adverbial-clause, and factive, "that," transformations) and in the total number of source sentences — 6 — within the textual sentence.

One such example does not make a case, and a much larger and statistically viable sample would be needed to arrive at any substantial conclusions. But this example does at least suggest that analyses of this type would be beneficial in investigating prose style.

BIBLIOGRAPHY

David DeCamp. "Sequence of Tenses, or Was James Thurber the First Transformational Grammarian?" *College Composition and Communication*, XVIII (February 1967), 7–13.

Nils Eric Enkvist, John Spencer, and Michael J. Gregory. *Linguistics and Style*. Oxford University Press, 1964.

Roger Fowler. "Linguistics, Stylistics; Criticism?" *Lingua*, XVI (April 1966), 153–165.

Morris Halle and Samuel Jay Keyser. "Chaucer and the Study of Prosody," *College English*, XXVIII (December 1966), 187–219.

Curtis W. Hayes. "Literary Analysis and Linguistics: A Study in the Prose Styles of Edward Gibbon and Samuel Johnson." Paper delivered before the fortieth Annual Meeting of the Linguistic Society of America, Chicago, Illinois, December 30, 1965.

Curtis W. Hayes. "A Study in Prose Styles: Edward Gibbon and Ernest Hemingway," *Texas Studies in Literature and Language*, VII, No. 4 (Winter 1966), 371–386.

William O. Hendricks. "Linguistics and the Structural Analysis of Literary Texts." Unpublished Ph.D. dissertation. University of Illinois, 1965.

William O. Hendricks. Review, *Language*, XLII (September 1966), 639–648. This review is of Samuel R. Levin, *Linguistic Structures in Poetry*, Janua Linguarum, Series Minor, No. 23. Mouton, 1962.

Archibald A. Hill. "An Analysis of *The Windhover*: An Experiment in Structural Method," *PMLA*, LXX, No. 5 (December 1955), 968–978.

Archibald A. Hill. "Some Points in the Analysis of Keats' *Grecian Urn*." Forthcoming.

Archibald A. Hill. "*The Windhover* Revisited: Linguistic Analysis of Poetry Reassessed," *Texas Studies in Literature and Language*, VII, No. 4 (Winter 1966), 349–359.

Samuel R. Levin. "Internal and External Deviation in Poetry," *Word*, XXI (August 1965), 225–237.

Samuel R. Levin. *Linguistic Structures in Poetry*, Janua Linguarum, Series Minor, No. 23. Mouton, 1962.

Samuel R. Levin. "On Automatic Production of Poetic Sequences," *Texas Studies in Literature and Language*, V, No. 1 (Spring 1963), 138–146.

David Lodge. *The Language of Fiction*. Columbia University Press, 1966.

Horace G. Lunt, ed. *Proceedings of the Ninth International Congress of Linguists*. Mouton, 1964. See section entitled "Stylistics," pp. 294 ff. See also Roman Jakobson's closing remarks, "Results of the Congress," pp. 1135 ff.

Louis Tonko Milic. "A Quantitative Approach to the Style of Jonathan Swift." Unpublished Ph.D. dissertation. Columbia University, 1963.

Richard Ohmann. "Generative Grammars and the Concept of Literary Style," *Word*, XX (December 1964) 423–439.

Richard Ohmann. "Literature as Sentences," *College English*, XXVII (January 1966), 261–267.

Thomas J. Roberts, compiler, "Literary-Linguistics: A Bibliography, 1964–1961," *Texas Studies in Literature and Language*, IV, No. 1 (Spring 1962), 625–629.

Charles T. Scott. "Persian and Arabic Riddles: A Language-Centered Approach to Genre Definition," *International Journal of American Linguistics*, XXXI, pt. 2 (October 1965).

James P. Thorne. "Stylistics and Generative Grammars," *Journal of Linguistics*, I, No. 1 (April 1965), 49–59.

17 MACHINE TRANSLATION

Winfred P. Lehmann

Many sentences in one language can be readily translated as entire units into another language. The German greeting which may be used when one meets a friend, *Guten Tag*, is translated not as two separate words but rather as the unit *Hello*. Greetings have been fixed by convention, and accordingly are translated automatically, almost mechanically. An English speaker would react strangely to the greeting *Good day!* He would also be surprised if a Japanese speaker parted from him with the words *if it must be so* (*sayonara*) rather than *Goodbye*. Conventional expressions are best translated by the equivalent convention in the other language, substituted mechanically.

Although greetings may be the most commonly used conventional expressions in language, they are by no means the only ones. Technical language especially — descriptions of experiments, reports of scientific research — uses many conventional constructions, and the question of translating scientific work by machine was raised shortly after the development of the first computer, about twenty years ago. Since then the necessary procedures for machine translation have been studied, and materials are already being translated by machine.

By far the greatest amount of material translated by machine will be technical. At school one deals with literary texts translated from all manner of languages — stories from the Persian of the *Arabian Nights*, from the Ancient Greek of Homer, from the Chinese of

Confucius — and may come away with the impression that most translations are literary ones. But technical publications — in physics, chemistry, economics, even in literary criticism — far outnumber the imaginative literature produced today or in the past. Scholars working on machine translation have about as much interest in translating imaginative literature as do contractors in building palaces; it may be amusing to contemplate, and even pleasant to plan, but the normal requirement is for ordinary, useful houses, and only one contractor out of thousands may ever design a palace. Literature is a refinement of language, much as a palace is an elaborate house. To direct one's efforts at learning to build palaces, or to translate literature by machine, would be unrealistic.

Furthermore, there is no tremendous haste to translate literature. If a professional literary translator delays his work for a week, a month, or even a year, no one is troubled. Technical materials, however, date rapidly. Scientists would like to know as soon as possible what their colleagues have discovered. For this reason alone it would be advantageous to have immediate translations of materials published in technology and the sciences. The promise of immediate access to foreign publications would of itself be an adequate reason for attempting to achieve machine translation.

While the rapid translation of technical and scientific materials is the strongest practical reason for interest in machine translation, the analysis of language necessary to bring it about leads linguists to a concern for it. Our understanding of language is still very poor. Most of us learn one language well as children, and pick up a smattering of others from teachers and grammars. The handbooks available to us fail to deal with many problems. Even well-informed foreign speakers often make mistakes in English, because of our inadequate grammars and dictionaries. They may, for example, use "information" in the plural, as a direct translation of the German *Kenntnisse* or *Erkundigungen*. Handbooks may not provide complete descriptions because we take our own language for granted. We fail to notice how we use words like *information* because we learned their uses thoroughly by taking them over from others, without observing the rules for those uses. But a computer will produce sentences only in accordance with the grammar and dictionary rules given it. Accordingly, these rules have to be complete. To the extent they are complete, a computer will produce correct sentences. For the first time linguists have an experimental tool to use in the study of language. Like the physicist who is performing an experiment, a linguist must specify precisely the procedures a computer will follow and the materials it will deal with. These procedures are the grammar of a language; the materials are its dictionary. Machine translation is based on the assumption that the grammar and dictionary of languages can be specified completely enough so that a computer can manage them. Besides providing such descriptions when using a computer for machine translation or any other linguistic processes, the linguist must frame a theory or a model of language.

A very simple approach to language, possibly too simple to be called a theory, sees it as a string of words. Actually the first applications of machine translation regarded language in this way, with very poor results. I have already cited greetings — simple forms of language that cannot be translated word for word. Translating longer sentences word for word brings up far more complex problems. In the simple German sentence *Diese kurze gemeinsame Ueberlegung ist eine Art Experiment mit uns selbst gewesen* for example, possibly the most serious problem is the position of the verb. The translation is *This short joint reflection has been a kind of experiment with ourselves* rather than *has a kind of joint experiment with ourselves been*. *Uns selbst* is translated *ourselves*, not *us self*. Clearly, a word-for-word approach is inadequate. In the course of devising adequate models, linguists have drawn on the work of scholars in other fields, notably philosophers who have concerned themselves with meaning and symbolic logic, and mathematicians who are interested in ways of precisely formulating rules for the formation of sentences. The interaction has led to various models of language. It will be some time before we can experiment adequately to test all of these, but the history of machine translation has seen increasing complexity in the models posited for language. As these approximate the system of communication controlled by a native speaker, translation by machine will be increasingly improved.

To examine briefly some of the difficulties these models must manage: Possibly the central difficulty of language is its structure as a series of layers or levels, which linguists often speak of as hierarchical structure. A simple example from English illustrates how language is hierarchically structured. Because of contrasting pairs like *sip:zip*, *hiss:his*, *race:raise*, *price:prize*, with differing meanings signaled by a difference between *s* and *z*, one has to assume that *s* and *z* are different items in the sound system of English. But an examination of the grammar of English shows that they may not be. The plural of *cat* is made with an *s*, that of *dog* with a *z*; accordingly here *s* and *z* are equivalent. That is, in making plurals, certain nouns use *s*, others *z*. Although *s* and *z* differentiate simple words, like *race* and *raise*, the plural of the noun *ray* takes *z*, as in *rays of the sun*. Similarly the third singular of verbs; one says *she pries into her son's affairs*, not [prays]. Because of this difference in the function of the same items in various portions of the language must posit various hierarchies, or levels. Language differs in this way from our system of numerals. In our numeral system, 3 always has the same meaning, whether it follows other numerals as in 23 or precedes them as in 32. Unlike *s* and *z* in the English language, 3 and 2 never have the same value.

While this hierarchical system makes language far more complex than the system of numerals — and far more difficult to manage, whether by man or by computer — it also accomplishes much with a small number of sound-classes. But although all of us use the complex structure of language with ease, linguists cannot yet describe it readily. One of the problems is the number of posited levels it demands. In English grammar, for example, there is the verb *go*. Although it has parallel meanings in many sentences — *He's going to town, He's going tomorrow, He's going home* — in the sentence *He's going steady* it has the considerably different meaning "being in love." And *He had to go* may have the totally different meanings "he had to leave" or "he had to go to the bathroom." To account simply for these differences in meaning, one may posit a semantic level and a grammatical level, comparable to the differing levels of sound and grammar.

When such different levels are assumed, there is the further problem of interrelating them. Some linguists have assumed a separate intermediate level between the level of sounds and forms; others treat the complexities in making plurals of *cats*, *days*, *rays*, and so on, as a subset of the grammatical level. These are theoretical problems which will occupy linguists for some time, including those who are working on the problem of machine translation. But if we as linguists wish to experiment with language by computer, we have to set up a hypothesis, test and refine or discard it — as is done generally in the sciences. In the course of these tests we may make our contribution to theoretical problems as well as to practical results.

It is especially necessary in machine translation to assume and follow a theory of language, for besides providing a guideline for the linguists engaged in a research project, a theory is also necessary to lay plans for the computer programmers who work with the linguists. The early work in machine translation demonstrated the advisability of having linguists and computer specialists deal separately with their problems — of separating linguistic analysis from computer programming. For if one tied the two together and programmed the linguistic analysis that seemed appropriate at any given time, the program would have to be changed if the analysis turned out to be inadequate, or wrong. Since no adequate analysis has yet been achieved for any language, there would be little likelihood of arriving at an adequate set of computer programs for handling, or translating language.

The system of analysis and programming being followed at the Linguistics Research Center of The University of Texas views language as a series of levels. The first of these we call the lexical. At this level we deal with the words of language. The next level we call the grammatical, or syntactic. At this level we bring units of form together. For example, in the German sentence discussed above, *ist . . . gewesen* is treated as a unit and translated *has been* rather than *is . . . been*. A further level we call the semantic. At this level we relate words to one another, translating *kurze* with *Ueberlegung* as *brief* rather than *short* or *curt*. Obviously, a semantic analysis would be very complex; we have barely begun to experiment with one.

Just as we cut up language into a series of levels, so we handle the programming problem as a number of separate processes. In doing this we may be remotely simulating the processes used by speakers in handling language, for there is a system of programs which perform a series of functions. One set manages the requests to the computer, insuring that they are in proper form. This set is a receptor, and can be roughly compared with the human ear. Another set manages the language material that is to be processed. A third set manages the grammar which has been developed and stored in the computer.

These three sets of programs handle the functions which correspond to the capability of man to listen to material in a language and proceed to match it with his knowledge of that language, that is to say, in accordance with a grammar and dictionary he has stored in his brain. Equipped with these potential capabilities, for one language or more, he uses them — in ways we can merely guess at — when he hears a sentence in a language he knows. But in our computer system we attempt to simulate the ways in which he manages the material he has heard and proceeds to understand it.

Basically the programs we use for this purpose have two aims: to analyze the material for its various levels, lexical, syntactic, and semantic; and to match the analysis with an expected analysis in a second language. This second aim is carried out by a fourth set of programs which consists of a transfer grammar; this transfer grammar is designed to carry out translation between two given languages. It moves from the input sentence to a sentence in the second language, synthesizing this matching sentence. If we were translating from German to English, the analysis programs would break down the German input sentence and prepare it for matching with English; the synthesis programs would produce an acceptable English output sentence.

A description of the process of linguistic analysis and synthesis would be very lengthy, for it is one of the characteristics of a computer that every step must be specified. When it has been specified, it can be carried out so rapidly that the tremendous number of operations are conducted with great speed. But although it is out of the question to describe here in any detail the processes involved in making a grammatical analysis of a sentence, I can indicate briefly the general procedures.

A sentence is analyzed in much the same way as it is in high school studies of grammar, though the symbols may differ. The basic procedure is to assume that each sentence is a unit, branching like a tree from a main trunk into various smaller entities. The branching may be simple; it is complex when the sentence is long and complicated.

For example: We present to a computer the simple German sentence *Diese kurze gemeinsame Ueberlegung ist eine Art Experiment mit uns selbst gewesen*. The sentence is first entered into the computer in such a way that it is accepted by the analysis programs. By these it is divided and subdivided into various segments; the segments next in size to the entire sentence are the words before *ist* and those that follow it; such an analysis can be made because *ist* is a verb, and in German verbs stand in second position in independent clauses other than questions and commands. The sentence accordingly fits one of the basic rules of the grammar. *S* (sentence) is made up of *NP* (noun phrase) and *VP* (verb phrase). Each of these components is analyzed in turn, and the elements are identified in the computer's grammar and dictionary. If the dictionary contains the noun *Ueberlegung*, it is identified as a noun of a class which requires any preceding modifiers to have certain endings. The program then examines these modifiers, *Diese kurze* and *gemeinsame*, finds that the endings on them are indeed the ones expected, and happily deals with the first four words as a subject consisting of a noun preceded by the limiting adjective *this* and two descriptive adjectives *brief* and *joint*. The predicate is similarly analyzed for its components, and ultimately each entity in the sentence is identified. The identification is expressed in a series of rules which deal with the smallest components of the sentence and its larger entities.

Each of these rules is matched against rules in the computer's English grammar: subject, for subject; nouns like *Ueberlegung* for nouns like *reflection*; and so on. Through such matching, the English counterpart is ultimately produced.

If the computer finds all the elements in a sentence, and if these fit into a regular construction, a sentence can be completely analyzed. If the grammars of two languages have been stored in the computer, and links provided between them, the computer can start with one language and translate sentences into the other.

When machine translation is discussed, trick sentences are

invariably cited, such as: *She drove into the bank.* From this sentence alone we cannot determine whether a lady driver was replenishing her supply of cash by driving to the teller's window of an outdoor bank, or whether she lost control of her car and hit the roadside.

There are several answers to this quandary. First, sentences generally occur in contexts from which one can determine the meaning of words that are difficult to identify precisely in isolation. A second, and better, answer is that a computer can readily provide both translations and let the reader choose the more likely one. Human translations are actually interpretations. If we do not have the original text in front of us, we have to accept the version given by the translator. Anyone who has ever translated materials knows that he always tries to make sense of them in the other language; in attempting to achieve a sensible translation he may even do violence to the original. A machine translation will always be brutally honest. If a sentence is not adequately translated, the computer will not frame a translation that looks attractive. By functioning so honestly and literally, it will not mislead the user, though it may not attract him with style.

Moreover, translations produced by computer will shortly be made available in ways different from those now in use to read texts. Rather than being provided only in printed form, the translations will be shown on terminals like television screens. More and more computers are being equipped with such terminals, on which the results of experiments and other data are shown. A great advantage of their use for machine translation is the possibility of giving the scientist the original text and various possible translations. If, for example, the sentence *She drove into the bank* were translated into German or Russian, both possible meanings could be shown. In this way the proper translation can be selected by the user who knows most about a particular context and field, not by the translator. Though a translator may have mastered two or more languages, he may lack the scientific command necessary to make proper judgments between various possible translations in such widely different fields as physical geology, atomic physics, molecular biology. Discussions of machine translation often fail to note the advantages which improved computer technology will bring to its users.

The translation which is being carried out by machine today is crude, so crude that it is edited before it is made available to users. After it has passed through this double process, its cost is somewhat higher than is that of human translation. But it is being continued, partly because the machine unfailingly turns out its quota of translation and partly because translations will be improved as linguists and programmers learn better how to handle language. And the cost is steadily being reduced.

I mentioned earlier that many problems remain to be solved. One of these is to produce machines that can identify equivalent sounds spoken by different speakers, such as a man and a woman. When we get a machine to understand oral language as well as a native speaker does, we can proceed to numerous other practical applications. We will for example be able to talk to a typewriter and have it type our sentences. More complex machines will be able to translate messages from one language into another.

Another problem for translation by machine is the semantic component of language. For example, when does *go* mean *proceed* and when does it have other meanings? The theoretical work on this problem is still in its beginnings. But when language can be handled in this way, machine translation will deal with the content of documents, and a computer will then be able to handle information, to make automatic abstracts, to answer individual questions about data in texts.

It will be some time before these and other problems are solved. When satisfactory solutions have been obtained for one or more languages, the necessary research can be carried out to achieve similar results with other languages. One of the large problems in keeping abreast of scientific developments today is the translation of technical works. A human translator may set out to translate a contemporary text in some complex branch of physics only to find, when he finishes his translation, that the text is outmoded. If instead of relying on a human translator we could use the paper tape which controls the original printing as a basis for immediately translating a text into other languages, if we could thus print it simultaneously in translation and the original, students throughout the world could keep abreast of modern developments.

Machine translation will accordingly have a tremendous number of uses and effects. But some of the ones which are occasionally hoped for may not materialize. For example, many students hope that machine translation will make unnecessary the mastery of more than one language. It may actually make unnecessary the reading of numerous languages; but anyone who wishes to communicate quickly will have to speak several languages. The direction of our foreign language learning may accordingly be shifted, but the problem will not be eliminated.

Thus far, work in machine translation has been a branch of applied linguistics — but its achievements have been largely in theory rather than in production. It has forced linguists interested in it to look at language as a whole and to devise comprehensive linguistic theories. It has brought linguists face to face with specialists in other fields: programmers, symbolic logicians.

It promises much: The manipulation of language by computer can bring about a change in handling information as profound as that caused by the printing press with movable type. The computer is a tool which will permit us to regain control of the masses of information now available in a great number of languages. Translation by computer is only one of the steps which will achieve this control. But it will remove one of the barriers that still blocks the rapid exchange of information.

18 COMPUTER LINGUISTICS

Wayne Tosh

One of the first problems which will confront the reader new to the area of computer linguistics is the variety of terms under which the same or related types of research are conducted. There are computational linguistics, mathematical linguistics, statistical linguistics, and mechanolinguistics, to name the more popular ones. The one element common to these closely related areas is the computer — algorithmic — techniques.

In this chapter I shall discuss various applications of the computer in linguistics, some of them real, some still conjectural. The premise is, at any rate, that computer linguistics is basically no different from any other kind, except perhaps in terms of explicitness and the degree of exactness induced by the need for explicitness. The computer is to be regarded as a valuable tool applicable to all areas of linguistic description which merit the terms "scientific" or "rigorous."

I shall discuss briefly the research being done by linguists in the United States in morphology and syntax, on dictionaries, in communications, in historical and comparative applications, in language pedagogy, and in other areas.

MORPHOLOGY AND SYNTAX

Computer-oriented studies in morphology and syntax received their initial impetus from research in machine translation.

The first such undertaking was made in 1956 by the Georgetown University Machine Translation Research and Language Projects, Washington, D.C., under the direction of Leon Dostert. Morphological and syntactic description was in the form of computer routines, or algorithms.

The first effort in constructing a linguistically oriented system was made by Victor Yngve while he was at the Massachusetts Institute of Technology. He developed a linguistic programming language known as COMIT which allows one to write immediate constituent parsing algorithms. He directed graduate students in experimental parsing of sentences in several languages to identify the constituent elements and correlate discontinuous elements. An example of this problem may be found in the verb expression *look over* as in the sentence *Will you look the list over?* Treatment of discontinuity remains one of the major problems in machine translation.

Another approach originated with Ida Rhodes of the National Bureau of Standards. The technique is known as predictive analysis and was further developed under the direction of Anthony Oettinger at Harvard University. This algorithm parses sentences by identifying the first component in a sentence and then predicting the permissible components which may follow. Researchers at Harvard have built elaborate descriptions of English and Russian in this system.

Another approach has been taken at the RAND Corporation, Santa Monica, California. A parsing program was developed which is known as the Dependency Analyzer. The program is modeled on dependency theories as expounded by David G. Hays in this country and Lucien Tesnière in France. The basic characteristic of the Dependency Analyzer is that it specifies the interdependence of sentence components, for example, the dependency of object on verb for case government, of subject on verb for number agreement.

Still another model of syntax is used in computer research by a group under the direction of Zellig Harris at the University of Pennsylvania. Complex sentences are analyzed to determine from which combination of simple kernel sentences they have been derived.

Research at the Linguistics Research Center of The University of

Texas in which I am engaged is based on a system of stratified models in which the morphological and syntactic description of a language resembles the phrase-structure component of a transformational grammar.

DICTIONARIES

Large dictionaries in computer form are one of the principal by-products of efforts in machine translation. During the time Georgetown University was active in this field, researchers there accumulated a Russian–English dictionary of 50,000 entries in chemistry, physics, and the biological and social sciences. The IBM Corporation compiled a bilingual Russian–English dictionary of over 150,000 entries, currently in use by the U.S. Air Force. Harry Josselson, Wayne State University, is compiling a Russian dictionary of similar magnitude. A. F. Brown, University of Pennsylvania, has compiled a word list in contemporary English which contains more than 350,000 entries. The contents of the Chinese–English dictionary published by the McGraw-Hill Company has been put into computer form and includes over 240,000 entries.

There are several advantages to having dictionary-stores like these in a computer system, aside from the requirements necessitated by application in machine translation. The most obvious and immediate advantage lies in the ability to revise the store continually and keep it up to date. One of the chronic problems in linguistic and language research is the delay between revised editions of any reference work. With the data in the computer the linguist has the latest information always at his fingertips.

There are other advantages as well. Dictionary-stores and other data collections of similar volume are often of sufficient size so that it is impractical to display the complete contents on every occasion. Now, if the data have been stored with information to identify certain subsets of data, it is possible to display just the fraction of the total store which is of interest. Thus, if we want to see those dictionary entries pertaining to a special discipline like nuclear physics, we request a selective display accordingly. We might well imagine a linguistic data-processing center which maintains a very large store of dictionary or other kinds of data which is never displayed in its entirety at any one time, but which is so constructed as to allow instant publication of specialized subcollections of data on demand.

COMMUNICATIONS

The computer is not only a tool for collecting and manipulating language and linguistic data, but also a medium for the communication of language and linguistic data. Two principal applications may be mentioned: machine translation and the retrieval of linguistic data. These two applications depend in one respect or another on all known aspects of linguistic science.

The problems inherent in these areas of research are very great. For this reason the support of institutions on the national level is needed. Among some of the government agencies which have expressed interest in these developments are the National Science Foundation, the Army, the Navy, the Air Force, the Central Intelligence Agency, and the National Security Agency.

The interest in machine translation arises from the need for high-speed translation of the virtually overwhelming volume of scientific publication. At the present time most countries engaged in this research are understandably interested in translating into the local language. In time the scientific community will perhaps also recognize the value of translating out of the local language into other languages for purposes of disseminating as well as collecting information. Transmission of information through translation is, however, only a part of the problem of communication. The information must also be pooled in a way that makes it easily retrievable and correlatable with other information. We shall consider now some details of these two problems.

About the problem of translation: There exists no completely satisfactory computer system performing automatic translation at the present time. The Mark II translation system, developed by IBM for the Air Force, produces an output of some 100,000 words per day of English translation from Russian. Machine translation output is available to scientists on demand from the Oak Ridge, Tennessee, laboratories, where the Russian–English system developed by Georgetown University is in use. The resulting translation is useful to scientists who want to determine whether a given article is sufficiently interesting to warrant a more accurate human translation. Otherwise the output requires post-editing to make it useful to the less technically sophisticated reader. Much improvement has to be made in the quality of machine translation. Nevertheless, progress has been made in the ten years since the United States effort in machine translation was initiated by Georgetown University in 1956.

Since that time many projects have come and gone. Among those recently active in the field are such groups as the one headed by Paul Garvin of the Bunker-Ramo Corporation, Santa Monica, California. Another group is the Linguistics Research Center under the direction of W. P. Lehmann. Mrs. Ching-Hi Dougherty continues research in Chinese–English machine translation. Her work was initiated under a project at the University of California at Berkeley directed by Sydney Lamb. Another group recently active is IBM's Thomas J. Watson Laboratories in Yorktown Heights, New York. Important contributions to research have been made by the RAND Corporation, Indiana University, Ohio State University, Harvard, MIT, Georgetown University, Wayne State, and the University of Pennsylvania.

Most of the effort in machine translation has been directed at the more well-known problems of describing the morphology and syntax primarily of English, Russian, Chinese, German, and French. The greatest number of problems remaining to be solved are in the novel area of semantic description.

The second major problem in a communication system is information retrieval. After the information in a technical publication has been translated, it must be stored with other information. Storage of linguistic data is, in itself, no great problem. Furthermore, if we assign to each batch of information to be stored certain codes, for instance the decimal classification of books in a library, it is not difficult to recall and display the information. The accuracy and the degree of refinement with which a computer can recall such information is entirely a function of the accuracy with which the researcher has assigned his retrieval codes.

There is, however, a more complex problem which is of great interest to us. At one time or another, we have all had the experience of asking someone for some rather specific information, whereupon we received not only what was asked for, if the other party is knowledgeable, but also related facts about which we may not have thought to inquire. Responses of this sort are referred to in computational circles as "associative retrieval." We would like to build the same capability into a computer. To do this, we must make use of the mechanisms required in the translation systems. The computer must, in effect, be made capable of analyzing the structure and content of inquiries and then searching its stores for both explicitly matching and implicitly related responses.

Perhaps one of the first sources of information which we linguists would like to consider automating is a linguistic bibliography, a comprehensive listing of publications in the field of linguistics. Information in the bibliography is arranged under certain subject headings, but because the annual bibliography must encompass so many titles, the extent to which a refined subject classification is realized is limited. Furthermore, the volume of linguistic publication increases yearly, as in most disciplines, making the task of keeping the bibliography up to date Herculean.

When the necessary support becomes available, automating the bibliography will expedite a finer cross-classification of titles and will yield a more rapid system for publishing supplements. The Center for Applied Linguistics in Washington, D.C., has expressed an interest in establishing a linguistic network in the United States, and outside it, which would feed linguistic information through the center as a clearinghouse to various regional processing centers, such as the Linguistics Research Center at the University of Texas. These regional centers would specialize in such tasks as the maintenance of large stores of language text in computer form, such as the tens of millions of running words of scientific Russian stored and processed by the RAND Corporation. Another specialty might be maintenance of a linguistic information retrieval system which would contain not only information like the linguistic bibliography but also linguistic descriptions or, say, rosters of language names as now being compiled at the University of Indiana.

Yet another specialty would be facilities for publishing information from the regional centers on demand. The University of Pittsburgh has computer facilities for accepting large stores of language data and photocomposing the data for printing in a wide variety of fonts. The Center for Applied Linguistics might then serve as the nerve center for a nationwide hookup of regional computing facilities to collect, correlate, and disseminate linguistic information.

COMPARATIVE APPLICATIONS

The comparative study of languages, whether for historical-genetic purposes or general typological purposes, lends itself to computer manipulation. There are forms to be sorted, statistics to be calculated. One study in which the computer would be a natural aid is the research of Joseph Greenberg, of Stanford University, who is interested in language universals and typology. Morris Swadesh of the University of Mexico carried out similar investigations based on his technique of glottochronology, which was designed to measure similarities or divergencies among languages. The Georgetown machine translation project did an experimental comparative study of Slavic languages for the purpose of developing an interlingua especially designed for this family of languages, although the results were not tested. The computer might be used in this case to test the adequacy of the set of constructions considered to be naturally applicable to the several Slavic languages, so as to avoid the necessity for a larger body of descriptive data entailed in the independent preparation of each language for the translation system.

Such studies as these lend themselves particularly well to computer treatment, since each study consists of a large, explicit data base. The problem then is one of data reduction, or comparison of elements for similarities and consequent abstraction of patterns.

An important detail is the accompanying arithmetical calculation of statistics, a relatively simple but often tedious task for the human researcher.

LANGUAGE TEACHING AND TESTING

The use of computers for teaching purposes is growing in popularity. This application has begun to spread into language teaching as well. Much of the programming at the present time is of the form which presents a series of interconnected problems to the student. As the student answers each question or solves each problem in the series, the answers are compared against a standard list for acceptability. If the student is correct, he is automatically directed to the next problem. The series is so constructed as to gradually increase the student's knowledge of some specified central issue. Whenever the student makes an error, the program directs him over the same ground again or, in more sophisticated programs, to an auxiliary, remedial series of problems. The student is thus rewarded immediately, or corrected and allowed to continue at his own pace.

Educators in many disciplines are beginning to experiment with such facilities. One such pilot project is being undertaken at The University of Texas by D. C. Travis of the department of Germanic languages and Wayne Holtzmann, chairman of the department of educational psychology.

In time the efforts of such men may be combined with those of researchers in machine translation, since the grammatical descriptions necessary for translation also have an application in language pedagogy. For example, we could allow the student in a foreign language program to construct answers freely in the target language in response to questions and problems posed in that language. Programmed-learning packages are at present limited largely to prespecified multiple-choice answers. With a grammar built into the machine the student could, in fact, compose essay answers. We would have a mechanical means of evaluating empirically many of the parameters of essay examinations which must now be evaluated largely on intuition. We would have the means for measuring exactly the student's vocabulary range and his ability in complex constructions in the language.

OTHER APPLICATIONS

There are many other linguistic uses to which we might put the computer. One of them is research on the signals which occur in speech, in which the computer could play a very important role in correlating and reducing the unimaginably large body of data created in converting the spoken continuum to discrete and processable forms. Another application is textbook evaluation — evaluation of the range and frequency of lexical items and syntactic constructions. There are applications in anthropological linguistics of the sort made by Duane Metzger who uses the computer to correlate the complex social patterns he derives from his field work in Indian communities of southern Mexico. Still another is in psycholinguistics, where we would like to manage the large volume of language data necessary to validate theories of cognitive processes and learning models. Finally, there are, each year, new programs in stylistic investigation, such as those carried out by Sally Sedelow of the University of North Carolina. Large collections of raw language data are necessary for these investigations and are being built up steadily. In addition to the store of scientific Russian text maintained by the RAND Corporation, there is a similar compilation of ten million words of contemporary English non-scientific text.

While much research and development in computer linguistics has been done in the United States much more of great challenge remains. Scholars have taught us much about the language and its nature in the last century, but much remains to be learned. The computer will be an important tool in investigation of language structure, of communication, and of many areas related to language and communication. Useful as we hope the computer will be in translation, that activity is but one phase, and perhaps not the most important phase, of its contribution.

19 SIMULATED SPEECH

Frances Ingemann

Were this chapter a spoken lecture, I could begin by playing a sample of artificial speech, produced by machine from line drawings which tell the machine what sounds to make. Since this chapter is to be read from print, I must content myself with pointing out that such an operation is readily possible and that the resultant speech is recognizable.

Such a simulation of speech is not to be confused with the sound reproduction of phonograph and tape recordings. In such recordings, the sound waves of speech are simply changed to a permanent form, from which the original sound waves can be re-created at any time. Speech simulators attempt to make speech by completely artificial means. To the extent that it is successful, it demonstrates our understanding of speech production. Through trying to correct our errors, we linguists gain additional information.

One of the most obvious ways to build a talking machine is to imitate nature. It is not surprising, therefore, that the earliest attempts at talking machines resembled the human vocal tract. The first well-documented such machine was that built toward the end of the eighteenth century by a Hungarian, Wolfgang von Kempelen. In his speaking machine, sound was produced by a stream of air supplied by a bellows, just as natural speech is produced by air coming out of the lungs. As the air went through a reed, it caused vibrations similar to those produced at the vocal cords. The air then passed through a resonating chamber which, like the mouth, could be varied in shape. Other passages were used for nasals and such fricative sounds as [s] and [š]. Considerable skill was required to perform the rapid manipulations necessary for making connected speech on this machine, but after much practice Kempelen was able to produce words and short sentences in French, Italian, Latin, and German. The machine was, however, not perfect, and Kempelen himself admitted that some words were understood more easily than others.

Several attempts at improving the mechanical model of the vocal tract were made in the nineteenth century, but gradually investigation along these lines diminished as attention turned to the study of the properties of sound waves. The development of electronic instruments in the twentieth century has permitted detailed acoustic investigation of speech. Quite naturally, investigators also became interested in using the results of their analyses to produce synthetic speech. Because of technological advances, it was now possible to produce sound electronically, without the use of mechanical vibrators, resonance chambers, and constricted passages. New synthesizers were developed which produced sounds at desired frequencies and intensities, without reference to the physiology of the vocal tract. The first such synthesizer which could produce connected speech was Voder, developed by Homer Dudley at Bell Telephone Laboratories and demonstrated at the 1939 New York World's Fair. Controlled by a keyboard and foot pedals, it was played like a musical instrument by operators who required a long training period.

Since then a number of other synthesizers have been developed in the United States and elsewhere to continue research on speech. Most recently, computer programs have also been devised for synthesizing speech without the need for constructing special equipment. An excellent summary of technical details of instrumentation is given in James Flanagan's *Speech Analysis, Synthesis and Perception*. Less technical descriptions can be found in papers published in the proceedings of the International Congresses of Phonetic Sciences.

One goal of speech synthesis could be to produce an utterance using every detail found in an analysis of natural speech. Such a task would demonstrate the correctness of the analysis and the ingenuity of the investigator in devising a machine or computer program that could duplicate the very complex wave forms of real speech. However, this type of synthesis does not reveal the role the various parts of the wave form play or the underlying principles which help organize and interpret the welter of detail.

Another approach has been to devise a synthesizer which is capable of producing speech with a limited number of variable controls (or parameters). This parametric approach was first used by Walter Lawrence working at the Signals Research and Development Establishment in England. He called his synthesizer PAT, from Parametric Artificial Talker.

The aim of the parametric approach is to build into the synthesizer as much as possible of the characteristics related to the production of natural-sounding speech. Ideally, the parameters should control only those aspects of the acoustic output a speaker uses to differentiate one utterance from another; everything else should be produced automatically by the machine. There is a highly sophisticated parametric synthesizer called OVE II, developed by Gunnar Fant and his associates at the Royal Institute of Technology in Stockholm.

Those working on parametric synthesizers have often been primarily concerned with deciding how many and what types of parameters are necessary to produce intelligible speech and with making the resulting speech more natural. To some extent this focus has come about as a result of a possible practical application of this type of synthesizer. Communication engineers are continually searching for more economical means of transmitting messages. If only a few parameters are needed to produce acceptable speech, these could be abstracted from an utterance and transmitted over a cable with a much smaller bandwidth than is required at present for a telephone conversation. If the bandwidth needed for a message could be reduced, more messages could be transmitted at once on the same cable, and thus the cost of each message would be less. For this kind of communication system, there must be not only an analyzer which abstracts the signals to be sent, but also a synthesizer which can reconstitute speech from them. Because communication engineers working on parametric synthesizers assume that the signals to control the parameters will come from the analysis of actual utterance, much of the work done with these synthesizers has involved copying the values for the parameters from an analysis of real speech. Furthermore, matters of timing have been little investigated because these are inherent in the transmission of the parametric signal.

Of special interest to linguists are the studies which have led to an understanding of the differences between speech sounds. As people looked at analyses of speech, questions arose about the role of the various parts in distinguishing one speech sound from another. Synthetic speech is ideally suited to investigation of these questions because it is possible to change one small part of the acoustic picture at a time, leaving everything else constant. Work in this field was pioneered at Haskins Laboratories in New York, where a group of engineers, phoneticians, linguists, and psychologists have, through extensive experimentation, uncovered a number of acoustic cues for the perception of speech sounds. Much of the impetus for this work came about as the result of the development of the sound spectrograph for the analysis of speech. Almost at once engineers set about to see if a machine could be developed which would convert spectrograms back into speech. Such a machine is the Pattern Playback, which was built at Haskins Laboratories in the late 1940s. By comparison with later synthesizers it seems rather primitive, yet its very simplicity, coupled with its reliability and ease of manipulation, make possible a kind of experimentation difficult if not impossible on other synthesizers.

The Pattern Playback is capable of producing pure tones at intervals of 120 cps in the range of 120–6000 cycles. Because this machine has almost no information about speech built into it, speechlike sounds will result only in so far as the investigator gives it the proper instructions. It therefore requires the investigator to make explicit everything about speech. For the purpose of producing synthetic speech, the lowest tone (120 cycles) can be regarded as the fundamental and each of the other tones as a harmonic of this fundamental. Each tone may be played as loudly or as softly as desired for any length of time, and any combination of tones may be played at one time. Thus, synthesizing speech on the Pattern Playback is equivalent to building it up harmonic by harmonic. Because tones occur only at 120-cycle intervals, the machine cannot produce pitch changes but speaks only in a monotone. There is also no provision for sounds not made up of harmonics (such as [s] and [š]), although these can be simulated to some extent by excitation of certain harmonics for very brief periods of time in a random pattern.

When the Pattern Playback was constructed, one of the first things done was to play back spectrograms of real speech. While the synthesized version has a definite machinelike quality, it is quite intelligible. The fact that this kind of synthesis is successful demonstrates that, for the most part, cues for the linguistically significant aspects of speech have been retained. Further experimentation revealed that the spectrographic input could be considerably simplified without much loss in intelligibility. At this point a series of systematic experiments was begun to determine the role which various acoustic components observable in spectrograms played in the discrimination of speech sounds.

The procedure was to select a variable the investigator had reason to believe played a significant role and then to vary it in steps. Groups of listeners, usually people who had no previous acquaintance with synthetic speech, were asked to identify the synthetic speech as speech sounds with which they were familiar. In this way cues for the perception of various speech sounds were determined. Because the listeners most readily available were speakers of American English, the sounds found in this language have been studied more thoroughly than sounds in other languages.

A description of second-formant transitions illustrates the kind of investigations carried out to determine perceptual cues. Vowels show up on spectrograms as dark horizontal lines indicating a concentration of energy at certain frequencies. These areas of concentrated energy are called formants, and each vowel has its own characteristic set of formant frequencies. Although several formants occur in real speech, most vowels can be unambiguously synthesized by means of the first two.

It was observed that when a vowel followed a consonant, the formants did not begin at the frequencies characteristic of that vowel but at other frequencies, from which they moved rapidly to those characteristic of the vowel. The portion from the onset of a formant to the place where it reaches the frequency characteristic of the vowel is called a transition. Investigations of these formant transitions were undertaken in considerable detail. A number of vowels were synthesized and formants varied systematically. When tested on listeners, the synthetic syllables were, of course, presented in random order. The results of this experiment showed that the second-formant transition signaled place of articulation. Thus, when the transition began substantially below the vowel frequency, the syllable was heard as [bæ]. When the transition began substantially above the second formant, the syllable was heard as [gæ]. When the transition began at the same frequency as the vowel formant or just above it the syllable was heard as [dæ].

Second-formant transitions do not begin at the same frequencies for all vowels, nor can they be characterized as simply beginning above or below the formant frequency. It was found that the starting point of the second-formant transition could be most simply specified if a frequency could be given for each consonant toward which the second-formant transition was assumed to point. The investigators at Haskins Laboratories have called this frequency the *locus*. It should be remembered that transitions only point to the locus and do not actually begin there. Second-formant transitions pointing to a locus of 700 cycles are heard as [b].

Second-formant transitions pointing to a locus of 1800 cycles are heard as [d]. Because this locus falls in the middle of the second-formant range for vowels, the second-formant transitions for vowels with a high second-formant begin lower than the vowel formant; for those with a low second-formant, the transition begins higher than the vowel formant; and for vowels with a second formant around 1800 cycles, little or no transitional change is required.

The situation is not as straightforward for [g]. For vowels with a high or central second formant, a locus of 3000 cycles can be used. However, vowels with a low second-formant [ɔ, o, u] have a second-formant transition starting at or slightly above the second formant of the vowel.

These same formant transitions which occur in initial position are appropriate for final position, although of course in that position the transition begins at the vowel frequencies and ends at a point midway to the locus. These second-formant transitions were found to be appropriate not only for [b, d, g] but also, in combination with cues for voiceless stops, for [p, t, k], and, in combination with cues for nasal consonants, for [m, n, ŋ]. Thus the second-formant transition is shown to be associated with place of articulation rather than with a particular speech sound.

Since the Pattern Playback cannot produce aperiodic excitation or pitch changes, another synthesizer, called the Voback, was used to study these aspects of speech. The Voback, really the synthesis part of an 18-channel Vocoder, consists of a bank of filters controlled by a hand-painted spectrogram similar to that used on the Pattern Playback. Either a periodic or an aperiodic sound source (usually referred to as "buzz" and "hiss" respectively) can be used, and the frequency of the buzz source can be varied, thus producing pitch changes.

The Voback has been used to study differences between fricative and affricate sounds. The difference between [s] and [š], for example, can be made by using hiss at a lower frequency for [š] than for [s].

The contrast between [ś] and [č], on the other hand, can be produced with identical hiss frequency and transitions, but with the hiss of [č] beginning more abruptly and lasting for a shorter time than for [š].

As a result of careful study of a number of cues, a considerable amount of information was amassed — enough, in fact, to be able to synthesize speech without consulting an analysis of the sentence to be synthesized. If we allow the investigator to put all his knowledge about speech to work in synthesizing, we produce rather high-quality speech.

Pierre Delattre's work on the Voback at Haskins Laboratories, for instance, is the creation of a highly skilled investigator with years of experience. He began by compiling a set of rules as simple as possible that would enable a person with no training to convert a broad phonetic transcription into speech. In the interest of keeping the rules minimal in number and complexity, naturalness had sometimes to be sacrificed. The reason for putting restrictions on the rules was the aim of producing instructions which would eventually be used in a reading machine, that is, a device which could read aloud from a printed page. Such a device has yet to be constructed, but the attempt at writing rules pointed up the extent of our knowledge about speech and the many areas still to be investigated.

A number of cues were found to apply to classes of sounds corresponding in general to those set up for articulatory phonetics in the dimensions of place, manner, and voicing. It was, therefore, more economical to give rules for classes of sounds than for the individual sounds. A sound was then synthesized by combining the rules for the classes to which it belonged.

The minimal rules I have been describing were originally written for synthesizing speech on the Pattern Playback at Haskins Laboratories. It was, however, possible to adapt them to other synthesizers.

A few words about the complexities of the cues used in the rules: First of all, because there is no one-to-one relation between the acoustic dimensions of frequency, intensity, and duration and the speech dimensions of place, manner, and voicing, it is not possible to say that frequency indicates place exclusively, that intensity governs voicing, and so forth. In addition, there was usually not just one cue to signal a class but several. While it was sometimes possible to find a single cue to be the decisive factor in distinguishing classes under certain conditions, another cue might be equally important under others. For that reason, the rules for a speech sound usually included several cues in order that they would be appropriate in many environments. Furthermore, successful synthesis must take into account more than isolated sounds. Although people may hear speech as consisting of discrete units, speech is in fact a continuum and rules must, therefore, make provision for the necessary linkage.

Other investigators have also devised sets of rules. J. L. Kelly and L. J. Gerstman at Bell Laboratories, for example, were the first to write a computer program for synthesizing speech by rule. None of these sets of rules is perfect, and all are complex. As research continues, we can expect continual improvement of such rules, but because there is no simple one-to-one correspondence between phonemes (or even the major allophones) and acoustic cues, some investigators feel that perhaps acoustics is not the best approach to a simple specification of speech, and in recent years there has been a growing trend to return to articulatory studies.

Peter Ladefoged and his co-workers at the University of California in Los Angeles have attempted to construct a replica of the vocal tract for speech synthesis. This replica would allow the independent manipulation of each proposed variable, thus testing the hypothesis that speech might be most economically and accurately specified in a limited number of articulatory terms. Unfortunately the attempt proved more difficult than originally anticipated because of the problem of finding construction materials which have the flexibility and firmness needed to perform the actions of human tissues. This attempt also pointed up the many still-unknown factors concerning shape of the vocal tract and stimulated research now being undertaken to gain further information by studying human articulation.

Still using the articulatory model, but taking advantage of advances in electronics and computer simulation, electrical analogs of the vocal tract have been created. Investigators at the Massachusetts Institute of Technology have been actively developing a dynamic vocal tract analog capable of producing connected speech. In this type of synthesizer, electronic circuits are built (or simulated on a computer) to have the resonance properties of sections of a tube. The circuits can be varied to represent different cross-sectional areas and thus approximate the configuration of the mouth.

Again, problems arise because so little is known about the exact configurations of the mouth in speech. While it is possible to make frame-by-frame studies of X-ray motion pictures, this is a time-consuming task and not as accurate as might be supposed. Another way of finding appropriate configurations is to make estimates of the proper values to produce a given sound and then compare the acoustic output with a spoken version of the same sound. However, even when these two match, there is no guarantee that the configuration of the vocal-tract analog is the same as that of the human speaker, since different configurations of the analog may produce similar acoustic effects.

One further approach which has been suggested by Franklin

Cooper, Alvin Liberman and their associates at Haskins Laboratories is a synthesis based on neuromotor commands. Because even articulatory descriptions are complicated, they theorize that the most simple and direct correspondence of the phonemes is to be found in the neuromotor commands that activate the articulators. Rules for a synthesis of this type would, they claim, be quite simple, and the complexities of converting these commands into speech would be built into the constraints on the synthesizer. They point out that this, in fact, parallels what happens in real speech, where the output is a result of the capabilities and limitations of the speech-producing mechanism. Synthesis of this sort has not yet been undertaken, but we may look forward to an attempt in coming years which will contribute still further to our understanding of speech.

Not much has been said about the relation of synthesis to the field of linguistics. This is because so much of synthesis is concerned with the articulatory mechanism as a whole and not just to those functional units we usually call phonemes. However, the results are of importance to linguists, since a phonological theory must not conflict with the physical facts, and the cues which are found to distinguish speech sounds can be used to specify either the phonemes themselves or distinctive features. On the other hand, linguistic structure needs to be taken into account in synthesis. Most progress has been made when engineers, linguists, phoneticians, and psychologists have worked together on their common goal of simulating speech.

In this brief survey it has not been possible to mention all the research carried out in the field of synthesis or all the investigators who have made significant contributions. While a large part of the work on synthesis has taken place in the United States, advances must be regarded as the result of international cooperation. Many of those who have worked in American laboratories are from other countries, and laboratories overseas have likewise drawn on the abilities of researchers from a number of countries, including the United States. It is to be hoped that this cooperation continues to stimulate research, so that we may gain an ever fuller understanding of the nature of speech.

BIBLIOGRAPHY

J. Anthony and Walter Lawrence. "A Resonance Analogue Speech Synthesizer," *Proceedings of the Fourth International Congress on Acoustics*, Copenhagen, 1962.

Cecil H. Coker, Peter B. Denes, and Elliot N. Pinson. *Speech Synthesis*. Bell Telephone Laboratories, 1963.

F. S. Cooper. "Speech Synthesizers," *Proceedings of the Fourth International Congress of Phonetic Sciences*, 'S-Gravenhage, 1962.

F. S. Cooper. "Instrumental Methods for Research in Phonetics," *Proceedings of the Fifth International Congress of Phonetic Sciences*, Basel, 1965.

F. S. Cooper, Alvin M. Liberman, Leigh Lisker, and Jane H. Gaitenby. "Speech Synthesis by Rule," *Proceedings of the Speech Communication Seminar*, Stockholm, 1964.

Gunnar Fant. "Acoustic Analysis and Synthesis of Speech with Applications to Swedish," *Ericsson Technics*, XV (1959), 3–108.

Gunnar Fant, J. Martony, U. Rengman, and A. Risberg. "OVE II Synthesis Strategy," *Proceedings of the Speech Communication Seminar*, Stockholm, 1964.

James L. Flanagan. *Speech Analysis, Synthesis and Perception*. Academic Press, 1965. Also "Kummunikation und Kybernetik in Einzeldarstellungen," Band 3, Springer-Verlag: Berlin, Heidelberg, New York, 1965.

Wolfgang von Kempelen. *Mechanismus der menschlichen Sprache*. J. V. Degen, 1791.

Peter Ladefoged. "Some Possibilities in Speech Synthesis," *Language and Speech*, VII (1964), 205–214.

Alvin M. Liberman. "Some Results of Research on Speech Perception," *Journal of Acoustical Society of America*, XXIX (1957), 117–123.

Alvin M. Liberman, Franklin S. Cooper, Katherine S. Harris, and Peter F. MacNeilage. "A Motor Theory of Speech Perception," *Proceedings of the Speech Communication Seminar*, Stockholm, 1964.

Alvin M. Liberman, Frances Ingemann, Leigh Lisker, Pierre Delattre, and F. S. Cooper. "Minimal Rules for Synthesizing Speech," *Journal of the Acoustical Society of America*, XXI (1959), 1490–1499.

Leigh Lisker, Franklin S. Cooper, and Alvin M. Liberman. "The Uses of Experiment in Language Description," *Word*, XVIII (1962), 82–106.

20 J. R. FIRTH AND BRITISH LINGUISTICS

J. C. Catford

The development of any discipline is influenced by the cultural and political setting in which it takes place; this is certainly true of linguistics. It is well known that the existence in North America of a large number of little-known and (from a European point of view) exotic languages was a powerful stimulus to the development of linguistics in the United States. American Indian languages have stirred the interest of anthropologist-linguists for nearly a century, and such great pioneers as Franz Boas, Edward Sapir, and Leonard Bloomfield all worked in this field.

In Britain, the growth of an overseas empire was one factor that stimulated linguistic studies. It was, for instance, an Englishman in the Indian civil service, Sir William Jones, who was the first scholar to appreciate the true relationship between Sanskrit and the ancient classical languages of Europe. In 1786, referring to this relationship, he stated that Sanskrit "bears a stronger affinity [to Latin and Greek] both in the roots of verbs and in the forms of grammar than could possibly have been produced by accident: so strong, indeed, that no philologer could examine all three without believing them to have sprung from some common source, which, perhaps, no longer exists,"[1] and he went on to suggest that "the Gothick" and "the Celtick" are also descended from the same source.

[1]Holger Pedersen. *The Discovery of Language*, trans. by J. W. Spargo. Indiana University Press, 1962, p. 18.

The study of Oriental and African languages continues up to the present to be a major preoccupation of British linguists. It is worth pointing out, however, that although this insight of Sir William Jones pointed the way to the great nineteenth-century development of Indo-European comparative philology and of the general principles of comparative linguistics, British linguists played a relatively minor role in these developments.

The British are reputed to be more concerned with practical things — with applications — than with theories. The elaboration of consistent theories about the nature and working of language in general, and about the principles of language analysis and description, was for long left to Continental (and, later, to American) scholars.

It was not until 1944 that the first chair of general linguistics was founded in Britain — appropriately enough at the School of Oriental and African Studies of the University of London. The first holder of the chair was J. R. Firth, a scholar who had a profound influence on the recent development of linguistic theory in Britain. Firth had a strong historical sense and was keenly aware of the development of linguistic studies in Britain. He himself pointed out that in the nineteenth and early twentieth centuries major British contributions to linguistics were in the fields of *lexicography* (the making of dictionaries), in *dialectology*, and, above all, in *phonetics*.[2] The monumental *New English Dictionary*, initiated by the London Philological Society in 1879 and later known as the *Oxford Dictionary*, set a new standard in lexicography; Joseph Wright's *English Dialect Dictionary* is another example, and one which links lexicography and dialectology.

The traditional British interest in phonetics is an important and characteristic component of linguistics in Britain even today. An interest in the sounds of speech has a long history in Britain, going back at least to the sixteenth century. Most of the earlier writers were chiefly concerned with describing the pronunciation of the English of their time, but some had wider interests, and it is interest-

[2]John R. Firth. *Papers in Linguistics, 1934–1951*. Oxford University Press, 1958, p. 92.

ing to note that Jones, the great Orientalist, was also interested in phonetics and the problems of transcribing and transliterating Asian languages.

A more general approach to the study of speech-sounds — a general phonetics — was developed in Britain during the nineteenth century. Among the leaders in this development were a remarkable Scottish family of speech teachers — the Bells — and Henry Sweet.

Alexander Melville Bell, the son of an Edinburgh specialist in speech correction, lectured on elocution at the University of Edinburgh in the mid-nineteenth century, and later in London. In 1867 he published a book entitled *Visible Speech, the Science of Universal Alphabetics*, a pioneering work on general phonetics. His son Alexander Graham Bell followed his father in the family profession; he emigrated to Canada in 1870 and in 1872 to the United States, where he is best known for his invention of the telephone. Both Melville and Graham Bell influenced Henry Sweet, who by the end of the nineteenth century was a specialist in phonetics with an international reputation, but scant recognition from his own university, Oxford. In 1902 Sweet, in a letter to the vice-chancellor of Oxford University, described his own subject, phonetics, as "one which is useless by itself, while at the same time it is the foundation of all study of language, whether theoretical or practical." This statement of Sweet's is important, since it expresses well a view which is still current in British linguistics: the importance of a thorough practical and theoretical knowledge of phonetics as the essential basis of all linguistic study.

J. R. Firth was very much in sympathy with some of these British traditions. He was deeply interested in Oriental languages — he had lived and worked in India and was influenced by the linguistic theories of the ancient Indian grammarians; and he believed that a thorough knowledge of phonetics was essential to the development of linguistic theory and linguistic description.

I can do no more here than outline some of the more characteristic features of Firth's theory of language: these include his insistence on what he called "the sociological component" in linguistic studies; his theory of *meaning*; his analysis of language in terms of *levels* and of *structure* and *system*; and, finally, his *phonological* theory.

Firth was deeply influenced by the Polish-British anthropologist Bronislaw Malinowski. Malinowski had found, in dealing as an anthropologist with the languages of remote preliterate peoples, special problems in translation. It was necessary, he found, to place words in the context of the whole utterance in its situation, in, as he put it, "the *context of situation . . .* which indicates on the one hand that the conception of *context* has to be broadened and on the other that the *situation* in which words are uttered can never be passed over as irrelevant to the linguistic expression."[3]

Firth adopted the term "context of situation" but, characteristically, he gave it a more general, more abstract, meaning. For Malinowski, the context of situation was the actual physical environment of an utterance. For Firth, it was a "field of relations" — relations between persons playing a role in society, the words they utter, and other objects, events, and so on, to which they are related.

The distinction between physical environment and the Firthian context of situation can be illustrated by imagining the following situation: Dr. John Robinson, physician, aged 37, enters the bedroom of a patient, Mrs. Elizabeth Smith, at 17 Main Street, Newtown, at 4:30 P.M. on December 17, 1967, and says, "How are we today?" It would be possible to go on describing this situation in more and more detail. But for purposes of linguistic description we *abstract* from the concrete, physical situation only those elements relevant to the utterance "How are we today?" These relevant elements constitute the *context of situation* for that utterance, and they do *not* include such details as the specific identity of the participants (Dr. Robinson and Mrs. Smith), the specific location, the time, and so on. They do include two *participants*, one of them a *doctor* and the other a *patient*, since the use of "we" in addressing someone is peculiar to speech in the doctor-patient relation — and so on.

For Firth, language had to be studied as part of the social process, as "a form of human living, rather than merely a set of arbitrary signs and signals." These words are taken from an article published shortly before Firth's death in 1960; but he had been emphasizing

---

[3]Bronislaw Malinowski. "The Problem of Meaning in Primitive Languages." Supplement I in C. K. Ogden and I. A. Richards, *The Meaning of Meaning*. New York; first published 1923, p. 306.

the importance of looking at language as a social phenomenon since the 1930s. In the same article he goes on to say, "As we go through life we have to learn our various forms of language in stages as conditions of our incorporation into our social organization. We do not mix up our roles and the various forms of language assigned to them in a kind of general mixed stew. Effective action and good manners require appropriateness of language in situational context. This leads to the adoption of the notion of *restricted languages*." And he goes on to point out that "the social person collects a varied repertory of interlocking roles without conflict or serious disharmony. . . . For the purposes of linguistics such a person would be regarded as being in command of a constellation of restricted languages."[4]

The Firthian concept of "restricted languages" related to the numerous roles played by the individual in society is an important one. The concept of a "whole language" is so vast and nebulous that we often cannot make use of it in linguistic studies. By relating any corpus of language material we may be studying to the social roles in which it is used we can justify our description of it as language. Firth criticized logicians for being apt to think of words and propositions as somehow having "meaning" in themselves, apart from participants in a context of situation. "I suggest," he says, "that voices should not be entirely dissociated from the social complex in which they function, and that therefore all texts in modern spoken languages should be regarded as having 'the implication of utterance,' and be referred to typical participants in some generalized context of situation."[5]

Firth's theory of meaning is a highly original and personal one; but perhaps the most striking thing about it is, simply, that it exists. The great American linguist Leonard Bloomfield took the view that the study of *meaning* is not a legitimate part of linguistics — that statements of the meanings of linguistic forms are the province of other sciences. After the publication of Bloomfield's book, *Language*, in 1933, this view was generally accepted in the United States, and it

[4]John R. Firth, "The Treatment of Language in General Linguistics," *The Medical Press*, August 19, 1959, p. 146.
[5]Firth. *Papers*, p. 226.

is only within the last few years that American linguists have begun again to make a systematic study of meaning within linguistic science.

In the 1930s Firth accepted the fact that linguistics is concerned with meaning, and by the 1950s was stating or implying that the statement of meaning is a major purpose of linguistics.

For Firth, meaning was the total network of relations or functions into which any linguistic item enters. "I propose to split up meaning or function," he said in 1935, "into a series of component functions. Each function will be defined as the use of some language form or element in relation to some context. Meaning, that is to say, is to be regarded as a complex of contextual relations, and phonetics, grammar, lexicography, and semantics each handles its own components of the complex in its appropriate context."[6] In a much later work, "A Synopsis," he explained: "To make statements of meaning in terms of linguistics, we first accept language-events as wholes and as repetitive and interconnected, and then we propose to apply theoretical schemata consisting of a framework of categories. . . . The 'meaning' in this sense is dealt with at a mutually congruent series of levels, sometimes in a descending order beginning with the context of situation and proceeding through *collocation*, syntax . . . to phonology and phonetics and sometimes in the opposite order."[7] Though he went on to talk about the "analytic dispersion of the statement of meaning at a series of levels," he was not implying that one must necessarily work through all the levels or that one must necessarily begin at one particular level. All these levels are abstractions and they are connected only by the fact that they all relate to the same bit of language. The only theoretical requirement is that the statements of meaning at the different levels be congruent and complementary.

We can give a clearer summary of Firth's view of meaning by making explicit a distinction inherent in his theory. The relations into which language items enter are of two kinds: *internal or formal*; and *situational*. *Formal* relations are those between one formal item

[6]*Ibid.*, p. 19.
[7]"A Synopsis of Linguistic Theory, 1930–1955." In John R. Firth, ed., *Studies in Linguistic Analysis*. Oxford University Press, 1957, p. 8.

and another, for example the relation between lexical items in collocation, or the syntactical relations between grammatical categories; the relation between terms in a grammatical system; the relations between one phonological unit and another; and so on. *Situational* relations are those between language items and nonverbal constituents of the situation.

Since language items enter into both types of *relationship*, they may be said to have both formal and situational *meanings*.

Collocation is one of the levels at which statements of formal meaning may be made. By *collocation*, Firth meant the habitual or characteristic associations of words in texts. Thus the word *cow* characteristically collocates with the verb *to milk*. In "A Synopsis," Firth said: "It can safely be stated that part of the 'meaning' of *cows* can be indicated by such collocations as *They are milking the cows, Cows give milk*. The words *tigresses* or *lionesses* are not so collocated and are already clearly separated in meaning at the collocational level."[8] Collocation is a purely formal relation: the fact that *cows* collocates with *milk* and that *tigresses* does not is thus part of the formal meaning of *cows* and *tigresses*. This is quite different from their situational meaning, which is their relationship to particular nonverbal constituents of situations, namely, particular kinds of animals.

Meaning at the grammatical level is another facet of formal meaning: it is essentially the "value" that any grammatical item or grammatical category acquires from its relationship to other items or categories, thus: "A singular in a two-number system has a different grammatical meaning from a singular in a three-number system or a four-number system such as in Fijian, which formally distinguishes singular, dual, 'little' plural, and 'big' plural."[9]

Firth would declare himself in a similar way about meaning at the phonological level: the "meaning" or a vowel, say [i], in a three-vowel system [i-a-u], is different from the "meaning" of the same vowel in a five-vowel system [i-e-a-o-u].

These "meanings" which language items acquire from their

[8]*Ibid.*, pp. 11–12. It should perhaps be added that the term which most often corresponds to *collocation* in American linguistics is *co-occurrence*.
[9]Firth. *Papers*, p. 227.

associations with other items are all examples of formal meaning. Situational meaning, on the other hand, is essentially what is most commonly regarded as "meaning": namely, the relationships between language items or categories and those elements *outside* the language in the situations in which language mediates between human participants in a social situation. It is not only lexical and grammatical items which have situational meanings. Phonological and phonetic features, and even orthographic features, may have a certain situational meaning. For example, the word *labor* written with-*or* rather than-*our* has a situational meaning even at the orthographic level: it means, in effect, "there's an American somewhere in the situation, either as author, reader, editor, or publisher."

In discussing meaning I have mentioned the "meaning" that language items derive from their membership in a system. The notion that language is *systemic* — is built up of systems of terms which supply each other with values derived solely from their mutual relationships — was basic to the European structural linguistics which developed in the 1920s and 1930s, largely on the basis of the work of the great Swiss linguist, Ferdinand de Saussure.

Firth made explicit for both grammar and phonology a useful distinction not always observed by European "structuralists" — namely, the distinction between *structure* and *system*.

Structure is a syntagmatic ordering of elements; systems are the paradigmatic sets of units which can replace each other at any place, or element, in a structure. In simpler terms, structures may be thought of as a "horizontal" ordering of elements; systems, as a "vertical" set of terms or units which can occur at any given place in structure. Thus, in phonology, C_1VC_2 (initial consonant–vowel–final consonant) is a *structure*, exemplified in English by such words as *pit, bit, pin, pen*; whereas the sets of specific consonantal or vocalic units which may occur at C_1, V, or C_2 are systems (thus in English we have a system of initial consonants: p, b, t, d, k, g, . . . ; a system of vowels: i, e, æ, . . .).

Firth was careful to point out that "elements of structure, especially in grammatical relations, share a mutual expectancy in an *order* which is not merely a *sequence*."[10] By this he meant that a gram-

[10]Firth. "Synopsis," p. 17.

matical structure, such as *SVO* (subject–verb–object) does not necessarily imply a specific sequence in time. In English, the grammatical relations implied by the structure *SVO* are, as it happens, most frequently expressed by the occurrence of subject, verb, and object, in that temporal sequence, as in *The boy loves the girl*. In some other languages, however, temporal sequence is much less closely related to structural "order." Thus, in Latin, the grammatical relations implied by *SVO* are the same whether one says *puer amat puellam*, *puer puellam amat*, or *amat puellam puer*. To use a term which has recently become rather popular in linguistics, Firth was careful to distinguish at the grammatical level between "deep structure" — which he called "structure" — and "surface structure," which was often simply the temporal sequence of linguistic units.

Firth's approach to phonology was equally original. It was characterized by two particular features, the "polysystemic" and the "prosodic." He distinguished between structure and system in phonology; but in doing so he rejected the theory of *phonemes*. He was, of course, perfectly familiar with the phoneme theory, which had been actively taught under Daniel Jones at University College in London starting about 1920; and Firth himself had been a lecturer there. What he objected to was, first, the idea that one could set up a *single* system of phonemes for the description of a language, and, second, that *all*, or almost all, the distinctive phonic features of a language had to be assigned to single segmental places.

The first objection arose from considerations such as this: In many languages the total number of segmental sounds which can occur at one place in structure is quite different from the number which can occur at another. In Javanese, for instance, there is a total alternance, a system, of eleven stop and affricate consonants in word-initial position — /p b t d ṭ ḍ tj dj k g ʔ/. In word-final position, however, only four stops occur — /p t k ʔ/. Then-current phoneme theory demanded that each of these four final consonants should be regarded as positional variants, or allophones, of some four, though it is not clear which four, of the eleven initial consonants. This led to problems in phoneme theory, necessitating the invention of "neutralisation" and "archiphonemes"; moreover, in Firth's view, assignment of the four final consonants to four of the others was unjustifiable. No term in an eleven-term system can have the same "value" as a term in a four-term system.

Firth's solution was simply to set up as many systems of *phonematic units*, as he called them, as there was need. Having first determined what structures occurred, one could then discover at what places in structure a different system had to be set up. This, then, was the *polysystemic* aspect of Firth's phonology.

Firth's second objection arose from the observation that, quite often, more economical statements could be made by abstracting from the phonic data of an utterance features which could be more than one segment in length. These he called *prosodies*. Phonological description was thus in terms of *structures* within which operated two types of element: systems of *phonematic units*, and *prosodies*. The domain of a prosody might be part of a syllable, a syllable, a word, a phrase, a sentence. Thus, in English, for instance, *intonation* has a prosody of phrase or sentence; in Thai, however, it has a sentence prosody, and *length, tone*, and *stress* have syllable prosodies. Often, a distinctive articulatory feature might be abstracted as a prosody, reducing the number of phonematic units. Russian, for instance, is traditionally described in terms of 5 vowel phonemes and 32 consonant phonemes: 12 of these 32 consonants are palatalized, that is, sounds like [p'æ] as opposed to [pa], [t'æ] as opposed to [ta], and so on. If we consider only the full system of consonantal sounds occurring initially and intervocalically, we can reduce the number of segmental units to 20 phonematic units, plus a single prosody of palatalization. The domain of this prosody is about half a syllable on either side of the consonant: consequently it affects a preceding or following vowel. Thus the Russian phonematic structure *dada* sounds like [dadə], while the same structure, with palatalization prosody superimposed $\left(\begin{smallmatrix} y...y \\ dada \end{smallmatrix} \right)$ sounds like [djædjə].

The brilliant and original ideas of Firth were often expressed in a language which was not crystal clear, and this is one reason why his influence was greatest on those who were his colleagues or students at the School of Oriental and African Studies. Linguistics in Britain today owes much to Firth, though few British linguists can now be said to practise a fully Firthian linguistics. Nevertheless, an interest in the sociological component of language, in restricted languages, in theories of meaning, in the distinction between structure and system, and in the acceptance of phonological theories in which the phoneme is not the only or the major unit — these are all character-istic of current British linguistics. The Firthian influence has been felt not only in theoretical linguistics but also in various fields of applied linguistics, such as translation theory and language teaching, where the idea of restricted languages and the Firthian view of meaning and of polysystemic and prosodic phonology have proved useful.

21 THE PRAGUE SCHOOL OF LINGUISTICS

Paul L. Garvin

To be invited to contribute a chapter on the Prague School to the current volume is a happy event for me, since Prague is a part of my background, though America is now my home. Thus my experience bridges Europe and America, just as nowadays the ideas of the Prague School can also be said to unite the linguistics of Europe and the United States.

Although I was raised in Czechoslovakia and spent my first university year in Prague, I did not become acquainted with the Prague School of linguistics until after I had arrived in the United States. At the time, Roman Jakobson, who is now a professor at Harvard and whom I had previously known in Sweden, encouraged me to take up linguistics and to enroll as his student at the École libre des hautes études in New York. The linguistics with which I was presented by Jakobson was of the Prague School variety. My contact with him was, however, not limited to linguistics. It introduced me to a group of exiled European intellectuals who, before the war, had been closely connected with the linguists of the Prague School. Having recently arrived from Europe myself, it gave me a nostalgic feeling of still belonging to the intellectual world of middle Europe of the late 1930s.

As I came to know more about linguistics and became closer acquainted with the work of the Prague School, I learned that my personal experience was not accidental: the impressions that I received during my casual contacts in New York turned out to reflect a typical characteristic of the Prague School. Unlike many other currents in linguistics, the Prague School is truly representative of the intellectual currents of its heyday, the 1930s. It was closely integrated into the intellectual life of its own country, which, as I remember from boyhood, in those days delighted in calling itself the "heart of Europe." As a major school of thought in linguistics, it was also part of a significant international development with echoes in a number of European countries. Its roots were not only domestic but also international: Jakobson, who had introduced me to the Prague School, is a Russian, and so were several other prominent representatives of this school of thought; others were Dutch and French. But the center of the Prague School was undoubtedly Prague.

This close integration of a group of linguists into the general intellectual climate of its time and place is quite remarkable from the vantage point of American linguistics. In this country, it is only quite recently that linguistics as a field has become better known and accepted by the general intellectual public. Until recently, linguists in America were a relatively small and isolated group trying to introduce new principles into the field of language study against very strong opposition from more traditional-minded students of language. While the linguists of the Prague School had their share of disputes with traditionalists, the isolation which was so characteristic for American linguists was lacking in Prague. The reason for this difference in the relation of linguists to their intellectual environment lies partially in the difference between the intellectual climates of Europe and the United States. In my opinion, it is in large measure also due to the differences in theoretical orientation between the Prague School and the prevailing currents in American structural linguistics. Unlike the earlier trend of American descriptivism, which is a further development of the work of Leonard Bloomfield (and also unlike the more recent, strongly model-oriented trends such as transformational theory), the Prague School approach to the study of language is characterized by a very strong emphasis on study of the functions of language. This emphasis on function includes both the function of language in the act of communication and the role of language in society, the function of language in literature and the problem of the different aspects and levels of language from a functional standpoint. It has brought with it a deepening and broadening of the interest in functionally significant problem areas in the study of language. The major areas of activity of the Prague School include the following: phonology, which is the study of the functional significance of the sound pattern within the over-all system of a language; the concept of functional sentence-perspective, which is a functionally oriented approach to the linguistic interpretation of the problem of style; the study of the esthetic function of language and its role in literature and the verbal arts; the study of the role of the standard language in modern society.

Aside from phonology, which is part of a world-wide development within linguistics, these functional areas of study have received much less attention by other schools of thought in linguistics outside Prague. Not unexpectedly, the nonphonological work of the Prague School is also much less well known among linguists elsewhere than is their phonological work.

I shall first discuss the concept of the functions of language held by the Prague School and then survey the application of their functional point of view to various aspects of linguistic study.

The most advanced and complete discussion of the functional theory of language in the 1930s was that by the Austrian psychologist Karl Bühler, who in his work on the psychology of language is considered a member of the Prague School. Bühler's basic conception is called by him "the organon model of language," using the Greek word for tool as a technical term to indicate a view that language, which is a system of signs, functions as a tool by means of which the one tells the other about things. This is in line with Buhler's philosophy of science, that of phenomenology. This conception stresses the importance of the situation in viewing an object of study. In the case of language, this means that in order to understand the function of language as a tool, it must be viewed in terms of the three basic factors of the speech situation in which it is used: the speaker, the hearer, and the things — in Buhler's terminology, the objects and "states of fact" — that are talked about. The linguistic sign is correlated with these three factors: it is correlated to the speaker, it is correlated to the hearer, and it is correlated to the objects and states of fact talked about. "Correlation" here means that if there is any variation introduced in the speaker, the linguistic sign will vary correspondingly; likewise, if there is any variation introduced in the hearer, the linguistic sign will vary; if there is any variation in the objects and states of fact talked about, the linguistic sign will vary with it. These correlations are considered by Bühler to be the basic functions of language. The correlation between sign and speaker is the expressive function; the correlation between sign and hearer is the appeal function; and the correlation between sign and states of fact talked about is the representative function.

Bühler's conception of the three functions was accepted by many important linguists of the Prague School. Most prominent among these was N. S. Trubetzkoy, who is known for his work in the field of phonology. His fundamental approach to the study of sound patterns takes into account the three functions. He distinguishes two major aspects of phonological study: the study of the role of speech sounds in carrying out the representative function of language, and the study of their role in carrying out the other two functions, namely the expressive and the appeal functions. The former field of study he calls *Phonologie*, a term which corresponds almost exactly to the current American term "phonemics." The second field of study is called phonostylistics. Most of Trubetzkoy's work is concerned with phonemics rather than phonostylistics. His fundamental conception of the role of sound patterns in language is that they serve to differentiate meaningful speech units from each other, without themselves necessarily being carriers of meaning. Thus, the minimal unit of the phonological pattern, the phoneme, is defined by its participation in the representative function — by its property of serving to distinguish different carriers of the representative function from each other. The basic concept in interpreting the functioning of phonemes in language is that of "phonological opposition": the critical audible differences by means of which phonemes are distinguished from each other and consequently are in turn capable of differentiating meaningful speech units. The classical American example of a phonemic difference illustrates the

Trubetzkoyan concept of the phoneme and the phonological opposition: in the two examples *pit* and *bit*, the initial consonants *p* and *b* are considered different phonemes because they serve to differentiate two meaningful speech units — in this case, words — from each other. They in turn are distinguishable from each other by means of the phonological opposition of voice: /b/ is voiced, /p/ is voiceless.

Trubetzkoy's work dealt largely with the discussion of the different types of phonological oppositions that he either considered logically possible or had observed in the languages of the world. Another important area in which the Prague School has applied and developed its functional point of view is in the differentiation of grammar from the study of style. The most prominent scholar in this area was Vilem Mathesius, who developed and applied the concept of functional sentence-perspective in his work on his own language, Czech, as well as on English and some other of the major European languages. This work has found a strong echo among the Prague School linguists, and Mathesius has a significant following to this day.

The essence of Mathesius' conception is the following: every act of speech is structured not in one but in two different ways. One structuring is given by the grammatical pattern of the sentence. Another structuring, which is not identical with the grammatical, is provided by what Mathesius calls "the information-bearing structure of the utterance." These are two different ways in which a language is capable of manifesting its functions. Mathesius thus describes the difference between the two types of structuring:

> The information-bearing structure of the sentence should be considered in opposition to its formal structure. Whereas the formal structure concerns the way in which a sentence is composed of grammatical elements, the information-bearing structure concerns the way in which a sentence is integrated into the factual situation during which it was produced. The basic elements of the formal structure of the sentence are the grammatical subject and the grammatical predicate, the basic elements of the information-bearing structure are the foundation of the utterance — whatever in a given situation is known or at least obvious and thus forms a point of

233

departure for the speaker — and the core of the utterance, that is, whatever the speaker affirms about the foundation of the utterance or in terms of it.[1]

(The terms "foundation" and "core" are replaced in current English writings of the Prague linguists by the classical terms "theme" and "rheme" respectively.) A very common form of expression of functional sentence-perspective in the languages of the world is word order. In ordinary unemphatic speech, the theme occurs first and the rheme follows after it. In the case of languages such as English in which word order has a grammatical function (that of differentiating subject from object), the word order required for functional sentence-perspective is achieved by using different grammatical ways of expression, such as the active as opposed to the passive voice. Thus, the active sentence *Professor Mathesius wrote this book on functional sentence-perspective* is differentiated from the passive sentence *This book on functional sentence-perspective was written by Professor Mathesius* in terms of different functional sentence-perspective. In the active sentence, *Professor Mathesius* is theme and *this book on functional sentence-perspective* is rheme, while in the passive sentence *this book on functional sentence-perspective* is theme and *Professor Mathesius* is rheme. One simple way of becoming aware of the theme and rheme of an utterance is to phrase the question to which this utterance would be a likely answer. The theme would be a definite nominal element of the question, and the rheme would be asked for by a question pronoun. Thus, to *Professor Mathesius wrote this book on functional sentence-perspective* corresponds the question "What did Professor Mathesius write?" *This book on functional sentence-perspective was written by Professor Mathesius* corresponds to the question "Whom was this book on functional sentence-perspective written by?"

While the study of functional sentence-perspective deals with the manner in which language manifests the three functions posited by

[1]Vilem Mathesius. "O tak zvaném aktuálním členení věty" ["On the So-Called Information-Bearing Structure of the Sentence"]. *Slovo a slovesnost*, V (1939), 171–174; reprinted in Vilem Mathesius, *Čeština a obecný jazykozpyt* [*The Czech Language and General Linguistics*] Prague, 1948.

Karl Bühler, another important aspect of the work of the Prague School concerns an additional, fourth, function of language which is not found in Bühler's writing. This is the work of the Prague School on esthetics and literary structure. This aspect of the work of the Prague School was pursued most intensively in the 1930s and early 1940s; its most outstanding representative in those days was Jan Mukařovský. The basic concept introduced into the study of esthetics and literary structure is that of the esthetic function. Mukařovský's conception of the esthetic function is approximately as follows:

Every object or action, language included, can be assigned a practical function — utilitarian for tools, communicative for language, and so on. If, however, an object or action becomes the focus of attention for its own sake and not for the sake of the practical function it serves, it is said to have an esthetic function; that is, it is responded to for what it is and not for what it is for. Thus, the esthetic function as such is not limited to works of art and literature but can appear in connection with any object or action. It comes about by virtue of what I have translated as "foregrounding," as opposed to automatization.

Automatization refers to the stimulus normally expected in a social situation; foregrounding — in Czech *aktualisace* — refers on the other hand to a stimulus not culturally expected in a social situation and hence capable of provoking special attention. To paraphrase a linguistic example given by Bohuslav Havránek:[2] If we translate the well-known Russian greeting *zdravstvuyte* into English by its functional equivalent *good morning*, *good afternoon*, or *good evening*, it will pass unnoticed as the normal greeting under the circumstances. If, on the other hand, we translate it literally as *be well*, it might still be understood as some kind of a greeting — that is, it might retain its communicative function — but it will in addition provoke special notice of some sort, perhaps causing some bewilderment about the intent of the translator or being interpreted as trying to convey the impression of a foreign environment. The free translation thus

[2]In Paul L. Garvin, ed., *A Prague School Reader on Esthetics, Literary Structure, and Style*. Selected and translated from the original Czech, Georgetown University Press, 1964, p. 9.

constitutes an automatization; the literal translation is an instance of foregrounding in which the wording itself, rather than the communicative content of the message, is responded to, and it is this property of stimulating a response in terms of itself that constitutes the esthetic function.

In regard to language, Jan Mukařovský refers to foregrounding as "the esthetically intentional distortion of the linguistic components."[3] To put this statement into its proper framework, we must understand that the scholars of the Prague School are followers of the Swiss linguist Ferdinand de Saussure. In the latter's conception, the linguistic pattern — *la langue* — is both a system of signs and a set of social norms. As a system of signs, the pattern has a certain flexibility allowing for variations within the units and in the choice and arrangement of units to the extent that it does not conflict with the requirement of intelligibility. As a set of norms, the pattern is more rigidly circumscribed in terms of the cultural preference for, and statistical frequency of, these allowable variations. Mukařovský's "distortion" is thus distortion of the pattern insofar as it is social norm, but still within the bounds of the pattern insofar as it is a system of signs, since the distorted, foregrounded units stem from the same system as their automatized counterparts or are borrowed into it and in terms of it.

The esthetic function is not limited to works of art and literature. What characterizes art and literature, as opposed to the random foregrounding which may occur in any social situation, is, in Mukařovský's words:

> the consistency and systematic character of foregrounding. The consistency manifests itself in the fact that the reshaping of the foregrounded components within a given work occurs in a stable direction; thus, the deautomatization of meanings in a certain work is consistently carried out by lexical selection (the mutual interlarding of contrasting areas of the lexicon), in another equally consistently by the uncommon semantic relationship of words close together in the context. Both procedures result in a foregrounding of meaning, but differently for each. The systematic foregrounding of components in a work of poetry consists in

[3] *Ibid.*, p. 18.

the gradation of the interrelationships of these components, that is, in their mutual subordination and superordination. The component highest in the hierarchy becomes the dominant. All other components, fore-grounded or not, as well as their interrelationships, are evaluated from the standpoint of the dominant. The dominant is that component of the work which sets in motion, and gives direction to, the relationships of all other components.[4]

As an instance of the dominant in poetry, Mukařovský gives what he calls the "prosodic line" of a poem, that is, the selection of the pro-sodic features, such as stress and intonation, that characterize a particular work of poetry. He shows how this prosodic line in Czech poetry is interdependent with word order. To demonstrate his thesis, he points out how, when the word order in a poem by a given Czech author is changed, without disturbing either rhyme or meter, the result is nevertheless a prosodic line that is characteristic of an entirely different poet.

Finally, there is an additional important area of research on which the functional point of view of the Prague School has been brought to bear. This is the study of the role of language in social differentiation. Here the function of language is studied not in terms of the speech situation, as it was by Bühler, but in terms of the social setting of the speech pattern as a whole. That is, study concerns what one might call the "sociological function" of language — its function of serving different strata of society.

The strongest concentration of Prague School work in this con-nection has been on the study of the standard language and its role in modern urban society, as in Europe.

The major principles of the Prague School approach to the question were formulated in the early 1930s. The scholars who con-tributed most to this formulation were B. Havránek and Mathesius. Their principles can be summed up as follows: A standard language can tentatively be defined as a codified form of language, accepted by and serving as a model for a larger speech community. The two basic properties the Prague School attributes to a standard language are flexible stability and intellectualization. The former is a goal to

[4]*Ibid.*, p. 20.

237

be achieved, an ideal property: a standard language, in order to function efficiently, must be stabilized by appropriate codification; it must at the same time be flexible enough in its codification to allow for modification in line with culture change. Intellectualization can be characterized as a tendency toward increasingly more definite and accurate expression, or, more specifically, as a tendency toward greater relational systematization and explicitness of statement, the former involving the grammar, the latter the lexicon.

The standard language is, in the Prague School conception, opposed to folk speech, which is the term applied to speech patterns not subject to codification. In addition to a study of the principles of language standardization, the Prague School has also been strongly interested in the interplay between the standard language and folk speech, particularly in the study of mixed speech patterns which contain elements from both sources.

Although the peak in the development of the Prague School was reached in the late 1930s, the theoretical frame of reference they have provided for the functional study of language remains important to this day. Roman Jakobson has developed many of his highly original ideas from a basis in Prague School thought and has brought much of this orientation with him to the United States; he has since been pursuing his own directions of thought. In Prague itself, linguistics continues to occupy an important place in the intellectual life of the city, and of the country as well, and linguists are not only attempting to keep abreast of international trends in linguistics but are also continuing to develop and spread internationally their own linguistic tradition. If I am enthusiastic about the work of the Prague School, I am so because that work has had a significant influence on my own thinking in linguistics. I find their basic concentration on the concept of function particularly productive, both for the theoretical interpretation of language phenomena and for the development of methods of linguistic analysis.

Steadily growing attention to function, widespread interest in the works of such scholars as Mathesius, Trubetzkoy, Vachek, and Trnka, even the detail that a prominent society of American linguists calls itself a "circle," as did the Prague group — all testify to the fact that American linguistics also finds Prague School approaches and principles productive.

22 AMERICAN SCHOOLS OF LINGUISTICS
(Other Than Generative-Transformational)

Eric P. Hamp

In this chapter I want to give a sense of the diversity of themes that characterize the current American scene in the field of linguistics. Some of these themes are implicit in other chapters of this book. The scholars presenting these topics — all of them Americans and practicing linguists — naturally deal with their material according to the theoretical views they themselves find defensible. At the risk of some repetition, I will not hesitate to highlight those aspects of material covered elsewhere that contribute to an understanding of the diversity of the field of linguistics in the United States today.

Furthermore, I omit from consideration one very important theme of current linguistics — generative-transformational theory. This large topic of very active current concern is treated separately in Chapter 24. Let us take a look, then, at trends other than the generative-transformational in current American linguistics.

Since the late 1940s scholars in other countries have tended to think of linguistics in America as a rather monochrome school, subscribing to a single set of premises, assumptions, and provisional results. No matter what the situation that gave rise to this impression, nothing could be farther from the truth today. Not only are there a wide variety of views; among specialists who share a basic point of approach there is also considerable divergence beyond their common ground and in the emphases and consequences they draw from the common ground. Moreover, it must be stressed that many of these

239

viewpoints are not exclusively American, but are shared by workers elsewhere in the world.

Thus, for the current American scene it is not accurate to speak of "schools" of linguistics in the traditional sense of the phrase; rather, there are characteristic themes which hold varying importance for different groups of scholars.

Perhaps the most important theme is one which divides all views into two sorts, taxonomic and nontaxonomic, to use terms that have recently gained currency. This distinction relates to the degree of importance attached by a scholar to our ability to assign portions of sentences we hear or read to discrete classes established by a given grammar of a language. The taxonomic view, in its extreme form, would insist that any linguistic feature be assigned its status and be classified solely on the basis of other audible or legible features which may be found in actual sentences together with the feature in question. A crude way of stating the taxonomic view is to say that all linguistic elements — both phonological and morphosyntactic — are to be classified by reference to the sounds they combine with. In this view, an English noun might perhaps be defined as a word found standing after the word *the* in a sentence in which it may be replaced by another word that also combines with a plural ending. One consequence often drawn from this view is the claim that an important aspect — or even the most important aspect — of linguistic behavior is the apperception by native speakers of elements and classes defined by this criterion. In such a view the speaking (or writing) human being is a highly sophisticated classifying mechanism, and cultures and languages are aggregates differing in their classification properties.

Nontaxonomic views do not necessarily resemble one another at all in their theoretical basis. A familiar instance of nontaxonomic theory is found in the traditional Western, or European-American, school-grammar on which many of us were raised and which is still frequently to be met with in our schools, despite repeated and differing criticism leveled at it by modern linguistics for the past four decades or so. This theory defines many of its grammatical relations on the basis of the supposed meaning, or content, or reference, or denotation, or designation of words. For example, "a noun is the name of a person, place, or thing." Of course, in many a sentence, such as *The singing of the chimera was beautiful*, one finds it insuperably difficult to decide whether *singing* is really a "thing," and whether a *chimera* for example is anything at all. In this view, the speaking human being is a mechanism that maps known logical and physical properties into sound; this would imply that all languages and cultures share the same internal structure, an implication that modern linguistics has rebelled against.

An entirely different nontaxonomic view places no emphasis on classification as such, and assigns status to members of sentences regardless of their appearance (or even nonappearance) in the sentence in question on the basis of abstract relations of strictly limited types which these members are found to bear to members of other sentences. Such a view plays an important role in generative grammar. Here the human being is viewed as a mechanism that produces, or generates, an indefinitely large number of different sentences. In this view, it remains to be shown whether or not all languages differ in or share some basic internal organization.

Linguistics in the United States has developed for more than a half-century in close association with anthropological studies. This association is an understandable reaction to the domination by traditional historical grammar in the study of the familiar languages of Western literature and of the classical cultures of Europe and Asia. This has colored the field of linguistics in several ways. An urgent and continually attractive problem for American anthropologists has been the study of the enormously varied cultures of the small residual numbers of American Indians. These groups still speak more than two hundred languages, though many will surely die out within a generation; the number of speakers of many of these languages was never large, and the urgency of the task has always been clear. An important consequence was the emphasis placed on problems and techniques of the collection of data — the activity which came to be known as "field methods." Many of the problems belonging properly to data collection were projected into the questions of analysis and presentation of results. On the other hand, theory construction in the absence of a large body of fresh data was characteristically viewed with suspicion. The extreme result of such views among some scholars was the rejection of the notion of constructing grammatical theories with explicatory aims, and the viewing of linguistic theory as frankly a method for rearranging data. Obviously, scholars sharing this point of view have differed considerably in the degree to which they have applied it in their work. But here we may see the source for the strong emphasis, which permeates so much of American work, on technique and method of compact statement; on meticulous formalism and on definitional purity. It is often thought that these habits of compressed, abstract statement and fondness for algebraic-looking symbols, which mark American linguists off from their humanistic (and anthropological) colleagues, derive from a preoccupation with mathematics, logic, or, more recently, computers. That is not so; these habits stem from the stress on elegance in rearranging anthropological data. Paradoxically, the abstract appearance of much American linguistic production comes from a desire to keep close to the observed facts gathered in the speech situation.

Another indirect result of the emphasis on data collection is the difference in outlook often referred to as "item–arrangement" and "item–process." Traditional grammar and the views of many scholars today depict a grammar as being supplied with a number, or inventory, of items (words, roots, sounds, and the like), and then applying processes to these items whereby they assume the shapes seen in sentences. The extreme form of the other view regards a grammar as being supplied with all the items actually seen in sentences, and then selecting from these the appropriate shapes by observing rules of arrangement, or distribution, without altering the shapes in so doing. The item–arrangement view — this latter one just mentioned — is doubtless closely related to the concern for not obscuring the basic data; it is another manifestation of the emphasis on an empirical approach, which shuns idealized forms that are considered not to occur as such in the raw data.

Still another recurrent theme stems from the history of the role of field data collection: namely, the debate on speech versus writing. Much of American linguistic scholarship insists that an adequate theory must recognize that speech is primary and writing secondary. The opposite view holds that language may occur in observed form both written and spoken, regardless of the history of traditions of writing. This difference in view at the same time reflects the outcome of yet another debate that I have already referred to: the rejection by modern linguistics of many positions taken by traditional school-grammar. Since that tradition favored classical and literary languages, it naturally favored written language; and it often mistook literary forms which were never spoken as being the preferred, correct, and only decent objects of study. Thus the rejection of written language has not necessarily been an end in itself (though it may have been for some scholars); but its rejection as a primary object of study reflects the attempt to rectify the more general error of emphasis. It is clear that one's approach to the analysis of written language will differ depending on whether one takes it to be necessarily secondary to, or on an equal footing with, the spoken form. On the other hand, a view of written language as not being subsidiary will alter some aspects of a theory of language change, for one must then treat with due prominence the intrusion of written forms into the spoken tradition.

The emphasis on data collection and consequently on the mode of arriving at an analysis which will not destroy, so to speak, the original data has led in another direction to a strong concern for making recoverable the steps whereby one arrives at the proposed analysis. This in turn has developed the doctrine of bi-uniqueness, which has occasioned much debate. "Bi-uniqueness" refers to the requirement not only that each symbol used in a transcription be convertible unambiguously in a given situation into the sound heard, but also that each fraction of sound, if heard clearly enough, be automatically assignable to one and only one symbol. Such a view greatly affects the status and definition of sound units; and various further doctrines — those of neutralization and the archiphoneme, for example — become possible or excluded depending on whether one rejects or accepts in a strong form the doctrine of bi-uniqueness. Not a few linguists contend that bi-uniqueness is not merely to be rejected, but is also technically impossible — it cannot be applied to real speech.

Still another consequence of the empirical approach has been the recurrent theme of rejection of language universals. All languages are to be analyzed in their own terms, without preconception; and therefore, a priori, anything is to be expected. Languages may thus differ unlimitedly. The opposite view claims that one must have some kind of expectation in order to approach the problem, and that linguists expect to find by successive confirmation universal features of language; that our most general starting theories include intuitions of these universals. The question of universals goes far beyond the consideration of linguists' preconceptions in approaching the analysis of a language or their construction of lists of features for an encyclopedic account of human language. It has an important bearing on how people learn languages and transmit their cultural tradition and on how bilinguals behave in situations of language contact.

There is currently much concern with the aims and form that a grammar must be supposed to have. The broadest claim has been that a grammar must enumerate and explain every sentence that may be said in the language. Any sentence, then, that may be spoken will be ipso facto grammatical, and thus very clear limits will be set for the characteristic of grammaticality. Others maintain that this is an unrealistic aim; that there is a twilight zone between grammatical and ungrammatical (or nongrammatical) that cannot be sharply delineated.

The notion of exhaustiveness has two decidedly different interpretations. One of the views just mentioned — the one that insists on accounting for every sentence that may be said — insists by implication that all future sentences (both uttered and possible) as well as recorded past sentences be accounted for grammatically. Another view contends that exhaustive accounting can be attempted only for past sentences — a given corpus of texts, as this body of sentences is sometimes called.

Then again, in lieu of determining the grammaticality of the competence of speakers, some contend that the realistic and more focused goal is the total pattern of the language, which will bring out its most prominent lines. This aim concentrates more on trying to highlight the most productive and noticeable features of a language, by one criterion or another, so that the search for exhaustiveness or predictiveness will not bury these main lines in detail. In this context, some linguists lay stress on the symmetrical, balanced characteristics linguistic structures often display. Some also view the role of a correct analysis as maximizing the statement of symmetries, and they see much historical change in languages as a process of filling gaps in temporary asymmetries.

Still others are less concerned with the form and aims of a grammar than with the idea that all thinkable approaches be dealt with even though not all resulting statements can be applied at once.

A further theme that has arisen in this connection is whether there may not be two different grammatical models that are applicable: one for the speaker and one for the hearer — that is, one that generates sentences and one that dismembers and classifies them. Against this is the contention that all normal persons are both hearers and speakers, and that therefore linguists must seek a model that embraces the total activity that switches back and forth. It has been further suggested that hearers "hear" and interpret by behaving in part as if they were speaking and then matching the result with the impulse actually received through the senses; if this is true, then there is strictly but one grammar.

A more specific theme which concerns the form of the grammar is the question of levels. Most agree that there is at least a duality in language: There are elements like words, usually with some sort of readily specified meaning (that is, morphemes, roots, stems, affixes, and the like), which are combined somehow into sentences, or clauses. And there are elements which build up the sounds whereby we can distinguish the words, or morphemes (that is, phonemes, phonological features, and the like). But there is disagreement whether these two spheres of integration are to be regarded as quite separate — analytically watertight — or whether criteria of the one apply in the discrimination of the elements of the other. One view claims that the spheres must be defined separately so that no definition risks being circular; such a view often claims also that thereby a sharper, cleaner focus is imparted to one's view of the machinery of language. A different view contends that the natural handling of language never makes distinctions on one level without clues from however many other levels coexist.

Moreover, there are those who will have more than two levels: Some have argued for the independence of a morphophonemic level, in addition to the phonemic and the morphosyntactic. Others regard morphophonemes as relational entities linking units in the phonemic and morphemic levels, but not themselves members of a self-consistent level. Two versions of a four-level model have been proposed: one with a lowest *phonic* level in addition to the phonemic, morphophonemic, and morphemic; the other splitting the morphemic level into two, one integrating morphemes into words and another building words into sentences. A five-level model has been proposed; it adds a semantic level to the others. No one seems to have suggested more than five levels.

The establishment of basic units of analysis for a language has occasioned a great deal of scholarly discussion. To some extent, such units depend for their status and definition on the number and nature of levels assumed; but they are also determined by intrinsic criteria. Opinions differ on the degree to which each kind of criterion applies. Within this debate the question of phonemes versus distinctive features has perhaps held a leading place and involves considerations both of the assumption or rejection of levels and of intrinsic properties. Not all linguists share the same view of distinctive features: For some, they are parameters defined by classes of phonemes; for others, they are the basic elements, and phonemes are complex units, bundles of distinctive features. A further conflict of assumption on these features of sound involves the question whether such features are general, universal, concretely phonetic features, a small number of which are found in all languages, or whether such *phonological features* (as they may also be called) are abstract features, drawn from such a universal set but specific to the language in question, and requiring further phonetic specification within the grammar of that language.

Along somewhat analogous lines the nature and status of morphemes, morphs, and morphophonemes have been intensely discussed. It has been asked whether one is related to the other by being made up of the other, or by representing the other; by relations of mapping, or by characterizing.

The doctrine known as *tagmemics* is an attempt to resolve some of the conflicts that arise from a rigid conception of levels and at the same time to bring out more flexibly the varying functions of the units of these restricted inventories — units assumed as basic in several theories just alluded to. It has long been noted that very different kinds of units or complexes of units may fill the same function, or be correlated in meaning, in a particular construction. In the tagmemic approach the correlation of a functional place, or *slot*, and its *filler* (that is, the class of items occupying the slot) is called a *tagmeme*. A slot is defined by privilege of occurrence in a larger tagmeme, or by class of fillers, or by semantic feature. Workers in this framework have now relaxed the earlier unnecessary restriction that a slot must have at least one filler which consists of a single morpheme; in many languages such things as verbs never occur without one or more affixes, and therefore could never themselves establish a syntactic slot with such a requirement, even though it would be natural to posit one in view of the rest of the syntax. Then there is a further debate on the insistence that a tagmeme is not a unit in the sense that other basic units are and that it is properly a relation among or a rule about units.

Another perennial theme has been the significance and role of distribution, or privilege of occurrence. This has led to two separate directions: The desire for abstract, formal definition has induced many scholars to attempt to define units extrinsically by criteria of distribution. In such discussions the classical notion of *syllable* has been pressed into service as a distributional unit in phonology; tagmemics has further placed its own interpretations on syllable organization. On the other hand, from such restrictions as one observes in distributional statements, others have sought descriptive economy and deeper explication by formulating the restrictions on occurrence as clues to redundancy.

The partitioning of syntactic structures into *immediate constituents* has long given rise to perplexity; experiments in mechanical translation have only served to underline the poor formulation of the problem. The doctrine of *string constituency* emphasizes that partitioning may be multiple and not binary. But constituents may also be discontinuous. Generative grammar has in particular addressed itself to the problems arising in giving a satisfying account of constituent structure.

The notion of *transformation* is not always used or understood in the

247

same sense: In addition to the conception basic to generative grammar, the term also applies to formulations which establish relations between already complete sentences.

The classical discipline of instrumental phonetics has neither stood still nor remained unaffected by theoretical currents. Although emphasis on field methods has lent prominence to unaided auditory techniques (often called *field phonetics*), sophisticated instrumental control has increased markedly in recent years. Just as phonological theory has introduced greater care in these applications borrowed from natural science, so instrumentation has imposed a healthy control on abstract theory. Scholars naturally differ in their emphasis on one or the other of these two modes.

The role of and approach to meaning in language is an important and vexatious theme of inquiry. Formerly, many American linguists, in a mood of strong rejection of traditional grammar and influenced by a rather extreme behavioristic position, viewed meaning with suspicion. This prevailing attitude has changed. But there are great differences among the hypotheses held. Some have said that meaning lies totally outside the linguistic system, that it is a sort of network between cultural systems; others say that it lies outside, but that linguistic meaning is ultimately a linguistic concern. Some feel that it is to be analyzed as a quite separate problem; others, that it must be constantly taken into consideration. For example, *idioms* have been called a part of grammar defined by criteria of productivity and semantic arbitrariness. Some of those who regard meaning as part of the linguistic structure regard it as merely another aspect of that many-faceted structure; others have assigned it a separate level, parallel to other levels. There is a general difficulty in successfully distinguishing subtle aspects of syntax (for example, animateness in English) from meaning (for example, the English terminology of politeness), and these from cultural value, or social use and situational difference. With the increased interest in and active debate on problems of meaning, a new common ground with the field of philosophy has been struck, and interest in an enlarging set of common problems has already emerged.

The themes of contemporary linguistics in the United States are various and sometimes intricately interwoven. In outlining those that have come to my attention as prominent, I have frequently sketched the extremist positions to put matters into bold relief. Scholars can be found whose views range all along the scale between these extremes, and no doubt some will be surprised at my compressions. But that is inevitable in the complex context of scholarly debate, where no views are immutable. And that is particularly as it should be in a lively field. I know of no American linguist who finds his scholarly life dull.

23 GLOSSEMATICS

Francis Whitfield

Thirty years ago, two Danish linguists — Louis Hjelmslev and Hans Jørgen Uldall — coined the term "glossematics" as the name for a new approach to the study of language which they had worked out in collaboration and which they saw as leading not only to a new kind of linguistics but, eventually, to a new organization of humanistic studies in general. Glossematics — the word is derived from the Greek *glōssa*, "a language" — was by no means the only term they coined. As their work progressed, they found that a number of new concepts demanded new names — or old names put to new uses — and their theory even acquired a certain notoriety because of its forbidding terminology. In spite of this, in the years just before World War II, glossematics became the subject of lively discussion at meetings of the Linguistic Circle of Copenhagen, where it had the benefit of detailed criticism from many different points of view. After the war, glossematic ideas came to be increasingly better known to scholars outside Denmark. In the United States — to take only one country — such linguists as Rulon Wells, Paul Garvin, Einar Haugen, and Sydney M. Lamb have made important contributions to international appreciation and criticism of glossematic theory.

Glossematics, then, is not to be thought of as a "Danish school" or a "Copenhagen school" of linguistics. Of course it is Danish in the sense that its progenitors are Danes — two more examples of how much the science owes to that small country that occupies such an amazingly pre-eminent place in the history of linguistics. It is also Danish in that it would be difficult to find a Danish linguist whose thinking has not been affected by it — even among those who have been most severely critical of it. But it is *not* Danish in any sense that would imply its being either a national monopoly or a provincial oddity. Even more important, it is not a "school," Danish or any other kind. I should be hard put to it to name anyone who considered himself a "glossematician." Those linguists who have taken a special interest in the theory and its applications simply do not think of themselves that way. Glossematics has neither a praetorian guard nor a priesthood sworn to the propagation of revealed truth. The reason is that, from the beginning, it was frankly proposed as a working hypothesis — something to be tested, not to be accepted on faith. And, from the beginning, it was recognized that by the very nature of the hypothesis, the work of verification would be a long one.

So far, I have been putting the emphasis on novelty. I have spoken of a new approach to language and the humanities, of new concepts, and of new terminology. There *is* a radical novelty about glossematic theory. Whoever studies it must be prepared for many surprises. But he should also be prepared to look behind the novelty and the surprises, particularly to see how glossematics actually returns to some age-old observations about language, how it tries to refine them, and how it tries to draw certain logical consequences from them. In this respect — despite the strangeness of its technical terms and despite its wholly justified claim that it proposes a revolutionary view of language — glossematics is one of the most traditional kinds of linguistics discussed in this book.

The most natural introduction to glossematics, then, begins with a sampling of the traditional observations that I have alluded to and then proceeds to show something of what glossematics does with them and with others of their kind. I shall almost entirely bypass such unfamiliar terms as are found in glossematic literature. Not that these terms are a superficial adornment — or disfiguration — of the theory; many of them would be practically indispensable in a more formal introduction than this one. But my first and most important purpose here is to show the general direction that glossematics follows in its investigation of language, and this can be done reasonably well without any special vocabulary.

The kind of traditional observations about language that can serve as an introduction to glossematics are reflected in all sorts of statements, definitions, and rules that most of us have encountered in ordinary school books when learning foreign languages or when studying the grammar of our own language. Some of them have become part of the common lore about languages in general, so that it would be impossible for anyone to remember where they originated. Take, for example, the distinction between vowel and consonant, which, in one formulation or another, reduces to the idea that a vowel can stand alone in a syllable while a consonant cannot stand in a syllable without an accompanying vowel. There are other rules from grammars of individual languages, for instance Latin: "An adjective agrees with its noun in gender, number and case"; "The prepositions *ā, ab, dē, cum, ex, ē, sine, prō, prae* are followed by the ablative case." They appear to be quite different kinds of statements. Some of them, like the distinction between consonant and vowel, seemed to lay claim to a general validity. Others obviously refer only to the particular language. Some are statements about sounds of speech or about letters of the written language. Others concern declension and conjugation, or the structure of phrases and sentences. They appear to be independent, unconnected nuggets of information.

Now glossematics begins by looking for a common element in these apparently quite different kinds of statements. It goes about this by first directing attention to the traditional concepts of grammatical agreement and government — concepts that have rightly been called the germs of glossematics. It tries to extend the application of these concepts, and it does so by analyzing them and by reformulating the traditional statements in a way that will reveal their fundamental similarities. Thus, instead of saying that the preposition *sine* is followed by the ablative case, one says, more precisely and, in a sense, more simply, "If *sine* is present in a phrase, then the ablative must also be present." One uses the same form of statement in describing grammatical agreement; for example, "If the accusative singular feminine form of an abjective is present in a certain construction, then a feminine noun in the accusative singular must also be present." And one can say, "If a consonant is present in a syllable, then a vowel must also be present"; a consonant, from this point of view, is seen to "govern" a vowel, just as a preposition governs a case.

These sample restatements are only rough approximations of the kind of formulas that glossematics uses, but they illustrate well enough a general form that will be found over and over again in glossematic descriptions and definitions: "If some element x is present in something, then some other element y must also be present." This kind of sentence is the cornerstone of glossematics, which deals at first with a very small number of possible relationships between elements — relationships that can all be expressed in simple terms. Another example: "If x is present in something, then y must also be present; and if y is present, then x must also be present." This is the form of statement one would use if, say, he were describing a language in which every syllable contained two elements — one that might be described from a phonetic point of view as a consonant, the other as a vowel. From a phonetic point of view only; such elements cannot be called consonants and vowels from a glossematic point of view. Glossematics uses the simple reformulations that I have talked about to *define* its elements. If "consonant" is defined as an element requiring the presence of a vowel in the same syllable, and "vowel" as an element not requiring the presence of any other element in the same syllable, then those terms cannot be used when describing a language in which no element can stand alone in a syllable and where, consequently, there are no vowels in the sense here given. And if there are no vowels, there cannot be any consonants either, since "consonant" is defined with the help of the term "vowel."

It certainly seems strange, at first, that a language might be said to have no vowels or consonants — especially strange, and even perverse, if one can plainly "hear" the vowels and consonants of the language when it is spoken. But such odd results of the glossematic approach are not at all hard to understand if one remembers that glossematics begins with certain relationships between elements and then proceeds to name the elements according to the relationships between them. All of its terms are defined in this way. Thus, it does not start by defining "vowels" as certain kinds of sounds and consonants as certain other kinds of sounds, and then talk about the distribution of those sounds within the syllables of a given language. Rather, it calculates the various possible relationships between the parts of a syllable. Parts that enter into certain definite relationships will be called vowels and consonants, whatever kinds of sounds may be involved. And it is up to the linguist who is studying any particular language to find out whether that language has consonants and vowels, as those terms have been defined. He may well discover that it does not.

At this point, the question that naturally arises is what conceivable advantage there can be in studying and describing languages in this way. What is to be gained from a method that frequently leads to such odd results and, at first view, may seem to be a mere playing with words? The first answer to this question in the literature of glossematics is that, if we succeed in applying such a method, we succeed at the same time in establishing an immanent linguistics, a linguistics that does not depend for its foundations on any other science — sociology, psychology, physics, or whatever else might be proposed. This aim of establishing an independent, immanent science of language has a particular importance for glossematics, which sees the various sciences as being themselves special kinds of languages. If this view is correct, it is the other sciences that require linguistics for their foundation, not vice versa.

But it is not yet necessary to look so far ahead to the furthest implications of the theory. There are problems arising much earlier in the study of language that lead to the search for an independent linguistics. At the very moment when we first encounter a language other than our own, we are forced to recognize that each language has its own way of dealing with the world — its own system of sounds and its own system of meanings. We find that, to learn the language, we must take our stand, so to speak, within the language. And there is no sure foothold for us in any science but the one that treats of the structure of language in general and the possible structures of individual languages. The phonetician can give us the most thorough analysis of speech, his instruments can help us to detect the finest distinctions between sounds, but what they cannot do (and were not, of course, intended to do) is to show us which distinctions are put to use in any given language and what kind of use they are put to. The physicist can provide the most refined analysis of the color spectrum, but it would be quite unfair to ask him how a natural language is going to divide up the spectrum by means of a small number of color words, as English does with its *red, orange, yellow, green, blue, violet.* If we do ask him, we have simply gone to the wrong man.

Traditional lore about language betrays, in fact, many instances of asking the wrong man for answers to questions. In order to recognize a noun, for example, some Americans have been taught that "a noun is the name of a person, place, or thing." *Peter, Paris,* and *pencil* are all good enough — but *privilege, picnic, poverty?* The world turns out to be full indeed of a number of things — presumably so classified by some droll ontologist. Actually, the more one thinks about it, the clearer it becomes that they are "things" only because they provide substance for nouns.

And this is just about the glossematic way of looking at matters — not so topsy-turvy or perverse as it may have originally appeared. First one finds out what kinds of elements the language has; one discovers and defines them by means of the simple relationships between them. Only after that does one describe the substance of these purely formal elements. To put it roughly, first one looks for the nouns, then one studies their meanings. First one looks for the vowels, then one studies the sounds that can serve as substance for the vowels — remembering always that the particular language one is describing may turn out not to have nouns or vowels at all, but, instead, units of content and of expression that have quite different formal definitions and must therefore be given different names.

Thus, the position of glossematics is that linguistics cannot find an anchor in some universal science of meaning or (and here lies the greater temptation) in some universal science of sounds. Each language provides two patterns of its own — one for the universe of meaning and one for the universe of possible speech-sounds or any other means (writing for instance) that is used for the expression of meaning. Notice, by the way, that all kinds of expression have

255

equal rights from this point of view. One can use the same strategy in analyzing written expression as in analyzing spoken expression. This is so because the essential part of a language is its formal structure — the network of relationships which connect its elements and by which its elements are defined — not the particular substance in which the elements are manifested.

What are some of the other consequences of this approach? I shall first note two immediate consequences for the work of the linguist who sets about to apply glossematic theory to the description of individual languages. I shall then speak briefly of some long-term consequences.

To return once again to some of the sample restatements considered earlier: "If a consonant is present in a syllable, then a vowel must also be present"; "If *sine* is present in a phrase, then an ablative must also be present" — in general form, "If *x* is present in something, then *y* must also be present." Observe now what was passed over in the earlier discussion, the third element in these statements, the "something" in which *x* and *y* are present. All such glossematic statements contain this third element, the unit within which the defined units establish their relationship. This can only mean that the larger unit must be defined before the smaller ones are. Glossematics accepts this consequence, beginning always with the largest possible unit — the undivided text, spoken or written, that it takes as object for immediate study — and progressively analyzing it into smaller and smaller units by the methods already described.

Another important immediate consequence is to be found in the very first division that glossematic procedure makes of any given text. This division is always of the same kind — a division into expression and content, the two largest parts of the text that are mutually defined by the fact that each requires the presence of the other. Like the general progress from larger to smaller units, this primary division into content and expression sharply distinguishes glossematic procedure from that of most other kinds of linguistics. It follows from the fact that a linguistic text cannot be a bare collection of sounds or of written marks; it must be sounds, or marks, or other possible elements of expression that are accompanied by meaning, or content. For glossematics, content and expression are the two faces of every linguistic sign, and both must be analyzed according to the same principles. When one speaks of consonants "governing" vowels, one is talking about expression elements; but when one speaks of a preposition governing the ablative, one is obviously talking about elements of content, not about the elements used to express the preposition or the ablative. In fact, it is only this dual aspect of the linguistic sign that makes possible an objective inventory of the elements in either content or expression. Thus, one cannot know that two different sounds are substance for two different expression-elements in a language unless one finds that the difference between them can imply a difference between two meanings — like the difference between the initial sounds of *pan* and *fan*. In contrast, many differences in sounds that I use when speaking merely show whether I have a cold in the head or am suffering from sinus trouble.

To trace some of the furthest consequences of the glossematic approach, let us look more closely at the primary emphasis that glossematics places on "form" as opposed to "substance." Formal elements are defined with the help of a severely restricted number of terms — such terms as "if," "then," and "is present." These terms have been chosen because they can be used in the kind of statements that linguists wish to be able to make about any language they may encounter and thus provide an instrument for calculating all possible formal linguistic structures and for thereby setting up a universally valid typology of languages. When a linguist studies a given language and describes it from a glossematic point of view, he may even think of himself as working to find out where that language "fits" — where it finds its match in one of the languages he is able to calculate as a possibility. He thus comes to view each language as the realization of something already foreseen as being realizable. Accordingly, while the objects he *studies* will be individual languages in the full richness and variety of their use, the object he *aims at* will be the formal structure of those languages and — through those structures — the structure of language in general. Glossematics aims at nothing less than a universal grammar, from which may be deduced the grammars of actually attested languages and, as well, the grammars of languages that remain only as possibilities. It is on this foundation that glossematics would proceed, in the manner of other sciences, to propose hypotheses about language and to suggest laws that can be put to objective test.

But the implications of glossematics do not end here. I have spoken about its search for an immanent linguistics. Strictly speaking, that search leads to the conclusion that there can be no immanent linguistics. The independent science that is sought turns out to be rather an immanent semiology — the science that studies semiotics, or sign systems in general. Natural language must be studied as a particular kind of semiotic whose specific features will be made more clearly evident by comparison and contrast with other semiotics that are not natural languages — such widely differing sign systems as, for example, those of symbolic logic, traffic lights, or military uniforms. I have already noted that glossematics views the sciences as also being languages or semiotics. It follows from this that linguistics in the broader sense — semiology — will be in the curious situation of being the only science that studies itself and provides its own definition. Far from being a loose agglomerate of sociological, psychological, physiological, and physical observations about human speech, linguistics thus assumes a central and organizing position among the sciences.

Such are the furthest horizons of glossematics. The journey toward them is a long one. For the present, as I stated at the beginning of this very general introduction, glossematics remains a working hypothesis only, which calls for long work of application and testing. If its fundamental theses are correct, the science of linguistics has hardly taken its first, faltering steps, but they are the first steps of a child that will be a giant.

24 GENERATIVE GRAMMAR

Robert P. Stockwell

The term "generative grammar" has come to refer to the research of a group of American linguists, and recently some others abroad, whose work depends on the theoretical advances made by Noam Chomsky. Chomsky teaches at the Massachusetts Institute of Technology, which remains the center of this activity even though several of the important scholars of this persuasion have been away from MIT for several years, and others never actually studied there at all but came into their generative convictions through Chomsky's published articles and books.

It is in fact a misnomer to refer to the work of this school of linguistics as "generative grammar," since the distinguishing claim of Chomsky's group is not that grammars should be generative but that a generative grammar should be of a certain form — namely, a type of rule known as a "transformational rule." Let us consider first what it means to speak of "generative grammar," in general.

The object of investigation of grammatical studies is sentencehood in natural languages. If it were possible to combine the words of a language in any way whatever in forming sentences — say, to select words from a dictionary list by some sort of random generating device — then grammatical studies would not be necessary, since there would be nothing to study except possibly the properties of random generating devices. But it is obvious that sentences are not formed by randomly stringing words together from a dictionary. There are exceedingly tight restrictions on what arrangements of words are possible in sentences. The grammatical study of a particular language is the attempt to characterize these restrictions in detail for that language. General linguistics is the theory of how such grammatical characterizations can best be achieved for all languages — that is, the study of the optimal form of grammars.

For the statement of such restrictions to be of scientific value, it must be absolutely explicit: it must make clear exactly what properties of the grammar of the language are covered by the descriptive account itself, as distinct from what information an intelligent human user of an *in*explicit description can infer about the language. To say that a descriptive account of the grammar of a language is "generative," therefore, is really to say no more about it than that it provides an explicit enumeration of its own claims about the structure of that language — such claims as what the sentences of the language are, what the internal structure of each sentence is, how each sentence is realized phonetically, how each sentence is interpreted semantically, which sentences are interpreted similarly, which ones are interpreted differently in spite of surface similarity, and so on — through a wide range of information about sentences that is clearly available to speakers and necessary for their understanding of the language.

"Generative" means, then, "explicit." But what is gained by such a term? What does the notion of generating sentences have to do with being explicit about grammatical structure? To answer this we must consider what possible answers there are to the challenge that the descriptive account must be explicit. We need consider only the absolutely minimal demand that can reasonably be placed on any grammatical study, namely that it should discriminate between those objects which are under study and those which are not — specifically, between strings of noises which are sentences of the language and any other object whatsoever, such as strings of noises which are ill-formed sentences of that language, strings of noises which don't belong to that language at all, and so on. It is immediately clear that the set of well-formed sentences of a particular language is a subset of the set of all sentences in all languages, and that both of these are subsets of the set of all strings of human communicative noises. It would be overwhelmingly difficult to define the set of well-formed sentences of a language by identifying all nonmembers of the set directly. What is necessary is the enumeration of the set of well-formed sentences for that language. One conceivable enumeration would be a list. A list is, at least, explicit. But there is no way to list all the members of a set which is indefinitely large (as is the case for the well-formed sentences of all natural languages). The only available alternative to a list is some rule or set of rules which has the mathematical property of *recursiveness* — the property of reapplicability indefinitely many times over, each successive application enumerating another member of the set. It is exactly in this sense that a simple rule for addition is said to generate, or enumerate, the infinite set of whole positive integers in mathematics.

To say, then, that a grammatical description is "generative" is only to say that it contains rules which formally enumerate the class of objects the description is about. This is equivalent to saying that the description is a testable one, since the objects it enumerates, along with their structural descriptions, can then be subjected to empirical verification with respect to such questions as the following: Are these hypothetically enumerated objects in fact sentences of the language, as claimed by the description? do they have the internal structure assigned by the description? are they interpreted in the way predicted by the description? do they have the phonological properties predicted by the description? It seems obvious that this property, the property of explicitness and therefore of potential empirical invalidation, is the least that can be asked of a scientific theory.

The use of the word "generative" by Chomsky and his group has been subject to deep misunderstanding among linguists all over the world, particularly among American "structuralists" but notably also in Great Britain and the Netherlands. The source of the misunderstanding seems to have been a confusion between the way a descriptive grammar generates a representation of the unconscious knowledge of the ideal speaker-hearer of the language, and the way an actual speaker-hearer produces his daily discourse (about which virtually nothing is known). That is, the grammatical description is an account of the intrinsic competence which must be assumed in principle to be available to the individual speaking the language if we are to explain how it is that he is able to do the subtle and intricate things he can in fact do with his language. This distinction of Chomsky's between *competence* and *performance* is a familiar distinction in general linguistics from quite early in the history of the science, one best known, perhaps, in the distinction made by the Swiss linguist Ferdinand de Saussure between *langue* ("competence") and *parole* ("performance").

Once it is clear that there is really no alternative to using recursive rules to characterize the structure of a natural language if the characterization is to be an explicit scientific account of the constraints on the formation of sentences in that language, the really interesting question arises: What is the form of the rules needed for this purpose? Prior to Chomsky's work, virtually no attention was given to this question in American linguistics. Chomsky's answers to this question have in effect revolutionized the discipline of linguistics, at least the discipline as practiced by the substantial segment of the academic community which has found itself persuaded by his arguments. Many assumptions and claims generally accepted before Chomsky's time have been challenged by the transformationalists, and as far as it is possible to judge in the almost total absence of serious replies to these challenges, have been successfully replaced by transformational views. The challenges strike deep into the basic concepts of earlier generations of structural linguistics — into such hallowed theoretical constructs as the phoneme, the regularity and independence of sound change, stratified levels within linguistic descriptions, and procedural requirements on description, and even into the sanctity of textual citation as supporting evidence for an analysis. The criteria that determine what constitutes adequate justification for an analysis are incomparably more complex after the transformational revolution, largely because a transformational grammar is interlocking and interdependent in its own structure to an extent hardly more than fractionally conceptualized before Chomsky's work. These developments of the past ten years are so extensive and range so totally through linguistic studies that here I shall only outline the aims of the rules in a transformational grammar and suggest the kinds of linguistic phenomena these rules are intended to account for explicitly.

In order to map a string of noises — represented as a string of phonetic symbols, or in any other representation appropriate to a basis for semantic interpretation — in order to understand an utterance of a language — a great many kinds of information must be available; and the converse of this mapping, namely taking a set of concepts and encoding them into a string of noises capable of receiving the intended interpretation, requires precisely the same information. This information may therefore be represented in a form which is independent of the manner or direction in which it is processed by the speaker-hearer. In this sense, then, a generative grammar, which is an abstraction of the information required for either of these operations as performed by people when they communicate by language, is totally neutral with respect to the manner in which the information is processed. In the following outline of the internal structure of the grammatical description, the sequence is a logical sequence only, though it is spoken of as a sequence of operations which follow each other as if through time. The grammatical description is an abstract characterization of the set of constraints under which the processing must be carried out; it is not a literal characterization of the way the constraints are processed in the act of speech, nor is there any assumption about the form the constraints take in the brain of the human being.

Let us consider, then, the kinds of information available in principle to the ideal speaker-hearer of a language, and the way in which the information is accounted for in a transformational generative grammar. First, in any sentence, words are grouped in two ways: by classes and by functions. Grouping by classes is a result of similarity in the way words combine with other words. For example, there is no sentence of the form* *he put it*, because one of the syntactic features of the verb *put* is that it must combine with a certain type of adverbial phrase, a *directional adverb*, as in *he put it into the garage*. To speak English one must know that there is such a class of verbs. In the grammar, these would be marked by having a certain syntactic feature, say [+Directional Adverb], as a property assigned to them in the lexicon. This syntactic feature is then a part of the syntactic definition of the verb *put*, and the rules of sentence formation are devised in such a way that this verb can be inserted in a sentence only if a directional adverb is combined with it. The classes to which each word of the language belongs are, then, the various intersections of the syntactic features required for the description of the way words can combine in that language. The combinatory properties of the verb *put* would be accounted for by the set of features [+Verb], [+Transitive], [+Directional Adverb], and so on. Any other verb with the same set of features would be identical in its combinatory behavior (total intersection of syntactic features), and other verbs would be similar to the extent that they shared any of these syntactic features (partial intersection).

But there must also be grouping by functions, since any single class can serve several functions. For example, a noun phrase may function as subject of the sentence or as object of the main verb. Function is a relational notion, each possible grammatical function being defined by a labeled branching-diagram which is generated by the first component of a transformational grammar, the base component, which contains what are referred to as the "branching rules," the "constituent structure rules," the "expansion rules," or the "phrase-structure rules." As these names suggest, these rules generate strings of words bracketed and labeled in such a way that the most closely related elements of the string are tied together as a unit, then the next most closely related elements, and so on, up to the final string of all items which are tied together under the label "Sentence." A function, such as "Subject of the Sentence," is assigned by virtue of the fact that the label "Sentence" appears directly above the topmost "Noun Phrase" in the usual diagrams.

The base component, then, generates the abstract structures which lie beneath the surface of sentences. These abstract structures, now commonly referred to as the "deep" or "underlying" structures of sentences, contain all the syntactic information required for the semantic interpretation of sentences (they also contain semantic information, perhaps in the form of atomized dictionary definitions attached to the atomic elements of the syntactic string). The deep structure specifies not only category information about words (the "syntactic features") and functional relations between words and phrases (by virtue of the labeled diagram), but also relations between the various simple sentences that may be combined to form a single more complex sentence. Thus a complex sentence like *The man who came to dinner ate the food that was on the table* is in some sense decomposable into a main sentence, *The man ate the food*, and two embedded sentences, one embedded in the subject — *The man came to dinner* — and the other embedded in the object — *The food was on the table*. The base rules for simple sentences in this case apply, recursively, three times. The intuition that the phrase *The man who came to dinner* somehow "contains" the simple sentence *The man came to dinner* is thus represented. There are infinitely many similar "containments." The great Danish linguist Otto Jespersen observed, for example, that an expression like *the furiously barking dog* somehow contained the sentence *The dog barked furiously;* similarly, *his shirt* somehow contains *He has a shirt*, and *his knowledge of her departure* contains both *He knows* and *She departed*, and so on. In these and all similar cases the deep structure would consist of a labeled branching-diagram where the simple sentences out of which the whole was composed would appear in their simple forms.

Perhaps an analogy will serve to make this conception of the deep structure of sentences clearer. Consider various aspects of a Bach fugue for organ. The score itself is the surface structure of the sentence, representing one output of the grammar of fugues. The performance of the fugue may deviate from the score in various ways, suggesting the distinction between competence and performance. The complexity of the fugue itself (that is, its internal structure as distinct from the performance of it) is the product of a number of essentially simple underlying structures: one, two, or three themes, introduced in a specific left-to-right temporal sequence, subsequently modified in accord with general rules about harmonic transition, rhythmic variation, partial repetition, and so on. The analogy with deep and surface sentence structure is not perfect, of course, because of such regular fugal features as recapitulation, rarely present in sentences though normal in discourse. But the analogy between simple underlying themes and their reformation, modification, truncation, and ornamentation in the fugue, on the one hand, and simple underlying sentence structures and their transformationally determined mapping into surface structure through such processes as reordering, partial deletion, and various kinds of linking may be illuminating.

A transformational grammar, then, may be said to enumerate the underlying structures of sentences of a language in its *base component*. The output of the base component is a labeled branching-diagram, of which the terminal nodes are formative elements contained in the dictionary. These formatives are simply the intersection of three sets of features: phonological features needed to map the sentence into a string of noises; syntactic features needed to map the deep structure into the surface syntactic structure; and semantic features needed to map the deep structure into the semantic interpretation. The *transformational component* of the grammar performs the mapping of deep to surface structure, and the surface structure in turn is the basis, along with the phonological features, for application of the rules of the *phonological component* which map the structure into the string of sounds that provide the basis for transmission of the message from one human being to others who speak the same language. The *semantic component*, about which very little is known yet, provides a mapping of the isolated minimal meaning-bearing elements into larger and larger units, related by virtue of the structure assigned to them in the base component, to, finally, the full sentence or larger unit of discourse.

What are some of the implications of transformational grammatical theory for the study of human behavior in a wider frame of reference? If Chomsky and his colleagues are right, ordinary, everyday communication in language — virtually every such act of communication — is a creative performance governed by rules of such abstractness and complexity that there is no reasonable likelihood that they could be acquired by a child unless he were born into the world with highly specific innate gifts for this particular kind of learning. Thus the notion that human beings acquire language merely as a set of conditioned responses — the notion that the use of language is habitual behavior in some meaningful sense of the term "habit" — is rendered quite improbable. On the contrary, the rationalist notion that this behavior is dictated by a set of prior, and uniquely human, mental capacities achieved by a million or more years of evolution is strongly supported.

The theory also provides intriguing speculations about linguistic change, and new insight into how it can come about that two people can readily communicate with each other even though they speak vastly different dialects — even though the surface structures of their utterances fail to correspond in any obvious way. Consider the second of these insights first, since linguistic change depends, in a rather direct way, on the existence of surface variation on underlying structures that are essentially identical. Suppose we consider a well-known dialect difference between British and American English, simplifying the details slightly. In American English, the normal answer to a question like *Have you lectured in Europe?* would be *Yes, I have,* or *No, I haven't.* That is, the answer would pick up the auxiliary element of the verb phrase in the question. Other examples, confining our answers to affirmatives:

Will you solve this problem for me?	*Yes, I will.*
Could you have written this essay?	*Yes, I could have.*

These same answers are possible also in British English, but very commonly one hears also the following ones:

Have you lectured in Europe?	*Yes, I have done.*
Will you solve this problem for me?	*Yes, I will do.*
Could you have written this essay?	*Yes, I could have done.*

This usage is not yet well attested in literary documents (as far as I know), because it is a syntactic change of recent origin, or at least of recent prominence in British colloquial usage. What appears to be involved is that whereas the American rule that operates to generate such tag responses requires simply that the first auxiliary element of the main verb be echoed, all the rest being deleted (*Yes, I will* being a truncated version of *Yes, I will solve this problem for you*), the British rule allows an additional optional choice of a dummy verb (*do*) to stand in, so to speak, for the main verb phrase that has been deleted. Since *do* is the normal dummy verb in other grammatical situations — in, for example, *What were you doing last night?*, in which *doing* stands in for some specific action verb (*I was working late, I was*

267

watching my favorite television show, I was trying to get out of a traffic jam on the freeway) — it is to be expected that *do* would drop naturally into this substitute function in the response to questions.[1]

Now this dialect difference — in this case a fairly trivial one which would never cause misunderstanding — is an instance of a difference which results from a very slight change (the addition of an optional replacement element in the rule that truncates the full-sentence response to a question) in the transformational rule which maps the deep structure into the surface structure. The deep structure is obviously the same for both dialects.

Consider now a more familiar kind of dialect difference: say, the British pronunciation and the Midwestern American pronunciation of the phrase *The panorama of the Far West*. A transformational theory would claim that these pronunciations have identical representations in the underlying phonological structure. In the case of British *far*, we must assume that an *r* is really present in order to explain the fact that in a phrase like *the Far East*, where a vowel follows the *r*, the *r* shows up in the surface phonetic form. In the case of *panorama*, we must assume that the penultimate vowel is really the same as the vowel of *cat* in order to explain the vowel in *panoramic*. Now it happens that historically the *r* in British but not in Midwestern American was dropped in all positions except where a vowel followed. And it happens that historically the æ vowel in British but not in Midwestern American was lengthened and changed to *ah* in certain environments and left unchanged in others. In a generative grammar, exactly these historical facts would be incorporated as late rules (drop the *r* and change the vowel) which would operate in British, but not in American — that is, Midwestern American English would lack these late rules, but the underlying forms would be the same for both dialects. Thus there is a sense in which the ordering of certain kinds of rules within a generative grammar recapitulates historical change and provides a principled basis for saying under what

---

[1]These descriptions are not intended to indicate actual historical developments. Consequently the reader is not to suppose that British English has at some time added a dummy verb to the American type. It should also be noted that other sentence types would be relevant to any historical discussion, namely, such forms as "Yes, I have done *so*" and "Yes, I have done *it*."

conditions differences between languages or dialects are relatively trivial, and when they are spread pervasively to such a depth within the grammar that the two dialects must be differentiated as distinct languages. Linguistic change may be specified in terms of rules added to and deleted from the grammar, with subsequent restructuring of segments of the grammar brought about by inconsistencies and unneeded complications in the total grammar which such additions and deletions may have created.

In sum, I believe that a scientific revolution of major import is occurring in American linguistics under the impact of the fresh views of Chomsky and his followers, and, further, that the implications of his questions and formulations are only beginning to be spelled out in detail. In one of his recent books, *Aspects of the Theory of Syntax*, Chomsky suggests lines of investigation — in both the psycholinguistic area and the unexplored field of the relations between the general theory of grammar and the specific facts of natural languages — in such richness that experimental activity could be directed toward these formulations for at least a generation. I do not think that linguistics has ever shown greater interest in, or given so much hope of success at, explaining facts of such general import for the understanding of human behavior.

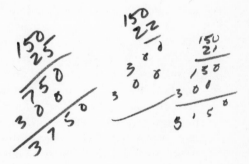

25 SUMMARY AND A PEEK AT THE FUTURE

Archibald A. Hill

This book has presented chapters by twenty-four different linguists, all now practicing their science in the United States, though the linguistic activities described are not thus limited geographically. One statement should surely be obvious — there is great diversity in the views of linguists now active. A second statement is probably by no means equally obvious. It is that there is a large body of views agreed on by all linguists. I shall begin by trying to demonstrate the truth of both statements, both the obvious one and the more questionable one. First, for diversity. A small but important example is the entity described by Martin Joos in Chapter 2, the plus, or internal, juncture (written +). Joos cites his own spectrographic investigations, which have led him to define the difference between such utterances as *writer* and *write 'er* as a physically observable difference in timing. Yet many (perhaps even most) linguists would say that the only important difference between these two utterances is that they contain elements of very different grammatical level and function. That is, the term "juncture" is used sometimes to mean a grammatical phenomenon which may be quite undetectable physically, and sometimes to mean a purely physical event, which may or may not be correlated with the occurrence of a grammatical event. Such difference in terminology is unfortunate, of course, but in a science still only in the early stages of vigorous development it is perhaps inevitable. The damage is greatest, certainly, when two speakers use the terms without being aware of differences in definition. For this reason I have made a determined effort to avoid using terms which are false friends. I do not use Joos's term "juncture" at all any more (no matter what I did earlier), but use the terms "physical separator" and "grammatical boundary." The terminology is clumsy, I am aware, but at least it helps to make clear which kind of item I am talking about. The disputes over the nature of entities such as junctures or separators illustrate the kind of divergence which is essentially terminological and no more — all disputants agree that physical differences may make two such utterances as those cited acoustically identifiable, and all agree that the different grammatical boundaries in *hoe-maker* and *home acre* may result in difference in pronunciation.

The differences are not, however, by any means always resolvable into disputes over terminology, as can be seen from Chapter 22, by Eric Hamp. But in addition to the issues there given, at least one more very real and very important point of controversy can be named. This is the matter of the so-called deep structure said to be back of surface structures that differ, as do such sentences as *John bought a book* and *A book was bought by John*. At present, these deep structures are being subjected to active speculation and exploration, and many have suggested the possibility that deep structure is universal and unchanging. If so, then deep structure is the structure of thought, and language is no more than the signal system into which deep structure is encoded. More conservative, or more Bloomfieldian, linguists are skeptical of such views, and would find the way into a knowledge of underlying, universal thought-processes not in manipulation of sentence types, but (if there is a way in at all) in the empirical and experimental procedures described in part in Chapter 15, by John Carroll.

What then of agreements? Are there any, after all, beyond the level of the most trivial kind of truism? There are many, I believe. What is perhaps the most basic is also remarkably ancient, since it was shared by the ancient tyrant Psammeticus, who attempted to investigate which of the world's then-known languages was closest to the original tongue of the first speakers. His method was experimental, since what he did was isolate two newborn infants and observe their babblings when they had reached the age at which talking could be expected. The experiment was cruel, and naive, but the important point is that it was an experiment. Psammeticus held the view that is mostly deeply embedded in all modern linguistics, that language is something which can be experimentally investigated.

The second agreement among linguists is closely related to the view of experimentalism. It is that any explication of the nature of language must present not merely the items of which it is made up, but also the complex relations which exist between them — that language is something in which not only the words but also the tune is important. Further, it is universally accepted that it is possible to judge between competing explications of language design, not always with perfect convergence in results but at least within rules on which all agree. The criteria are that all statements of design must be complete, consistent, and simple. That statement which most nearly fulfills these criteria is the best, though no statement can be expected to fulfill them uniquely and irreplaceably. Though it may amount to reviewing the obvious, it is worth spending a sentence or two on these criteria.

Completeness is simple enough to understand, since it is mere common sense to say that any set of data can be explained in any way at all if enough is left out. Consistency is also easy to comprehend, since again it is clear that nothing can be brought about equally well by the presence and absence of whatever may be the cause. Yet consistency is not always achieved. That it is recognized as a criterion of excellence, however, is shown by the fact that the theory of one unfortunately romantic historical linguist came to be an occasion for general amusement. This was the theory that Indo-European gender distinctions could be explained as a sort of folk-poetry, in which (for instance) nouns tended to be feminine if they were small and weak or if they were, contradictorily, large, enveloping, and strong. Simplicity of statement — which is not at all the same thing as ease of comprehension — is familiar under its other name, parsimony of hypotheses. It can be observed in use in almost any of the polemics about grammatical or phonological analysis and theory. Perhaps as clear an example of it as can be found is the use made of simplicity in the statement of the historical development of the pronunciation of words such as Modern English *day* formulated more than a generation ago by the great Danish Anglicist Otto Jespersen. He observed that the Middle English ancestor of *day* had a diphthongal vocalic element and that *day* now has a diphthongal vowel nucleus. Therefore, he said, it is uneconomical to suppose that the Middle English diphthong became a long simple vowel in Early Modern English and then once again a diphthong in contemporary speech.

It should be clear what these several agreements amount to. They add up, of course, to an agreement that a science of language is possible. Note also that some of the secondary conditions often thought to be necessary before any activity can be called a science are also agreed on, though usually in a form adapted to linguistics as a special area of science. Among these other characteristics of a science possessed by linguistics is the possibility of verifiable prediction. Prediction in linguistics does not mean that such-and-such a development in language will take place at a future date, to be verified with passage of time; it usually means that a design has been partially observed and that predictions are made on the basis of these incomplete data. The predictions are then corroborated or denied by the observation of further data. In practice this kind of prediction is a constant tool for field workers in linguistic analysis. Thus I once looked at my own field notes of the phonology of an American Indian tongue and observed that I had recorded a number of forms with an initial /h/ — the sound in English *home*. Looking further, I saw that I had systematically recorded a set of front stops and spirants in contrast with back stops and spirants. My /h/ recordings were suspect because they were not in keeping with my recording of other consonants, so I went back to my informant and asked for further examples. My suspicion was fully borne out — the sound that I had recorded as /h/ was really two contrasting sounds.

Another criterion of scientific status is that all true sciences develop generally applicable statements, held to be true at all times and all places. In short, sciences develop laws. Most modern linguists would agree that laws of sound change, such as Grimm's law, are not general statements in this sense. They are, rather, statements applicable within strict limits of time and place, and would need a good deal of restatement before they could yield anything like a general formulation of the development of language sounds. Truly general statements, perhaps many of them, may certainly emerge from the current concern with deep structure and language universals; but at present the general statement must be regarded with some caution, if for no other reason than that consideration of these matters is only beginning. A safer example, less far-reaching it is true, but more generally acceptable, is what is known as the Joos law, applicable to that form of semantics which can be called translation or paraphrase. The law states that of the possible meanings for a given unknown item, that meaning is best which contributes least to the meaning of the total context. As Joos has pointed out, the law has been followed, though not always consciously, by lexicographers and ordinary men at all times. Further, it is followed by learners of language in all societies whenever the learner is faced with a new term. The law is, in short, truly general in its application and not limited either by time or place.

A characteristic of at least those sciences which are past their earliest stages is that they are shown not to be merely trivial, as a science of wallpaper might be said to be trivial. A nontrivial science has results which throw light on other areas of knowledge and inquiry, thus establishing a network of relationships and ties with the sum total of human knowledge. Such ties are evident today in the relations of linguistics with anthropology (explored by Norman McQuown in Chapter 14), literary criticism (treated by Curtis Hayes in Chapter 16), psychology (developed by John Carroll in Chapter 15), language teaching (discussed by David DeCamp in Chapter 13), and other fields not developed in the limited scope of this book. Prominent among these other ties is the exploitation of linguistic and paralinguistic analysis in psychiatric diagnosis, an activity within the area of paralinguistics described by Henry Lee Smith, Jr., in Chapter 9. It is worth noting that some of these ties and relationships are quite practical — the use of the findings of linguistics in language teaching, the techniques of linguistics in psychiatric diagnosis — while others are much more theoretical and less obviously and immediately useful. Among these latter pursuits is the use of linguistics in the study of literature. Another is the recently awakened interest in the process by which a child forms the collection of rules which enables him to produce grammatical sentences throughout his life and to understand all the sentences he will hear in his life; this theoretical relation of linguistics to the study of man and man in culture is, of course, one of the major contributions of generative grammatical analysis, ably described by Robert Stockwell in Chapter 24. Yet whether one considers only the practical applications of linguistics, or only its theoretical implications, or both, there has been a striking change and a striking development within a single generation. In the 1920s, when I turned to linguistics as a sort of refuge from what was perhaps an excessively historical study of literature, I would have been hard put to it to justify the study of linguistics on any other ground than that it was fascinating. Today it is perhaps easy to say that the findings of linguistics are wrong or that linguistics is a science directed toward areas in which science should fear to tread; but it is no longer possible to say that linguistics is trivial or useless. And if the results of linguistics continue to be used in other inquiries, it will be less and less possible to say that these results are wrong or that language is not properly a part of the domain of science.

So far, I have been concerned primarily with the disagreements and agreements among linguists currently practicing. Furthermore, I have tried to show that there is a large area of agreement among them which can be summed up in the simple statement that linguistics is and ought to be a science, showing many of the characteristics of other sciences, but with special goals, techniques, and results of its own. Yet while the disagreements have been amply described in the earlier chapters, it seems to me that it would be well to say at least a little about the various schools of linguistics now active, not so much to discuss how they disagree or agree as to explore the different approaches used by each and to suggest how it is possible that some of these schools may be concerned with what can be described as differing faces of the same reality.

It ought to be clear that the major division among linguists today is that between the school of neo-Bloomfieldians, or structuralists, and the school of transformational generative grammarians who follow Noam Chomsky. Relations between the two groups have not by any means always been amicable, since the transformationalists resent the fact that they were not given a full hearing immediately in earlier days when the neo-Bloomfieldians were dominant, and the neo-Bloomfieldians (I am afraid) often feel themselves committed to positions stated almost a generation ago and resent the necessity of change. Yet by and large the two schools are complementary rather than contradictory. The neo-Bloomfieldians concern themselves with the identity of linguistic items — with taxonomy, in fact. In arriving at identity, neo-Bloomfieldians observe the phonological, grammatical, and syntactic characteristics of all items and insist that the tokens (to use a bit of technical jargon) can always be divided into "sames" and "differents." The neo-Bloomfieldians insist that it is possible to rely on juries of native speakers for the decision that two items are "differents," as we would still rely on a jury to show that English *bat* and *pat* are different. Yet the neo-Bloomfieldians are never equally effective in dealing with "sames." For instance, do *is* and *are* contain an instance of "same," and if so, what is it? The jury test and the notion of contrast or difference remain the principal investigative tool contributed by the structural school.

The transformational school has been, in general, less interested in the jury test and the notion of difference, but has been greatly interested in the notion of the well-formed sentence. They have often spoken, somewhat unfortunately, of the "grammatical sentence," a term which should have been avoided, since the notion "grammatical sentence" is so confused by notions of socially approved and disapproved ways of talking that it can scarcely be understood. What is really meant is that if the identity of items is assumed, and is stated to be without change, then certain transformations and rearrangements are impossible because they would result in sentences not well formed. Thus, if it is established that *vanish* is an intransitive verb, we cannot quarrel with the statement that such pseudo sentences as *The mouse vanished the mountain* and *The sun vanished the rain*, are other than well formed. Yet if we look up *vanish* in *Webster's Third*, we find a sentence in which vanish is transitive — *You can vanish the coin completely* — quoted as observed data. Since we are — acting as a native jury — usually sure that *vanish* with an object is ungrammatical (unless it is sleight-of-hand which is being talked about), we have then no real choice except to say that *vanish* in the sentence in *Webster's* is not the same item as *vanish* in *The sun vanished behind the clouds.* That is, we have used grammaticality to add a further test to those used for identity by the neo-Bloomfieldians. It would seem to me that these tests are all there are, and that if two slightly differing items undergo the same sets of transformations, substitutions, and additions, they are then surely instances of sames, and the neo-Bloomfieldian difficulty is solved. That is, *wen-* in *went* is the same with *go*, because *go*, when it becomes *went*, undergoes a modification closely similar to the modification shown by *send* when it becomes *sent*. Such identification of *go* with *went*, though it has never troubled the traditional grammarian, is difficult for the neo-Bloomfieldian, since there is no phonetic similarity between the syllables *go* and *wen-*. I think, therefore, that a wise use of the tool of grammaticality enables the analyst to go on into syntax as those structuralists who are too narrowly concerned with phonological sames and differents never could. At the same time, however, the successes of transformational analysis in the realm of syntax have sometimes led to a certain carelessness in the establishment of identity of items. A sound taxonomic foundation is the necessary basis for all the more operative types of scientific analysis.

One of the other very vigorous American schools of linguistics is that called tagmemic, briefly described in Chapter 3, by Carleton Hodge. One feature of this approach which sharply differentiates it from others currently in use is that it has a strong pragmatic basis, since its practitioners wished to develop a means whereby teachers and missionaries dealing with exotic tongues could acquire not merely a structural understanding of these tongues, but a structural understanding which would lead as quickly as possible to a practical command. Tagmemic analysis assumes, perhaps as a product of this practical viewpoint, that the basic phonological entities are the classes of sounds which occur in identified meaningful units, rather than bundles of recognizable features of contrast which serve to make meaningful units recognizable. In this view, tagmemic analysis is close to transformational generative grammar in that both work downward in analysis from identified large units. Tagmemic analysis is like neo-Bloomfieldian structuralism, however, in making full use of contrastive differences, such as those in *bat* and *pat* — differences which are obscured in generative phonology. Generative phonology assumes that binary distinctive features are much the same in all languages of the world, with the result that it becomes unimportant to observe whether a given language employs such a vocalic difference as grave versus acute distinctively, or merely redundantly. In at least some features of syntax, however, all three schools seem to meet. That is, structuralists, tagmemicists, and transformationalists all recognize — to use a relatively simple example — that certain modifiers, such as definite and indefinite articles, can occur only before the noun, so that there must be a position which is sometimes filled, sometimes left empty; and that the entities which fill this slot make up a class. It does not make much difference whether we speak of this correlation of slot and filler as a tagmeme, or call the fillers determiners, or speak of a position which can be filled by various entities including zero. However we do it, we are describing a phenomenon in much the same way.

The newest American school is one which has not yet gone beyond an essentially programmatic stage — that is, its founder, Sydney Lamb, and his followers have not as yet gone beyond the stage of discussing theoretical procedures in linguistic analysis and statement, and have not yet produced an actual description and statement of language pattern in these terms. Lamb — the author of Chapter 4 (he does not develop there his general analytical approach) — quarrels with both structuralism and transformational analysis. He attempts to rescue the phoneme from the Chomsky–Halle attacks, which suppress a phonemic level between the binary distinctive features and morphemically ordered classes of sounds; he attempts the rescue by splitting the phoneme and morpheme into yet more levels, or strata. The school is interesting, though not as yet presented clearly enough for full evaluation of its results.

The great European tradition of scholarly philological analysis and description is of course still practiced in the United States, which has produced at least one great practitioner of it in William Dwight Whitney. At least one of the scholars represented in this volume — Hans Kurath, the author of Chapter 7, on the history of English — can be said to belong to this tradition, though it is not at all true that he belongs to this tradition alone. It should also be pointed out that the European scholarly philological linguists were one of the bases on which anthropological linguists like Boas, Sapir, and Bloomfield built their work, and that a recent generation of scholars including Edgar Sturtevant and Franklin Edgerton carried on distinguished work, largely within this tradition. The fact that this scholarly philological tradition lives on, untroubled by the alarms and excursions of the last thirty years, is after all a proof of the vitality and continuity of the science.

About schools based abroad I shall be brief. One close to American points of view is that of Firthian linguistics, as practiced in the British Isles, represented in this collection by Chapter 20, by J. C. Catford. Firth made extensive use of "contrast," as do American structuralists. What seems to me to be the principal difference is the Firthian insistence on multiple systems within language and the ultimate incomparability of items from one system with those from another. Yet in practice the difference is often less startling than it appears to be. Firth insisted on simultaneously occurring signals from sets he called "prosodies" and "phonemes proper." One set was typically made up of such things as stress and pitch, the other of vowels and consonants. When Firth spent a summer in Ann Arbor together with American structuralists, the relations were amiable, and most of the time the terms "prosody" and "phoneme" could be easily translated into the American "suprasegmental phoneme" and "segmental phoneme."

An extremely vigorous and fruitful group of linguists outside the United States is the Prague School, whose activity is described by Paul L. Garvin in Chapter 21. The relations between this school and American structuralism and transformational analysis have been extremely close, though there are ways in which all differ. Structuralists, for instance, in contrast to Prague School theorists, and to Firthians, tend to want to group linguistic entities from different environmental sets together, so as to reduce the number of classes. Thus J. C. Catford points out in Chapter 20 that Firth insisted that the sets of word-initial consonants and word-final consonants in Javanese could not be equated because there was a large number in the initial group, but only a few in the final group. Prague School theorists talk of "neutralization of opposition" in such cases, saying that the opposition (or contrast) between sets of initial consonants is neutralized or made impossible in final position. American structuralists generally make a determined effort to classify the members of the smaller final group with the nearest member of the larger initial group. Yet once again the difference is less important than it seems. The justification for the Firthian position is that American attempts at such cross-system classification have not resulted in complete convergence, so that whatever system the analyst follows, he ends with having to describe each environmental set fully and having to state the oppositions found in each.

Another European school discussed in this book is that of glossematics, described by Francis Whitfield in Chapter 23. The school (essentially the work of Louis Hjelmslev) is particularly interesting in that Sydney Lamb has said that his own stratificational linguistics is largely a reworking of the theories of Hjelmslev. A very brief characterization of glossematics is that it is an analysis of language which starts with the notion that the most obvious and basic dichotomy of parts in any linguistic item is that between form and content. The school has proved acceptable to many, therefore, to whom the structuralist nervousness about statements having to do with content — or meaning — has been repellent. The interest in content, and the insistence that content can show structure just as form does, is ultimately responsible for the kind of structural semantics successfully developed by Lamb in Chapter 4.

This summary in once-over-lightly fashion is perhaps striking in that I have in some measure been rewriting the first chapter of this book, that by William G. Moulton on the nature and history of linguistics. Yet my remarks have been quite different; Moulton is concerned with the long-range history of linguistic science, whereas I have been concerned with the similarities and differences between currently active schools, and with trying to show that all are no more than mansions within the house of the same science. I shall also go somewhat beyond Moulton's formulation, since I think it is at least possible to make some predictions about the future. The predictions fall into two groups: one covering relations between the various schools which we have been discussing, and a second taking up the activities within linguistics which can be expected to concern linguists in the next generation or so.

First, on relations between the schools: With some confidence I predict that linguistics is ready to enter a period of synthesis like the one it experienced when such structural linguists as Henry Hoenigswald were taking pains to show that the findings of pre-phonemic linguists (Grimm for example) could still be regarded as valid structuralism in spite of the absence of terms like "allophone" and "complementary distribution." This prediction is based on a long-range view of the nature of scientific revolutions: They begin with a period of violent argument and name-calling and then proceed to a stage in which both the triumphant insurgents and the surviving members of the old guard make a determined effort to review all past statements, searching out areas of agreement. The insurgents hunt for those passages in which the earlier establishment seemed to be saying things which foreshadowed the revolution, and the survivors of the old guard hunt for those passages from statements of the insurgents which seem to show that some at any rate of the earlier formulations are still valid. "Period of synthesis" suggests a prognostication of peace and good will, but I predict that any such period will certainly be short. From the neo-grammarian revolution to the emergence of structuralism was a lifetime. From the emergence of structuralism to the transformational revolution was less than thirty years. And if stratificational linguistics proves to be a genuine revolution, the period from transformational linguistics to stratifica-tionalism is less than ten years. As in all other activities, in linguistics the rate of change has been enormously accelerated in this most hurried of centuries.

As for the activities within linguistics about which it is possible to make predictions, once again I think they fall into two classes: Those in which it is unlikely that any great amount of change will take place in the immediate future and those in which increased activity, and thus great change, is probable. Among the areas of linguistic investigation and speculation which are not likely to produce much more that is new is that of the origin of language, covered in Chapter 5, by Harry Hoijer. Had I been writing this chapter a century ago, I would have made the same prediction, and I would have been wrong. Yet the recent formulations derived from new understanding of the nature of human language and of what differentiates it from animal communication seem at this minute to exhaust all the evidence there is on the origin of speech. If, however, there is a further breakthrough in man's understanding of how language works, further conclusions about its origins will become inevitable.

It is also probable that further change in the description of the history of our own family of languages (see Chapter 6, by Henry M. Hoenigswald) will not take place soon. Structural phonetics had a great impact on notions of change in sound, and transformational analysis is having a similar impact at the moment. The most startling claim made by the current avant-garde is that sound changes do not follow blind phonetic laws, as the neo-grammarians claimed. Yet it would seem that even this claim will fail to shake the firm conviction of most scholars that whatever the cause and channel of changes in sound, they are essentially systematic. It would seem, therefore, that there will be a period of stock-taking and synthesis in historical studies before there is a completely new formulation.

Studies of dialect and attention to usage are two areas which can be easily lumped together. As Raven I. McDavid, Jr., has shown in Chapter 8, nonstandard dialects have their own structure, and though it is unlikely that the layman will ever become completely tolerant of dialectal difference, it is certain that tolerance will increase, paradoxically because of the effort to study nonstandard dialects so as to be able to spread the adoption of standard speech. In matters of usage, covered by Thomas Pyles in Chapter 12, it is to be hoped that increasing instruction in the linguistics of English, not merely for experts, but for all students, will at least accomplish the task of making the unnecessary violence of disputes over dictionaries less likely in future. It is also to be hoped that teachers of the native language, as Albert H. Marckwardt tells us in Chapter 11, will be able to make more use of linguistics and be more friendly to it than they have been in the past.

In Chapter 10, Einar Haugen describes for us one of the practical uses of linguistics new in our century, the creation of national languages out of divergent dialects or artificially revived older tongues. With the great upsurge of nationalism, this activity is certain to increase, and more principles about how to do it will emerge.

One final area of linguistics for which I predict increased activity and consequently great additions to knowledge is machine linguistics. For instance, synthetic speech, described by Frances Ingemann in Chapter 19, holds out the hope of a solution to the nagging lack of correspondence between what can be called the cues in speech recognition — the things which tell us what we are hearing — and the distinctive features as tabulated either by Jakobson or by an articulatory phonetician. Computer linguistics, discussed in Chapter 18 by Wayne Tosh, can control masses of variables, far more than any human calculator can handle; for instance, it is likely that computer analysis will be able to simulate the conditions of communication within a speech community over a period of time, and thus throw rich new light on how language changes. As for machine translation, discussed by Winfred P. Lehmann in Chapter 17, promising successes, limited it is true but nonetheless real, have already been achieved.

I have said enough, I hope, to demonstrate that linguistics is an active, flourishing science, young in its vigor at least. I venture one final prediction about it. In that distant future when linguistics is as fully developed as chemistry or physics and has become a science in which so much is known that the apprentice will need years of study before he reaches the edges of knowledge, linguists will look back at the twentieth century as the golden age of linguistics, and say with Wordsworth:

> Bliss was it in that dawn to be alive,
> But to be young was very heaven.

Index